CELEBRATING THE EARTH

An Earth-Centered Theology
of Worship with
Blessings, Prayers, and Rituals

Scott McCarthy

Resource Publications, Inc.
San Jose, California

Editorial director: Kenneth Guentert
Managing editor: Kathi Drolet
Copy editor: Elizabeth Asborno
Production artist: Ernest Sit
Illustrations: Patricia Kay Shubeck

Part I, Part II, and Appendix A were originally published as
Creation Liturgy: An Earth-Centered Theology of Worship,
© 1987 Resource Publications, Inc.

Reprint Department
Resource Publications, Inc.
160 E. Virginia St., # 290
San Jose, CA 95112-5848

Library of Congress Cataloging in Publication Data

McCarthy, Scott.
    Celebrating the earth / Scott McCarthy. --Rev. ed.
    p.
    Rev. ed. of: Creation liturgy. c 1987.
    Includes bibliographical reference.
    ISBN: 0-89390-199-7
    1. Nature--Religious aspects--Christianity.   2. Worship
programs.
I. McCarthy, Scott. Creation liturgy. II. Title.
BT695.5.M39 1991
264--dc20

Printed in the United States of America

95 94 93 92 91 | 5 4 3 2

To my parents, John and Margaret; to my brother, Anthony; and to those people of every faith and good will living within the area of the Diocese of Monterey in California; and, in a special way, to the Native Peoples of North America: Hecel lena oyate kin nipi kte, "That these People may live."

You can see that Yahweh your God is the true God, the faithful God who...is true to his covenant and his faithful love for a thousand generations as regards those who love him and keep his commandments (Dt 7:9).

Contents

Preface

Jesus Christ is Lord: Lord of the Universe, Lord of all time and space, the Alpha and the Omega. His redemptive presence is revealed in time and space, yet it is also veiled as a result of these dimensions: "Now we see only reflections in a mirror, mere riddles, but then we shall be seeing face to face" (1 Cor 13:12). We believe in a God who is present to us in the creation, but we also believe in One who speaks to us by means of "spatial signs" that have been put into our world: water, oil, flowers, bread, and the like. God also gives us other "temporal signs" of spiritual presence: the seasons, the weeks, the days, the life cycles of fauna and flora, the flow of the tides, the life-span of men and women with its birth and death and new life. Throughout all of this creation is the redeeming rhythm of the Christ: "Look, I am making the whole of creation new..." (Rv 21:5).

Now is the time of our salvation. We are saved *in tempore*. Time is precious; time is sacred. In our modern desire to dominate the earth, we have misused space and forgotten about sacred time. We have interfered deeply with the ecology of our world. The seasons, four special signs of God's love for us, seem to mean very little to us any more. Our preoccupation with technology has alienated us from a healthy knowledge and experience of the presence of the Lord in nature.

God loves us "with an everlasting love" (Jer 31:3). This love redeems us in Jesus. Time, like everything else, is sanctified by the presence and action of Jesus. The redemption is an ever-present reality because Jesus has made time a medium which expresses the fact of redemption for all people. The cycle of the seasons expresses the rhythm of natural life. For the person of faith, the cycle of the seasons becomes the cycle of salvation. The ordinary year becomes the year of the Lord, a year of liturgy, a year in which each recurring season manifests some new aspect of the mystery of Christ living in our world. People breathe the life-giving atmosphere of the Spirit and are able to raise their hands in praise and adoration of the Father for time and all eternity.

The more fully that we live our lives, the deeper will be our experience of the Lord. The deeper our experience of the Lord, the more we will share in his paschal mystery, his death and rising. The ebb and flow of daily life is the milieu in which we individually and communally die to selfishness and sin and rise to the glory of the sons and daughters of a smiling heavenly Father.

The seasons speak of life on two complementary levels. As they flow into one another, Spring, Summer, Autumn, and Winter describe the rise and fall of life forms. The cycle perpetually repeats itself and life is continually assured. This could be called the first level of life. The seasons declare the ceaseless abundance of life; it not only exists, but it also comes as a gift from the Creator. A gift is both given and received. As one gives a gift, one empties oneself of that gift so that another may gratefully receive; as one receives a gift, one is filled with a sense of joy and thanksgiving. God offers the gift of new life in Christ in the second level of life.

Although each of the four seasons contains elements of *kenosis* and *plerosis*, emptying and filling, giving and receiving, one might regard the seasons of Spring and Summer as special times for receiving God's two-fold gift of life and new life in Christ. They are the seasons of germination and growth. Autumn and Winter might be regarded as special times for giving back to God the gifts the Creator has given—not only an emptying of the earth symbolized by harvest thanksgiving celebrations, but also an emptying of ourselves, the gradual fading of selfishness in preparation for again receiving the gifts of life and new life in Christ. The themes in the Christian mythology of creation and redemption can easily be celebrated in the context of the seasons.

I have chosen to develop liturgically the four seasons because I believe that they have been neglected to a certain extent by liturgists in the past, and even now there seems to be no great abundance of theological thought on the subject. Part One of this work is investigative. The first chapter inquires into the concept of liturgical time as lived out in various religious cultures; the second chapter discusses the seasons and their connection with human and spiritual growth; the third chapter concerns the ways that people of different times and places understand the sanctification of the day and the year. As a complement to the third chapter, a fourth looks to the use of matter as it is variously religiously experienced; and a fifth chapter discusses technology, the four seasons, and the need for a revitalization of worship that is in keeping with the Christian tradition and true to our present experience of the world. Part One concludes with a rationale for liturgical celebrations which take into account the four seasons.

Part Two contains four liturgies, one for each season, that attempt to celebrate what has been proposed in Part One. They are efforts to utilize in worship those elements that are special to the seasons (allowing, of course, for the fact that various parts of the United States and the world experience the seasons differently). A specific natural setting (such as snow, a river, a beach) is given in each worship service; however, other settings are just as adaptable for celebration, depending upon the creative ability of the liturgists involved. The liturgies are distinct from each other in order that their adaptability might be seen. Two are eucharistic liturgies led by a priest; two are not. Two endeavor to express *kenosis*, and two try to manifest *plerosis*. They are simply to be paradigms for other kinds of Christian celebrations. They endeavor to describe, to point to, and to help celebrate the presence of the Saviour of the world.

Part Three contains various kinds of liturgies and rituals, both personal and communal. They are offered as examples of how we might better involve ourselves with God's Creation, our Mother Earth. The reader, the celebrator, is always invited to glean the traditions and to explore the possibilities with the help of God's Holy Spirit, for

> we are well aware that God works with those who love him, those who have been called in accordance with his purpose, and turns everything to their good (Rm 8:28).

I have tried throughout to avoid sexist language, except in the quotes from sources and when speaking of God.

Acknowledgments

This book is the result of many years of travelling, reading, thinking, meeting people, celebrating, and silently and prayerfully reflecting on the gift of Life.

Many people, especially friends in California, have helped me to gradually understand this Great Mystery.

I thank these kind people, who are too numerous to mention here.

I also thank the authors and publishers who gave permission to use material from their publications:

From Casimir Kucharek, *The Sacramental Mysteries: A Byzantine Approach*, Alleluia Press. From Walter M. Abbott, *The Documents of Vatican II*, reprinted with permission of America Press, Inc., 106 West 56th St., New York, NY 10019, © 1966, all rights reserved. From Henry J. M. Nouwen, *With Open Hands*, copyright © 1972 by Ave Maria Press, Notre Dame, IN 46556, Used with permission. From A. Bugnini and C. Braga, ed., *The Commentary on the Constitution and on the Instruction on the Sacred Liturgy*, copyright © 1965, Benziger Publishing Co., New York. From John R. Wilch, *Time and Event*, used by permission of E. J. Brill, Leiden, Netherlands. From Louis John Cameli, "The Spirituality of Celebration," *Chicago Studies*, copyright © 1977 Civitas Dei Foundation, Mundelein, IL. From Paul Neuenzeit, "Time," *Sacramentum Verbi*, vol. 3, copyright © 1970, reprinted by permission of The Crossroad Publishing Company. From Thomas Aquinas, *Summa Theologica*; from Walter Harrelson, *From Fertility Cult to Worship*; from Henri J. M. Nouwen, *Aging*, Doubleday & Co., Inc. From Franz Cumont, *The Mysteries of Mithra*, © 1956 by Dover Publications, Inc. From Christopher Hollis, *The Achievements of Vatican II*, © 1966 by E. P. Dutton, Inc. From George A. Lindbeck, *The Future of Roman Catholic Theology*, Fortress Press. From Warren G. Hansen, *St. Francis of Assisi: Patron of the Environment*, © 1971 Franciscan Herald Press, Chicago, IL. From *The Sacred and the Profane* by Mircea Eliade, copyright © 1957 by Rowohlt Taschenbuch Verlag GmbH, translated by Willard R. Trask, copyright © 1959 by Harcourt Brace Jovanovich, Inc., reprinted by permission of Harcourt Brace Jovanovich, Inc. From Teilhard deChardin, *Science and Christ*, Harper & Row, Publishers, Inc., © Georges Borchardt, Inc. From Harvey Cox, *The Feast of Fools*, Harvard University Press, reprinted by permission. From Franklin Edgerton, *The Bahagavad Gita*, copyright © 1974 by the President and Fellows of Harvard College, © 1972 by Eleanor Hill Edgerton. From *The Collected Works of St. John of the Cross*, copyright © 1979, Washington Province of Discalced Carmelites ICS Publications, 2131 Lincoln Road N.E., Washington, DC 20002. Excerpts from the English translation of *The Liturgy of the Hours* © 1974, International Committee on English in the Liturgy, Inc. (ICEL). Excerpts from the English translation of *Rite of Christian Initiation of Adults* © 1974 ICEL, all rights reserved. From Mary Reed Newland, *The Year and Our Children*, P. J. Kenedy & Sons. From Gerard A. Pottebaum, *The Rites of People*, copyright © The Liturgical Conference, 806 Rhode Island Ave. N.E., Washington, DC 20018, all rights reserved, used with permission. From Michael Marx, ed., *Protestants and Catholics on the Spiritual Life* copyright © 1965 by the Order of St. Benedict, Inc., published by The Liturgical Press, Collegeville, Minnesota, used with permission. From *St. Benedict's Rule for Monasteries*, copyright © 1948 by the Order of St. Benedict, Inc, published by The Liturgical Press, Collegeville, Minnesota, used with permission. From Lewis Browne, *The World's Great Religions*, reprinted with permission of Macmillan Publishing Company, copyright © 1946 by Lewis Browne, renewed 1974 by Rebecca Tarlow. From Theodore Gaster, *Festivals of the Jewish Year*, William Morrow and Co. From Aylward Shorter, *African Culture and the Christian Church*, Orbis Books. From Lawrence Cunningham, ed., *Brother Francis*, © 1975 by Our Sunday Visitor, Inc., reprinted by permission. From William O'Shea, *The Worship of the Church*, © 1957 by Darton, Longman and Todd, London, reprinted by permission of Paulist Press. From Mary Evelyn Jegen and Bruno V. Manno, ed., *The Earth is the Lord's*, © 1978 by Paulist Press. From F. C. Happold, *Mysticism*, p. 29, © 1964, Baltimore, reprinted by permission of Penguin Books Ltd. From Raymond Brown, et al, *Jerome Biblical Commentary*, © 1968, Prentice-Hall, Inc. From "Morning in April," published in *Sightseers into Pilgrims*, © 1973, Tyndale House Publishers, Wheaton, IL 60187, used by permission of Luci Shaw, editor. From Joseph deGuibert, *The Theology of the Spiritual Life*, used with permission of Sheed & Ward, 115 E. Armour Blvd., Kansas City, MO 64141. From Mircea Eliade, *Patterns in Comparative Religion*, used with permission of Sheed & Ward, 115 E. Armour Blvd., Kansas City, MO 64141. From Victor Solomon, *A Handbook on Conversions to the Religions of the World*, Stravon Educational Press. From Clark Tibbitts, ed., *Handbook of Social Gerontology*, © 1960 by the University of Chicago Press. From Rev. Louis Bouyer, *Liturgical Piety*, © 1955 by University of Notre Dame Press. From Frank Waters, *The Book of the Hopi*, © 1963 by Frank Waters, reprinted by permission of Viking Penguin Inc. From Kenneth W. Morgan, ed., *The Religion of the Hindus*, copyright © 1953 The Ronald Press Co., reprinted by permission of John Wiley & Sons, Inc. From Andre Dumas, "The Ecological Crisis and the Doctrine of Creation," *Ecumenical Review*, © 1975 World Council of Churches, Geneva, Switzerland.

Acknowledgments for the Revised Edition

As this second and enlarged (and renamed) edition of *Celebrating the Earth* goes to press, I would like to take the opportunity to especially thank and honour within these pages the following people for their labours of love:

Gay (Howard) Pollock, for many, many hours of typing and revising the original manuscript;

Maria Rosa Gonzalez, for her patience and prayers;

Toni Hunt, for typing and re-typing the material for this edition;

Juan Mancias, for his critiquing expertise;

John Grinnell, for research assistance;

Dennis Meza, for his continual encouragement;

and also those who have in many important ways shared in various aspects of the liturgies within this book: Genaro Arista; David Bobardt; Robert and George Carmona; Cristina and Herman Celaya; Paul Kay; Andrew and Anthony Lilles; Berto Lopez; Alvaro, Johnny, and Aaron Lopez; Martin Marroquin; Frank Martinez; Martin Munoz; George and Jesus Rocha; Hector Rodriguez; Irma and Ernie Serna; John Shubeck; Jeremy Two Feathers; Norman, Angeline, and Rhonda Whiteman; and others too numerous to mention here.

Thank you! Gracias! Ahoo!

Scott McCarthy
Pryor, Montana
February 15, 1991

PART ONE

1

Time

Introduction

Suspended between time and space, humankind at some time or other contemplates its presence in the universe. Whether religious or not, people are definitely aware of time and its effects wherever they are. It cannot be escaped, for it is the occasion of our existence. For centuries philosophers and theologians alike have attempted to understand the context of the time-space continuum. Material creation, of which we are a part, is in perpetual motion—is passing through time. One has only to observe nature to see definite change in the passage from Spring on through Summer, Autumn, and Winter. Time seems to be one of those mysterious things about which everybody knows but which nobody really ever properly explains.

Philosophical definitions of time abound. Time is variously described as: "the moving image of eternity," according to Plato; or "the number of motion according to before and after," as stated by Aristotle; or, in Augustine's view, a distension of the soul with future and past segments stretching bilaterally from the distended present of attention.[1] One could also delve into the concept of time from many other points of view. Religious people would see holiness in each moment as it relates the individual to eternity. For the average American business person, the epithet "time is money" would hold true. "Lived-time" is that sense of duration experienced by an individual or a nation. This is a sense of past events that are significant for shaping the future. An example of this is the celebration of the American Bicentennial. A biologist would notice that time regulates the buildup and breakdown of living tissues. A mathematical-physical notion of time would insist that there is a metric intersubjectivity applicable to every change in the universe.[2]

The philosophical concept of time is derived from an awareness of change in the person or in the objects apprehended. Although there is no special sense that perceives time the way that the eyes perceive color, it is said by psychologists that we have a "time sense." Quite often we are able to "clock" ourselves and be fairly accurate without the aid of certain mechanical devices. We are all familiar, as well, with the speed with which time seems to pass when we are enjoying ourselves and how slowly it seems to pass when we are bored or are waiting for something special to happen. The old saying "a watched pot never boils" would hold true in relation to this kind of psychological time.

Time, then, for the purposes of this study, may be divided into two forms: ordinary time and sacred time. Ordinary time is the experience of one moment to another; it is the period between two events during which something happens. Ordinary time is profane time in that the actions performed within the duration do not have a religious meaning. Sacred time, holy time,

liturgical time, on the other hand, represents the reac-
tualization of a sacred event that occurred in a mythical
past, *in initio*.[3]

Sacred Time and Profane Time

One can speak of ordinary profane time and sacred
time. A religious person is aware of both types of time,
but a person who is not religious experiences reality
only in a "secular" manner. The God-dimension is not
present for that person. The passage of time simply calls
for the functioning of the human person on a variety of
physical and psychic levels: certain types of behaviors
that bring degrees of fulfillment. It is difficult to imagine
an individual stripped of religion, one who is not, at the
very least, vaguely religious. Surely, if one does not
believe in God, he or she at least has a "God-object,"
someone or something that is considered to be greater
than the individual.

By means of liturgical rites, people pass from ordinary
time to sacred time and back again safely to ordinary
time.[4] They "come apart for a while" to celebrate their
participation in an event that transcends the mereness
of ordinary profane time. Sacred time is the time of the
participants' full communion with cosmos and Creator.

> Seasonal rituals are functional in character. Their
> purpose is periodically to revive the topocosm; that
> is, the entire complex of any given locality con-
> ceived as a living organism. But this topocosm pos-
> sesses both a punctual and a durative aspect,
> representing not only the actual and present com-
> munity, but also the ideal and continuous entity of
> which the latter is but the current manifestation.
> Accordingly, seasonal rituals are accompanied by

4

myths which are designed to present the purely
functional acts in terms of ideal and durative situations. The interpenetration of the myth and ritual
creates the drama.[5]

It is impossible to celebrate time without attending to
matter as well. Time has no meaning in and of itself unless it is coupled with the "stuff" of the universe, which
is matter. Time, it might be said, flows through nature.
Seasonal rituals

fall into the two clear divisions of *kenosis*, or
emptying, and *plerosis*, or filling, the former repre-
senting the evacuation of life, the latter its
replenishment. Rites of kenosis include the observance of fasts, lents, and similar austerities, all
designed to indicate that the topocosm is in a state
of suspended animation. Rites of plerosis include
mock combats against the forces of drought or evil,
mass mating, the performance of rain charms and
the like, all designed to effect the reinvigoration of
the topocosm.[6]

The Four Seasons and Rhythmic Time

The four seasons demonstrate rhythmic time, especially to *homo religiosus*. Spring is that time of year in
which plants begin to grow after lying dormant all
winter; it is that period between the vernal equinox and
the summer solstice; it is a time of beginning, of new-
ness. Summer is the warmest part of the year; it is the
time between the summer solstice and the autumnal
equinox; it is a season of growth, of development, and
of fulfillment. Autumn, the time before Winter, is a time
of maturity or of beginning decline. Winter is the

coldest season of the year; it is that period between the Winter Solstice and the Vernal Equinox; it is a time of decline and dreariness.

Nature herself illustrates the seasons dramatically and in a most wondrous way. Light and temperature bring about changes in plants and birds and beasts. Nature seasonally displays her multicolored raiment. Perhaps the poet best speaks of the kinds of changes that take place throughout the year:

> It rained last night, a mighty, gasping rain.
> The buds flew open like surprised mouths.
> The solemn trees turned virile green again.
>
> Oaks sprawl above the fields, and to the south
> birches fence away infinity.
> The sky lies over all like a white cloth.
>
> And the galvanized moon above the tree
> is like a nail pounded with some tool
> to hold the sky in place, wrinkle- free.
>
> I sit by the window, a stage-struck fool,
> watching the color of the grass, beyond
> propriety. Green does not follow rules,
>
> nor does God damn it to. Forever on
> the script that moves the world are written all
> the possibilities in every lawn.
>
> I'm less than an observer. Who would call
> the grass, the world, God's will? I only know
> that grass has always greened, and that oaks sprawl,
> that on some mind was written this last night:
>
> Rain fall.[7]

Sacred Time in Nature Religions

Taken as a whole, humanity is religious; however, there are different types of religious belonging. The relationship between people and Divinity belongs to the categories of either "natural" or "revealed" religion. Natural religion concerns a mystical ascent to God by means of nature and cosmos. Revealed religion, on the other hand, is about God first speaking to people by means of a special intervention into the existing state of affairs. An excursus into a few types of natural religions to see how the people experience sacred time might well illustrate the importance of the seasons in worship.

In the mystery cults, the god was always put on a pedestal equal with nature. The celebration of resurrection was not the occasion for recalling an actual historical event as in Christianity, but was more of a reminder of a process that was repeated annually with the seasons.

The mysteries of the Mother Goddess Cybele and Attis, her shepherd lover, developed in Phrygia before Christianity. The followers of Cybele and Attis began very early to believe in the immortality of the soul. Just as Attis died and came to life again every year, these believers were to be born to a new life after their own death.

At the festivals, priests called *koribantia* worshipped with cries and shouts accompanied by clashing cymbals and drums, especially during the great Spring festival. On the twenty-second day of March, a pine tree was cut down in the woods and brought into the sanctuary of Cybele, where it was treated as a divinity. On the second day of the festival, there was ceremonial trumpet music. The third day of this five-day festival was known as the Day of Blood; on this day the high priest and other minor ministers drew blood from their arms and presented it as an offering. This rite formed a part of the mourning for Attis.

But when night had fallen, the sorrow of the worshippers was turned to joy. A lamp was lit and the god's tomb was opened; he was declared to have risen from the dead. As the priest touched the lips of the worshippers with balm, he softly whispered the glad tidings of their salvation. This ceremony and other public rituals were performed for the sake of good crops. But more private ceremonies were aimed at the union of the individual with the god so that salvation would be assured. Ceremonies were always held in the Springtime, the season of regeneration.

It could be said that a Native American spends about one-half of waking hours in religious activities; just about everything that is done is bound up religiously. Very little time goes by without some ceremonial event enacted to bring good weather, to keep the crops growing, or to bring blessings and health to individual and clan. Hopi ceremonials are good examples of the four seasons being celebrated religiously by a Native American tribe.

Hopi mythology concerns four creations by Taiowa the Creator worked through his nephew Sotuknang: *Tokpela* (Endless Space); *Tokpa* (Dark Midnight); *Kuskurza* (no direct translation); and *Tuwaqachi* (World Complete). *Tokpela* was good. People were good insofar as they kept open the invisible spiritual door at the top of their heads so that they could receive life and communicate with the Creator. People and animals were in harmony and concord, but they turned to evil ways, and the successive worlds (*Tokpela, Tokpa,* and *Kuskurza*) were each destroyed. A remnant was saved and entered the fourth world, which was *Tuwaqachi*. The people dispersed and migrated to different parts of the world to claim it for Tiaowa. Here Hopi history begins.

Three great liturgical celebrations describe the creation, and these rites are celebrated outside as well as within the *kivas*, the underground ceremonial chambers that represent the womb. One goes to and from the world outside by means of a ladder coming out of the *kiva*, which symbolizes the umbilical cord.

The first of these celebrations, *Wuwuchim*, lays out the pattern of life development for the coming year. The second, *Soyal*, accepts it, and the third, *Powamu*, purifies it.[8] At the end of these ceremonies, both priests and people watch the sunrise with prayerful concentration. They greet it together and try to let the glow fill their bodies and their minds.

They ceremonially re-enact the three-part drama of creation.[9] In the first phase, *Wuwuchim*, the humans made their emergence into the new world (*Tuwaqachi*), the first fire was lighted, and life was germinated. In the second phase, *Soyal*, humankind's dwelling-place was erected on the earth, the sun was redirected on its course to give warmth and strength to the germinated life, and the *kachinas* arrived to consecrate its growth. With the third phase, *Powamu*, plant life made its appearance; humankind, as children, was initiated by the *kachinas*, and the entire Road of Life throughout the worlds was purified.

All of these phases of creation are endlessly repeated in annual cycles of germination, growth, and harvest. The ceremonies also plan, confirm, and help to carry through the agricultural cycle upon which all life depends. Moreover, creation is reaffirmed with the dawn of each new day, and the ceremonies reaffirm with endless repetition a persistent faith in the manifold meaning of the emergence into reality: the reality of birth, death, and rebirth.

Oceangoing peoples celebrate sacred time in ways proper to their cultures and environments. Hawaiian ritual was always closely connected with their divisions of time. Like all Polynesians, time was reckoned by lunar months of twenty-nine and thirty days alternately. The New Year began with the month Makalii (about November 20). The five months beginning with our January were war months, but during the remaining seven there could be no war. During each month there were four taboo periods of two nights and one day, each dedicated to the four great gods. During taboo periods, the king and the priests held certain rituals; women were forbidden to enter canoes or to have intercourse.

The other gods gave the people many things: bananas, useful plants, trees, and fish. Some were gods of professions: fishing, hula dancing, farming, and homemaking. There was a whole host of deities residing in volcanoes, trees, the sea, and in other places. Each deity had to be appeased at special times. The day was sanctified by activities that, because they were taught by the gods, were considered to be holy. Thus the Hawaiians were conscious that their work was prayerful and wholesome because it allowed them to be in touch with the gods. Even the sacred action of fishing was regulated by the "holy times."[10]

Ancient Hawaiians constantly waited for an auspicious time to hold a sacred ceremony. For instance, a shower of comets or other unusual cosmic phenomenon would be considered as a sign from the gods that a sacred event should be held. The marriage of an important tribal member, for example, would be the occasion for special ceremonies. A shrine would be built for the ceremony, only to be abandoned soon afterward; for the Hawaiians of old, holy times took precedence over holy places.

The Sonjo of Tanganyika are an agricultural people who also herd goats and sheep. Their religion centers on a deity named Khambageu. They practice a cult of ancestral spirits who must be sacrificed to and who have something to do with human fertility. Each village has two temples dedicated to Khambageu tended by priests and elders, as well as several shrines and other sacred places like groves of trees and rock formations.

This is their mythology: Khambageu came to exist as an adult without a mother or a father. He was poor and worked at a village in very menial jobs. Because he refused to do some irrigation work, he was sentenced to death. He escaped, but was pursued. He arrived at a new village, Soyetu, was offered sanctuary and given a position of honor. He married and then performed many miracles throughout his life. Then he decided to move on to Rokhari. The two villages began to quarrel over him. When he was old, he announced that he would die and gave directions for his burial. Instead of obeying his requests, the people of Rokhari buried him immediately. When the grave was opened by the people of Soyetu, nothing was found except his sandals; he was subsequently recognized by all to be God. His story is strikingly similar to the life of Christ.

A number of rites are performed at specified times. There is a harvest festival, *Mbaribari*, which is celebrated for four days at all the villages in rotation, so that the cycle of this feast lasts a month or so. Prior to the festival itself, a delegation of ritually pure men and women march in procession to Rokhari, the locus of the main temple, bearing gifts for Khambageu. They spend the night in the temple precincts, and if favorable omens are obtained, the delegation returns to its village with news that the festival may begin the following day. The festivities start in the early morning each day with rites performed at the holy springs and temples.

The second festival, *Mase*, which is also celebrated for four days at each village, concerns the special visit of Khambageu in person to the particular village. His presence is made known by the sound of a concealed horn. The dancing is slow and is accompanied by hymns. There is no drunkenness or laughter or loud talking: only an atmosphere of intense piety. Rituals by priest and elders are enacted before dawn each morning and the whole village greets the rising sun with a hymn. At that time goats are brought to the temple for sacrifice. Once in a while, the dancing is interrupted while an elder chants a prayer on behalf of a supplicant, beseeching Khambageu for specific blessings such as the birth of children or health of good crops. The chant is answered by the sound of a horn, indicating that Khambageu has heard the prayer.

The third festival, *Mbori-ya-bura*, lasts one day and is celebrated when the crops are half-grown. The warriors dance through the fields and goats are sacrificed there to ensure that there will be a good harvest. In the winter there is a women's fertility celebration. All of the women gather at one of the temples at dawn, and there they pray and dance and sing until noon. During this time the men must vacate that part of the village. Then the women process to the village square and give a public performance of folk dancing and singing.[11]

> To live here and now is the most important con-
> cern of African religious activities and beliefs. There
> is little, if any concern with the distinctly spiritual
> welfare of man apart from his physical life...God
> comes into the picture as an explanation of man's

> contact with time. There is no...apocalyptic vision
> of God stepping in at some future moment to bring
> about a radical reversal of man's normal life.[12]

For African traditional religion, times of prayer relate to the symbolism of the various times of the day. For example, the hours of sunrise, midday, and sunset refer to sun symbolism in the worship of the Creator. The occasion of prayer is often that of a disaster or misfortune affecting the individual or the group. Private prayer is known, but community prayer is more typical.[13] For the worshipper in a traditional African society, as it is for peoples of other cultures, "any time is a good time to pray."

Jewish Sacred Time

"Worship is an ordered response to the appearance of the Holy in the life of individuals and groups."[14] And as such, the worship of God, if it is not to remain vague and indefinite, finds expression through certain elements belonging to the senses, such as signs and words, and it is connected to places and times. By the changes of day and night, seasons and years, Creation calls upon people to raise their minds and hearts, indeed their very selves, to God at stated times in order to commune with their Creator.

One might say that in the so called "nature religions" the year is important, while in Judeo-Christianity it is the day that is important because each day is the day of the Lord, the *dies Domini*.

The Israelites celebrated the actions of God in their own historical presence. They believed the year and the month and the day to be holy because Yahweh had created them in order to give them to his people; they were holy because Yahweh was holy. Three important agricultural festivals were celebrated during the Jewish year. They were the Feast of Unleavened Bread (a Spring festival of the barley harvest), the Festival of the Weeks or Pentecost (a feast occurring seven weeks later when the wheat was harvested), and the Festival of Ingatherings or Booths or Tents, which took place in the Autumn. These three divisions of the calendar all seem to have been adopted from the Canaanites.[15]

Israel's life of worship included far more than the temple cult; it penetrated into the daily life of each Jew. The sanctification of each day and the praise of Yahweh was an obligation that was in no way restricted to the priestly caste. The spirit of sacrificial prayer eventually found its home in synagogue worship and in personal and domestic prayer rituals. The *Shema* was recited, one might say, "at all times and in all places."

The Israelites, like their pagan neighbors, evolved over the years from a nomadic people to an agrarian people. "Each of these cultures possessed its own rites. The rhythm of the nomadic world was marked by the worship of the moon, that of the agrarian world by harvest and vintage worship."[16]

The year was divided into two seasons: the winter, *horeph*, and summer, *qays*, corresponding roughly to the cold and hot seasons, the seedtime and the harvest. This simple division corresponds to the climate of Palestine where the hot, dry season and the cold, wet season succeed each other fairly quickly, leaving no distinct sensation of Spring and Autumn as in other more temperate countries.[17] Originally a nomadic people who travelled by night, the Israelites followed a lunar month. The time period for observing the moon in its various movements is called a lunation. As a lunation takes twenty-nine days, twelve hours and a fraction, the lunar months had twenty-nine and thirty days alternately.

Following is an ancient Israelite calendar, found at Gezer near Jerusalem, attributed to the 10th century B.C.E.:

2 months: *'sp* = Ingathering

2 months: *zr'* = Seedtime

2 months: *lqsh* = Late Seedtime

1 month: *'sd psht* = Flax Gathering

1 month: *qsr s'rm* = Barley Harvest

1 month: *qsr wkl* = Wheat Harvest

2 months: *zmr* = Pruning

1 month: *qs* = Summer Fruits

This is not a memorandum of tasks to be carried out in the different months of the year, but a concordance table between twelve lunations and the periods of the agricultural year, which the workers named after the tasks they performed in them.[18] Since then, other calendars have come into existence to regulate Jewish activity and worship.[19]

The weekly Sabbath "...reflects a method of measuring time in sequences of seven days."[20] It was devised independently of the phases of the moon.

> On this day the conforming Jew will abstain from all kind of work, labor, or business occupation, from traveling or handling any tool or working implement, except in cases of danger to life, when all Sabbath laws are set aside...It is a memorial of the Creation, serving to impress upon the mind man's dependence on God for all he has, including the

work of his own hands; and it is also celebrated as a reminder of the great deliverance from Egyptian bondage, and as such is a symbol of human equality and freedom.[21]

The various positions of the sun during the seasons of the year were carefully watched by the Hebrews.[22] The re-emergence of the sun, especially in the Spring, was an obvious date from which to reckon the renewal of the world's vitality,[23] while the decline of the sun was a natural occasion from which to date the eclipse of such vitality.[24]

We can speak of nomadic and agrarian rhythms.

...the feasts of the astronomical order honored the order of the created world, the regular rhythm of its evolution, man's submission to the dominion of "the elements of the world"...Here we find ourselves in the heart of a natural religion where man is aware of his solidarity with the elements of creation and makes this solidarity the object of his praise and prayer.[25]

The Hebrews were originally a nomadic people. They bred sheep and goats because these animals were quite well adapted to the terrain where they lived. When the Chosen People finally conquered the Promised Land of Canaan and settled down, they took over and "baptized" certain pagan feasts of their proximate neighbors.

Like any people who had once been herders, the Israelites finally came to settle down: they built towns, raised crops, and bred cattle along with their sheep and goats. They became more and more attached to a definite piece of land instead of wandering all over the creation.

Feasts of both nomadic and agrarian origin had been happily combined at the moment when Israel itself had come to the end of its nomadic life and had entered the land that it was now to cultivate as a farmer. From the nomadic rhythm, came the feasts of the new moon, the new year, and the strangled lamb rite. From the agrarian rhythm, came the feasts of the offering of first fruits of field and vineyard, feasts of harvest followed by merrymaking.[26]

The rhythms of herding and farming speak of two different ways of looking at life; the story of Cain and Abel brings out some of the tension between these two basic styles of life.

The nomad is full of fear. He is afraid of his god and seeks to conciliate him. He looks on a feast as a means of achieving harmony with nature, adapting to its rhythms with as little difficulty as possible, avoiding all causes of disturbance. When nature is hostile, he shields himself from danger with the rite of protective blood. The man who cultivates the soil, on the contrary, has greater self-confidence. He sings the praises of his work and offers it proudly to his god. He is rich, and the nomad seems to be poor. While the nomad tries to live in harmony with the laws of nature, the farmer rejoices over the control of nature by his work. The former is passive, the latter is active. The former is more interior, the latter needs to express himself, to rejoice more, to dance and to offer holocausts.[27]

The Hebrew Festivals

The main seasonal festivals celebrated by Jews even down to the present day are: Passover, *Pesah*, which in ancient times was a ritualization of thanks for the Spring

17

barley harvest; Pentecost, *Shavuoth*, which was a celebration of the end of the barley harvest; and In-gatherings, *Succoth*, also called the feast of Tents or Booths or Tabernacles, which celebrated the reaping of summer fruits at the beginning of Autumn. The ceremonies that celebrate the divisions of holy time represent the mechanism by which, at a primitive level, society seeks periodically to renew its vitality and thus ensure its continuance.[28] The Israelite seasonal ceremonies are no exception in this matter. These three feasts evolved in the following stages.

1. The time of the patriarchs and judges: this roughly was the time of nomadic pastoral life.

2. The time of David and the Monarchy until the Babylonian captivity: this roughly was the beginning of organized agricultural life in Israel.

3. The time of the rebuilding of the Temple under Nehemiah until the coming of Christianity: this roughly was the time of historicizing the feasts as celebrations of the Covenant.

4. The apostolic era to the present: this is the era of abolishing the feasts, for now all feasts of Israel continue in the person of Jesus, the Feast of Feasts, the Feast toward whom all other feasts were tending.[29]

Passover, *Pesah*, is a combination of two early elements: the rite of unleavened bread and the rite of the protecting blood of the lamb. The Hebrews believed in the divine power contained in the substance of blood. In their nomadic phase, the Hebrews had taken over a blood ceremony that had been practiced from of old by their neighbors to ensure safety from evil spirits. Sprinkled blood was thought to have a preservative power. "Even today the rite of the lamb is classic among nomadic tribes. A lamb is immolated, its flesh is not necessarily eaten, but its blood is always sprinkled on the tent pegs to ward off evil spirits."[30]

The agricultural rite of unleavened bread also was borrowed from the Canaanites. It "...is an expression of the farmer's anxious care not to mix flour made from new grain and old."[31] The old grain was considered to be empty of its "divine power"; hence the need for the new grain given by Yahweh. It could be said that

> ...in very early times this Canaanite festival was related to Passover by the wandering tribes in their movement into the settled land at the time of spring. They consummated their pastoral period with the Passover celebration and initiated their agricultural period with a festivity at the time of the barley harvest. And they probably did so near the Jordan ford at which was commemorated their entrance into the Land of the Promise.[32]

These two rites came to be blended together, and in the course of time, probably during the Exile, Passover became historicized as did the other feasts of Judaism. It came to be celebrated in memory of the Egyptian bondage, the exodus, and the birth of the nation. At the time of the reform of Josiah, about 640 B.C.E., the people had begun to eat the paschal lamb as well:

> You must sacrifice the Passover not in any of the towns given you by Yahweh your God, but in the place where Yahweh your God chooses to give his name a home; there you must sacrifice the Passover, in the evening at sunset, at the hour when you came out of Egypt. You will cook it and eat it in

the place chosen by Yahweh your God, and in the morning you must return home and go to your tents (Dt 16:6-7).

"Time changes things," as the saying goes; time also changes the meanings of liturgical celebrations. Or, one might say, time heightens the meanings.

Before this time the rite consisted merely in the immolation of the lamb and the sprinkling of its blood...If, on certain occasions, the lamb was eaten, the meal formed no part of the paschal rite which was simply a meal of unleavened bread. But after the days of the Deuteronomist...the paschal lamb meal becomes more important...No longer does the symbolism of the rite matter most (that is, the repetition of what was done in time long past) but rather the attitude of soul that the memory of the event recalls...The eating of the lamb better expresses the personal participation of the faithful in the feast than did the immolation of the lamb...The Deuteronomist legislation no longer requires that the blood be sprinkled on tent pegs or door lintels: to eat a lamb—and in this way to eat the lamb of the original event—supposes and signifies a far deeper, personal involvement.[33]

The Last Supper was most likely a celebration of the Passover.[34]

In its early agrarian phase, the Feast of Weeks or Pentecost, *Shavuoth*, was "simply the end of the barley harvest...and its distinctive feature...the presentation of an offering consisting, according to one version of the Law (Dt 16:10), of whatever one feels prompted to give, or, according to another (Lv 23:17), of two loaves."[35] The presentation of first fruits was no mere token of thanksgiving or mere submissive rendering of tribute. It

20

was the payment to God of the dividend on his invest-
ment, and to withhold that payment was an act of em-
bezzlement.[36] The feast began the day after the sabbath
on which the first wheat sheaf was presented and seven
complete weeks were reckoned to the day after the
seventh sabbath: fifty days in all; hence the Greek name
for "fiftieth,"[37] *pentecoste*.

To the feast was imputed later covenantal significance;
thereby it was historicized.

> ...the natural and historical aspects of this festival
> run parallel to each other. For if the former marks
> the end of seven weeks' collaboration between God
> and man in the reaping of material harvest, what
> the latter celebrates is the end of a corresponding
> spiritual harvest, which began with the deliverance
> from Egypt and reached its climax with the con-
> clusion of the Covenant...Moreover, if, in the primi-
> tive agricultural rite, man offers to God two loaves
> of the new bread as a symbol of cooperation, in the
> historical counterpart...God offers to man the two
> tablets of the law.[38]

But the apostolic church saw a deeper meaning in this
feast beginning on the day of the new Pentecost when,
as recorded in Acts 2:1-41, Peter, under the influence of
God's Holy Spirit, stood up and proclaimed Jesus as the
fulfillment of this feast.

A third important celebration for the Jews is the Festival of Tents, *Succoth*. "In the pre-monarchical period
its character was two-fold, so far as can be determined; it
was at once the time of the fall fruit harvest and the time
for the reaffirmation of the covenant between God and
people."[39] This "fall festival concentrates attention upon
the story of the patriarchs, the giving of the land as
Yahweh's special gift, and the decision for the covenant

God, with emphasis upon covenant law."[40] The twenty-fourth chapter of Joshua sets the scene for such a covenantal reaffirmation. But it was originally a celebration held while the grapes, olives, and fruits were being harvested. People actually dwelt in huts or booths or tents made from tree-boughs and vines and simply ritualized their joy and feelings of thankfulness for all that Yahweh was giving them.

Like many feasts, both Jewish and other, some, which were originally nature feasts, came to lose their primitive meanings and became expressions of an historical event. By the time the people had settled in their towns, the feast "no longer symbolized the rhythm of nature but the development of history guided by the hand of God."[41] Because of the booths in which it was celebrated, this Feast of Ingatherings came to be associated with the wanderings in the wilderness when the Israelites could claim no settled homes. This new historical association did not necessarily wholly displace the agricultural character of the feast,[42] but it did give new depth of significance.

To repeat, the Feast of Ingatherings evolved from an agrarian feast to one celebrating a historical event; it also acquired an eschatological meaning. One of the prophets' roles was to keep the people's minds on the future because the future days also came from Yahweh. Isaiah prophesied:

> The desert becomes productive ground, so productive you might take it to be a forest. Fair judgement will fix its home in the desert, and uprightness live in the productive ground, and the product of uprightness will be peace, the effect of uprightness being quiet and security forever. My people will live in a peaceful home, in peaceful houses, tranquil dwellings (Is 32:15-18)

These tents will be signs of eschatological happiness.[43] The Feast of Tents was a celebration for the moment when the seed had come to the end of its slow development and the harvest was assured.[44] In looking at the feast eschatologically, and from a Christian stance, one can see that this world is still in the process of accepting salvation; our faith tells us that a bountiful harvest is assured indeed.

Hebrew Notions About Time

The Hebrews, unlike their neighbors, were wont to not put their faith in what might be called cyclic time: cycles of history returning endlessly to their starting points. Neither did they understand time to be merely linear time: time thought of as being like a straight line of limitless extent which, when viewed from the present, extends backward through past events and forward through future ones. However, they could comprehend time that was "filled," time "for" something.[45] Such an understanding

> is based on the underlying psychology of the two Semitic or Hebrew tenses, which appears to recognize only two kinds of past, namely that of the completed event (perfect, *factum*) and that of the still uncompleted event (imperfect, *fiens*), in addition to the present and the future. Time, therefore, is conceived of subjectively from the standpoint of the beholder of history, who divides it according to the events which he himself regards as significant.[46]

Significant times for the individual were applied to the actions of Yahweh on the individual, the nation, and the universe. All events, whether they were human or cosmic, owed their existence to Yahweh, who permitted any and all events to happen.

Thus there is a time for every matter under the sun which humans have to use and which imparts a rhythm to this life. The individual history of a man's life is made up, therefore, of the total sum of these rhythms in time...The sum total for the salvific deeds of God in the life of the chosen people constitutes the time of salvific history in its total extent,...considering these events in their relevance to the present life and worship of the individual Israelite.[47]

The Hebrew notion of time includes participants: Yahweh and the creation (including men and women). Time has to do with "the specific, definite occasion of Yahweh's intervention."[48] God has cut across history with a two-edged sword and has divided all time. For Christians, the point of the sword's entry is the moment of the conception and birth of Jesus. He is Yahweh's anointed, "the Alpha and the Omega, the First and the Last, the Beginning and the End" (Rv 22:13).

The Christian Notion of Kairos

We are living in the era of salvation, the *Annus Domini*. A Christian tries to understand time in reference to the point of view of God and divine activity. God is beyond time, but time is also one of God's creations. If one is to understand time at all, God must be included in a definition of it; God cannot be excluded. The Scriptures and our Christian Tradition are the two sources for our knowledge of how God redeems us in time. Christ's coming ushers in a new age for all of creation:

He will make his home with them; they will be his people, and he will be their God, God-with-them.

> He will wipe away all tears from their eyes; there
> will be no more death, and no more mourning or
> sadness or pain. The world of the past has gone.
> Then the One sitting on the throne spoke. Look, I
> am making the whole of creation new. Write this,
> "What I am saying is trustworthy and will come
> true." Then he said to me, "It has already hap-
> pened. I am the Alpha and the Omega, the Begin-
> ning and the End" (Rv 21:3-5).

In speaking of a New Testament notion of time, it is
important to understand the *kairos*, that is, the time
which has as its content the work of Jesus and the
decision of men and women to accept or to reject this
salvific event.[49] Such a time concept makes God the
giver and demands

> that men shall lay hold of this offering of salvation
> on God's part...and this *kairos* of God gives certain-
> ty. In this it is unlike cosmic or human *kairos*,
> which has to remain in a constant state of readiness
> for all possible opportunities even when they are
> only remote.[50]

For Christians, "now" is the time of salvation; the hour
of decision is taking place now. The Good News is that
Jesus is "taking time out of itself so that it is becoming
more fully in Him." Everything ultimately fits into God's
plan of salvation, a plan which is lived out in history.

> This *kairos*...is not at all to be understood as an
> "hour" in the sense of a discrete unit of time
> measured along a line of temporal succession. It is
> determined uniquely by the events which take
> place, events which are brought about by God and
> impinge on the life of men.[51]

25

Luke, in his Acts of the Apostles, speaks of times and seasons, *kairoi*: "It is not for you to know times or dates that the Father has decided by his own authority..." (Acts 1:7). So does Paul: "About times or dates, brothers, there is no need to write to you for you are well aware in any case that the Day of the Lord is going to come like a thief in the night." (1 Th 5:1-2). At this very moment, God is saving the whole of creation: individuals, humanity, the world. As the universe flows through time, it is being directed to God and by God, who is its fulfillment. The New Testament authors knew well

> ...that he who comes, the judge who exercises cosmic judgement, is not only already victor and Savior of mankind, but a person familiarly known from the Gospel record of his earthly life of humiliation and suffering. The Old Testament Day of Yahweh, in consequence, has been transformed into the Day of Christ; and its nature has been essentially revealed to men by Jesus' life, death, and resurrection. Indeed this Day is not so much something ordained to be the termination of this world, but rather a reality already dynamically present in history. And thus history becomes fundamentally salvation history; for the value of the present time, as also the significance of the future, has been created and revealed to us by Jesus Christ.[52]

The apostolic church was well aware of the meaning of time. They believed themselves to be living in the eighth day, which lasts forever (the seven days of the week plus the day of resurrection). The church in patristic times also recognized time as being "of the Lord." There was a great desire to hold fast to the *paradosis*, the transmitted truth. In working with the heritage of the Scriptures and apostolic tradition, the Fathers of the first few centuries of Christian life stressed the idea of redemptive history.

Sacred history was an important element of theological controversy; the Fathers often held divergent views of such a history. For instance, Origen focused his entire method of exegesis on the tension between the shadow of the Jewish past and the image and reality of the Christian epiphany that would come, while Irenaeus taught that the Fall was an historical event which took place as described in the Book of Genesis and that the entire purpose of redemption was the restoration of the divine image lost, or at least stained, by Adam's rebellious acts.[53]. The Fathers, by means of images and figures, tried to relate the idea of redemptive time to the ordinary experiences of the faithful.

In his Sermon XCI, Leo the Great attempted to induce his flock to a prayerful way of life. Leo draws upon their experience of time to stir their memory to the fact of God's plan, which unfolds every day. The great love of God, as it is exhibited daily by the elements of the cosmos, should behoove men and women to worship with great praise and thanksgiving. He said:

> For the very elements of the world also minister to the exercise of mind and body in holiness, seeing that the distinctly varied revolution of days and months opens for us the different pages of the commands, and thus the seasons also in some sense speak to us of that which the sacred institutions enjoin.[54]

Thomas Aquinas, a medieval master of philosophy and theology, taught in his *Summa Theologiae* that time helps us to learn about eternity.[55] Time was also important to Thomas More, who lived and died in sixteenth century England. In a meditation entitled "On the Remembrance of Death," he expresses the belief that time permits us to move toward death and resurrection.[56]

We might consider the time-notion of a man of this century. Pierre Teilhard deChardin does not consider time in the traditional sense, a homogeneous quantity that is capable of being divided into parts. Instead, he sees time as somehow containing the means of development within itself. In *The Future of Man,* he says,

> ...why not define Time itself as precisely the rise of the Universe into those high latitudes where complexity, concentration, centration and consciousness grow and increase, simultaneously and correlatively.[57]

Teilhard deChardin says that time should be thought of as being dynamic, and not static. For him, as for Henri Bergson, duration could be understood as "existence continuing itself."[58] Jesus Christ is considered by Teilhard deChardin to be not only Lord of the Cosmos, but also truly Lord of the cosmogenesis: he is the principle of all movement and the unifying centre of the world.[59]

> Since Jesus was born, and grew to his full stature, and died, everything has continued to move forward because Christ is not yet fully formed; he has not yet gathered about him the last folds of his robe of flesh and of love which is made of his faithful followers. The mystical Christ has not yet attained to his full growth; and therefore the same is true of the cosmic Christ. Both of these are simultaneously in the state of being and of becoming; and it is from the prolongation of this process of becoming that all created activity ultimately springs.

> Christ is the end-point of the evolution, even the
> natural evolution, of all beings; and therefore
> evolution is holy.[60]

Time and space, according to this Jesuit, are joined so
as to weave the stuff of the universe. All that exists has
an irreversible coherence[61] which is Christ. A Christian
holding to a Teilhardian sense of time would see that
evolution offers a magnificent means of feeling more at
one with God and Creation. It helps one to say to God:
"I love You, not only with my body and my heart and my
soul, but with every fibre of the unifying universe."[62]

For Christians, the Scriptures, the sacraments, and the
apostolate are the human activities that constitute the
instruments for the sanctification of that one unique
time period called the *Annus Domini*.[63] Christians must
constantly be careful not to abstract themselves from life
and human experience as they live out the days of the
Lord.

The Christian Sanctification of Time

The whole mystery of Christ, from his Incarnation to
the day of Pentecost and the expectation of his coming
again, is brought to mind by the Church during the
course of the year.[64] Redeeming the time by distinguish-
ing phases in the ecclesiastical year is an ancient and
hallowed tradition. Borrowings have been made from
both Jewish and pagan sources. From time to time, the
Church has found it necessary to reform the ecclesiastical calendar because the principal mysteries of the
redemption had lost their proper place to special
religious devotions. In our own century, in 1969, Pope
Paul VI approved a new Roman Calendar. The purpose

of the restoration of the liturgical year and the revision of its norms is to allow the faithful, through their faith, hope and love, to share more deeply in the whole mystery of Christ as it unfolds throughout the year. By means of devotional exercises, instruction, prayer, and works of penance and mercy, the Church, according to traditional practices, completes the formation of the faithful during the various seasons of the liturgical year.[65] A revision of the calendar demanded a revision of other areas concerned with the Church's life of prayer. Therefore the Liturgy of the Hours, which will be discussed later in this book, also took on a new format that is in keeping with the new calendar.

The liturgical year opens to the people the riches of the Lord's power and merits so that these are in some way made present at all times, and the people are able to lay hold of them and become filled with saving grace.[66] The church year has several seasons.

The season of Advent is a period of preparation for the coming of Christ. Nowadays the first part focuses on the glorious return of the Lord, his *parousia*, while the second part accents the preparation for the Lord's birth, his incarnation. Yet it is not so much a preparation for Christmas or an expectation of the second coming as it is an anticipation of Christmas and a celebration of the incarnation. It is not so much a reliving of history, but, rather, it is the celebration of a mystery: a present reality containing and mediating salvation.[67] The term "advent" originally had a secular reference to the official reception of royalty to a locality.[68] The celebration of Christ's birth is a festival that came into the Church's liturgy relatively late.[69] The festival of Epiphany commemorates several events in the life of Jesus by which he manifested his divinity: his baptism in the Jordan River by John, the visit of the wise men, and the miracles at the Cana wedding feast.[70] At his birth Christ was seen by a few people. At his epiphany he was seen by others besides his own people; hence he is the manifestation of God's love for all peoples.

The season of Lent is especially a period of introspection and a reflection on the realities of daily life: it is a way of seeing how Christians have been giving and taking. The custom of preparing for the Easter Celebration by fasting developed early. The purpose of Lent has always been two-fold: the people's spiritual renewal by penance, prayer, fasting, and almsgiving, and the preparation of the catechumens for their Easter Vigil baptism. Since the seventh century, Lent has begun on Ash Wednesday.[71] It ends on Holy Thursday.

The Easter Triduum (Holy Thursday, Good Friday, and Easter) is a celebration of Christ's resurrection as well as the feast of our redemption. Easter was already being celebrated during the first and second centuries.[72] The Easter Season, Eastertide, lasts for fifty days until Pentecost, which closes this one single length of festival time. Ordinary Time fills out the remaining weeks in the church year.

In all feasts, pagan, Jewish, or Christian, there is a continuity between the human action and the religious significance of that ritual action. One moves from a natural level to a supernatural level. One might say that

> ...feasts entered the calendar only after dying with Christ and being reborn to a new existence in the Christian Sunday. At any rate, it cannot be denied that the Jewish feasts which were incorporated into the Christian liturgy were at first connected with Sunday. The Sabbath was associated with Christ's death because the rest it prescribed recalled Christ's rest in the tomb so that He might be reborn

31

on Sunday. Even Easter and Pentecost came into Christianity only in connection with the Sunday on which they were celebrated.[73]

The relationship between Sabbath and Sunday and between Jewish and Christian feasts is strong indeed. Perhaps the best way to relate the transition of pagan and Jewish feasts into Christian feasts is to use a chart (see Appendix A).

The Christian liturgy can be regarded as a demonstration of Christian lifestyle and faith. The liturgical year with its several seasons presents the panorama of the historic faith of Christianity throughout the centuries in such a way that it matches the inner experiences of the worshipper.[74]

2

The Seasons and Human Life

Introduction

Men and women celebrate God's presence in their lives at times appropriate to their own growth during their pilgrimage through life. Ancient rites of passage are common to all religions. It is through the initiation rites that someone in a traditional society comes to know and to assume identity.[75]

> The term initiation...denotes a body of rites and oral teachings whose purpose is to produce a decisive alteration in the religious and social status of the person to be initiated. In philosophical terms, initiation is equivalent to a basic change in existential condition; the novice emerges from his ordeal endowed with a totally different being from that which he possessed before his initiation; he has become *another*.[76]

Rites of Passage

Scholars distinguish three basic types of initiations that people may undergo. In most cultures there is some sort of movement from childhood or adolescence to adulthood accompanied by rituals. These "puberty rites" or "tribal initiations" are endured by all the members of that society. Usually some kind of ordeal must be suffered by the initiates, such as circumcision, separation from the mother or the tribe for a period of time, fasting, and the like. The act of initiation is a religious experience by which the initiate is said to undergo an ontic change.

A second type of initiation has to do with individuals entering a secret society or confraternity. Such a society possesses a secret lore, and membership is usually limited to one sex.

There also exists a third level of initiation, and it has to do with an individual's mystical vocation of medicine person or shaman.

> ...we can say that those who submit themselves to the ordeals typical of this third kind of initiation are—whether voluntarily or involuntarily—destined to participate in a more intense religious experience than is accessible to the rest of the community.[77]

Usually there are several phases in an initiation ceremony:

a) the preparation of the "sacred ground," where the initiates will remain in isolation during the festival;

b) the separation of the male novices from their mothers and, in general, from all women;

c) their segregation in the wilderness, or in a special isolated camp, where they will be instructed in the tribal religious traditions;

d) certain operations performed on the novices, usually circumcision, the extraction of a tooth, or other tortuous ordeals.[78]

> The experience of initiatory death and resurrection not only basically changes the neophyte's fundamental mode of being, but at the same time reveals to him the sacredness of human life and of the world by revealing to him the great mystery, common to all religions, that man, with the cosmos, with all forms of life, are the creation of the Gods or of Superhuman Beings.[79]

Other religions (Hinduism, Buddhism, the Greek mystery religions) also have forms of initiation. One can speak of the *Upanayana*, the *Diksha*, or the Tantric Meditations. The *Upanayana* is a puberty rite by which a novice becomes a Brahman of the three highest castes in India. In this ritual the novice is symbolically changed by the teacher into an embryo and is kept in his belly for three nights. The teacher conceives when he puts his hand on the boy's shoulder, and on the third day the boy is reborn spiritually as a Brahman.[80]

In another Brahmic initiatory ritual, the *Diksha*, priests make the candidate into an embryo again by sprinkling him with water (symbolizing sperm); they conduct him to a special shed (symbolizing the womb), cover him with a garment (symbolizing the caul), and dress him in a black antelope skin (symbolizing the placenta). The initiate then closes his hands, casts off the animal skin, and enters the bath and is reborn.[81] Such initiations are a way of "re-doing" things spiritually and symbolically so that new life will be present.

One other type of initiation, which is common to Buddhistic Tantrism, is not so much performed bodily but rather is acted out by the mind in a form of meditation and concentration. The initiate goes through a meditation in which he/she imagines being stripped of flesh and becoming only a skeleton.[82]

> The novice submits himself to an initiatory ordeal by stimulating his imagination to conjure up a terrifying vision which he masters by his power of thought...This is at the same time a post-mortem experience...but through it the novice realizes the emptiness of all posthumous experience, so that he will feel no more fear at the moment of death and will thus escape being reborn on earth.[83]

By means of such rites, a youth is admitted to the society of adults. At the same time, one becomes worthy of some spiritual teaching and spiritual values. The rites prepare one for the new life to be lived. Without the ceremonies one is unable to attain this new mode of existence.

Christianity is no exception to the use of passage rites. Ritually speaking, baptism is the sacrament that permits one to enter a new mode of existence so that one may celebrate the other sacraments of Christian life. Initiation into the Church through baptism must be understood as the beginning of a process by which a person becomes a member of a world-wide society extended throughout time and eternity: the Church in all its fullness. This Church is the people who follow Jesus Christ as he leads them to their destiny: total human fulfillment in God.

Christian baptism has some things in common with other religious rites. There is a period of preparation: catechesis. There is the use of matter: the pouring of water during the recitation of the trinitarian name. During this moment the initiate dies to selfishness and sin and is reborn to new life in Christ. The font has a double symbolism of tomb (death) and womb (the new life of Christ); there are anointings with the holy oils; there is the use of candlelight. All of these symbols speak of a tradition of initiation that has developed throughout the years. Each Rite of the Church, however, has adapted the preparation and actual ceremony according to its own local or regional conditions.

Seasons in the Life of an Individual

One might also speak of the "seasons" in the life of an individual. Just as each season brings about changes in nature, each season of human life also brings its own significant changes. As one develops from infant to child to adolescent to adult to middle-aged adult to senior adult, many important changes are experienced.

> The early years...are characterized almost entirely by growth of the organism and by enlargement, differentiation, and refinement of capacities. The middle and later years are often characterized by the terms "involution" or "senescence," which imply decline, decrement, or loss of function.[84]

Whether by choice, by chemical make-up, or by societal expectations, one responds to life in certain ways at various times.

> The aging individual is, in effect, a responsive and responding nexus for social and sociological judgments. He plays a series of roles, in part determined by age, set out for him by society which has formu-

lated certain expectations of behavior...These roles are played with varying degrees of success and cognition.[85]

It is at the root of Christian faith that there is one life to live—and that life is lived forever. Coming

> into the world we are what we are given, and for many years thereafter parents and grandparents, brothers and sisters, friends and lovers keep giving to us—some more, some less, some hesitantly, some generously. When we can finally stand on our own feet, speak our own words, and express our own unique self in work and love, we realize how much is given to us. But while reaching the height of our cycle, and saying with a great sense of confidence, "I really am," we sense that to fulfill our life we now are called to become parents and grandparents, brothers and sisters, teachers, friends, and lovers ourselves, and to give to others, so that when we leave this world, we can be what we have given.[86]

The psalmist was well aware of the ages of an individual. Poetically, and very beautifully, the writer compares the ways of a child to childlike trust in God:

> Yahweh, my heart is not haughty,
>   I do not set my sights too high.
> I have taken no part in great affairs
>   in wonders beyond my scope.
> No, I hold myself in quiet and silence
>   like a little child in its mother's arms,
>   like a little child, so I keep myself.
> Let Israel hope in Yahweh
>   henceforth and for ever (Ps 131).

And then in old age, despite its physical, emotional, and societal problems, the psalmist continues to trust in God:

> Take pity on me, Yahweh,
>   for I am in trouble.
> Vexation is gnawing away my eyes,
>   my soul is deep within me.
> For my life is worn out with sorrow,
>   and my years with sighs.
> My strength gives way under my misery,
>   and all my bones are wasted away.
> The sheer number of my enemies
>   makes me contemptible,
> loathsome to my neighbours,
>   and my friends shrink from me in horror.
> When people see me in the street
>   they take to their heels.
> I have no more place in their hearts than a corpse,
>   or something lost (Ps 31:9-12).

Religious people, especially Christians, have often traditionally expressed their spiritual life as a pilgrimage through the city of people to heaven, which is the city of God. The Church is a people on pilgrimage reaching out and longing for the heavenly Jerusalem.[87] In this life one prepares for heavenly life by enjoying, by using well, the things of this world because, for the person of prayer, they have eternal value. Even the "little moments" of life lead to salvation, as do the "peak moments," which are the sacraments. Sharing in ordinary conversation, or pouring a friend a cup of coffee, or anxiously doing homework problems are some of these moments. A Christian lives these moments with an underlying consciousness and faith that ultimately they will lead to heavenly fulfillment. For the Christian believer, all of life has something to do with the spiritual life.

"There is no absolute way in the devotional life; there are only different ways."[88] Just as all flowers are not the same, so too the approaches to the spiritual life vary. A certain rhythm, a certain movement, flows through every Christian as he or she travels the road to paradise.

Living Spiritually

God leads people to perfection by the influence of the Holy Spirit so that they might live their lives as disciples of Jesus. One can speak of the "degrees," or stages, within the spiritual life. These degrees are similar to the seasons, which follow one after the other; yet the degrees are different as well. They are points of spiritual process within the context of a person's life with Christ. The natural seasons of Spring, Summer, Autumn, and Winter begin at certain determined times within our yearly calendar. One can say, "Spring has come because the calendar says that the vernal equinox is here." But when one is observing a person's spiritual progress, one cannot say, "Obviously you are on the purgative level because you are twenty years old. By the time you're forty years old you should be on the illuminative level." The spiritual life just does not work quite that way. Great care must be taken by a spiritual director in helping someone to discern where he or she is on the spiritual spectrum at a particular time in life. As there is within the rhythm of the natural year a unit of time that contains the four seasons, so too in the context of a person's whole life there is a rhythm of spiritual progress.

The degrees that one goes through in the ascent to perfection have been classified by one spiritual writer, Adolphe Tanqueray, as the purgative way, the illuminative way, and the unitive way, "...three marked degrees, by which souls who generously correspond to divine grace traverse in the spiritual life."[89] These stages might be compared to a person beginning, advancing toward, and attaining a goal. By a prayerful life, one is able to "pass over" from one degree to the other.

The purgative moment in a person's life, like the other moments, has no specific temporal period; "...the soul's progress...is a vital action, with its ebb and flow; at times the soul presses onward, at times it recedes."[90] To use traditional Roman Catholic language, beginners in the purgative state "habitually live in the state of grace and have a certain desire for perfection, but...have...attachments to venial sin and...fall now and then into grievous faults."[91] Prayer and discipline help beginners on this stage of spiritual existence.

Those in the second degree, the illuminative way, "struggle to adorn themselves with Christ's virtues."[92] They recognize that Jesus is the real center of their lives. Prayer becomes all important.

The third degree, the unitive way, leads to an habitual and intimate union with God through Jesus. Christians in this degree hope to be able to truly say with Saint Paul, "Yet it is no longer I, but Christ living in me" (Gal 2:20). Contemplation, the profound experience of feeling God present in one's whole life, is the goal of the unitive way.

But contemplation is not always easy. It assumes faith in the abiding presence of God. Pierre Teilhard de-Chardin, I believe, was a man who practiced intense contemplation. He recognized God's creation as "the divine milieu" and he was aware of the spiritual power of all matter. For him, the incarnation of Jesus Christ was not something to be relegated to theological discussion only. For him it was a reality to be daily experienced, as this prayer of his clearly indicates:

> Jerusalem, lift up your head. Look at the immense crowds of those who build and those who seek. All over the world, men are toiling—in laboratories, in studios, in deserts, in factories, in the vast social crucible. The ferment that is taking place by their instrumentality in art and science and thought is happening for your sake. Open, then, your arms and your heart, like Christ your Lord, and welcome the waters, the flood and the sap of humanity. Accept it, this sap—without its baptism you will wither, without desire, like a flower out of water; and tend it, since, without your sun, it will disperse itself wildly in sterile shoots...Now the earth can certainly clasp me in her great arms. She can swell me with her life, or draw me back into her dust. She can deck herself with every charm, with every honor, with every mystery. She can intoxicate me with her perfume of tangibility and unit. She can cast me to my knees in expectation of what is maturing in her breast...She has become for me, over and above herself, the body of Him who is and of Him who is coming.[93]

Contemplation means to live as a creature as the best way of achieving illumination. When God the Creator is known, one consents to become with God and through God a creator of oneself, of others, and of the world. This knowledge is at the same time contemplation and love, prayer and action; it is life. To live as a creature is to live together, to *live with* everything else: "All belong to you" (1 Cor 3:23). It means that one is able to regard all creatures as God the Creator regards them[94]; it means that these words of Saint John of the Cross become one's own:

Mine are the heavens and mine is the earth. Mine are the nations, the just are mine, and the sinners. The angels are mine and the Mother of God and all things are mine; and God himself is mine and for me, because Christ is mine and all for me.[95]

The spiritual life is at the same time simple and complex. Prayer is that which allows one to live the spiritual life. "Prayer is watchfulness, docility, openness, and a valiant effort to bring all things back to their source in God.[96] Prayer enables one to pass from degree to degree.

A man who prays is a man standing with his hands open to the world. He knows that God will show himself in the nature which surrounds him, in the people which he meets, in the situations he runs into. He trusts that the world holds God's secret within it, and he expects that secret to be shown to him. Prayer creates that openness where God can give himself to man.[97]

The rhythm of the spiritual life has been perceived in other ways as well. Referring to spiritual growth and its relation to charity, Saint Thomas Aquinas says,

...in spiritual growth the different degrees of charity are made evident by the perceptible effects which charity works in him who possesses it. The first effect of charity is...that man withdraws from sin, and thus the mind of one who possesses charity is mainly intent on becoming cleansed of past sin and avoiding future sin. And because this charity has this effect it is called incipient charity. The second effect is that one who is assured that he is free from sin, exerts himself to achieve good; this is...called progressive charity. The third effect is that one who has been well nourished on the good, comes to

regard it as his natural food and takes pleasure in it
and is satisfied by it. This is perfect charity.[98]

Saint Bonaventure recognizes three degrees of perfection: the lowest, which concerns observance of the commandments; the middle, which has to do with the fulfillment of spiritual counsels insofar as evil is avoided, good is done, and trials are borne; and the highest degree, which has as its goal the deep fruition of eternal joys.[99] A contemporary spiritual writer, Father Henri Nouwen, sees the spiritual life as existing in three moments: the moment between loneliness and solitude when one reaches out to one's innermost self; the moment between hostility and hospitality when one then reaches out to others; and the moment between illusion and prayer when one reaches out to God instead of chasing after vain strivings.[100]

Sacraments are times for worshipping God, for building up the body of Christ, and for making people holy. They have a double, inward-outward character: "...like the Church, the reality of the sacraments is both visible and invisible, a combination of an outward, visible sign which is perceived by the senses and an inward, invisible grace which is not."[101] Christian faith and tradition tell us that the sacraments are visible signs by which God "pours grace into the soul of man, if man places no moral obstacle to that grace. These seven signs contain the grace which they signify, and they confer it through the performance of the rite."[102] The grace of the sacraments helps us to live out our lives as people centered on Christ the Lord.

All the sacraments with their proper catechesis may be considered to be passagelike in nature. Baptism, confirmation, and eucharist together make up the sacraments of Christian initiation:

> The sacraments of baptism, confirmation and the eucharist are the final stage in which the elect come forward and, with their sins forgiven, are admitted into the people of God, receive the adoption of the sons of God, and are led by the Holy Spirit into the promised fullness of time and, in the eucharistic sacrifice and meal, to the banquet of the Kingdom of God.[103]

Candidates move from the catechumenate stage to full sacramental fellowship with the Church. Penance brings one from the moment of individual and community sinfulness to reconciliation with God and the people, to wholeness. Holy Orders intensifies one's commitment to serve Christ and his people in a ministerial way all the days of one's life. Matrimony brings one from the single state to a new life of love in Christ with and for another and others. Anointing of the Sick celebrates the fact of Christ's power over sin and death; the healing ministry of Christ and his people strengthens and prepares one for the life of the resurrection. The sacraments, then are dynamic, not static moments; they are special encounters with the Lord while one is moving, while one is on pilgrimage. They bring one from ordinary time to sacred time, from temporal existence to heavenly existence.

While we live we pass over from one stage of earthly existence to another. John Henry Cardinal Newman once declared that to grow is to change and to have changed often is to have become perfect.[104] We are creatures of great complexity, and therefore our passages are many and varied. We become incorporated into communal and religious living. We recognize that we are more dynamic than static. Our body cells change with the passage of time, and so does our outlook on life. The seasons bring about change and development in nature. The seasons in our lives also speak of transition from one way of thinking and acting to another. And all this happens as the cosmos groans and travails as it gives birth to new forms of existence:

> We are well aware that the whole creation, until this time, has been groaning in labour pains. And not only that: we too, who have the first-fruits of the Spirit even we are groaning inside ourselves, waiting with eagerness for our bodies to be set free (Rm 8:22-24).

3

Worshipping in Time

Introduction

Daily prayer, both public and private, is a vital and necessary element in most religions, and it is offered throughout the course of the day, the week, and the year. Each religious tradition has set times for celebrating its special spiritual truths. Most religious peoples have their own calendars or certain ways of reckoning the proper times for prayer. It would be worthwhile to describe the times of prayer for a few religious cultures in order to see how the day is divided and what kinds of prayer accompany the divisions.

Hindu Prayer

A Brahman's days are filled with prayer and devotion to the deities. At sunrise such a person goes to a stream and touches the purifying waters before worship. This man or woman sits facing east and sprinkles water on the head. After bathing, he or she sprinkles more water on the ground to make it into a "holy seat," and then offers food, flowers, and sandalwood paste sunward. The worshiper celebrates the glory of the deity with a *mantra*, the chanting of a holy text from the Vedas. Upon returning home, the Brahman makes the morning *puja*, or act of worship, to a favorite deity. The family performs *puja* before every meal in order to sanctify the food. The details of the ritual vary according to the particular deity worshipped. *Puja* is performed before midday; late in the day, a temple may be visited where offerings may be placed on the altar. Evening worship is done at sunset; as a sign of respect, the Brahman will touch the floor with the head and slowly depart, walking backward so as not to offend the temple's reigning deity.[105] Generally speaking, Hindus do not usually gather for liturgical prayer at times other than the special festival celebrations. Hinduism is more of an individual religion. Yet in this Hindu way of doing things, devotion, *bhakti*, leads to knowledge and enlightenment. Every time that a devotional exercise is performed during the day, the worshipper is conscious that he or she is one step closer to enlightenment. The *Bhagavad Gita* says:

> Through devotion he comes to know Me,
>   What my measure is, and Who I am, in very truth;
> Then, knowing Me in very truth,
>   He enters into (Me) straightway.
>
> Even though all actions ever
>   He performs, relying on Me,
> By my grace he reaches
>   The eternal, undying station.[106]

Time is an important element in Hindu worship: a well-timed offering is considered to be more effective than a multitude of ill-timed ones.[107] Special injunctions set the proper times of holy days for beginning and ending fasts, taking ceremonial baths, and giving gifts.

> Auspicious times for fulfilling vows, going on pilgrimages, and for all ceremonies must be observed, taking into account the moment, the lunar mansion, the conjunction of the planets, the hour of the day, the day of the month, whether it is bright or dark, the fortnight, the season, and the half year.[108]

The Hindu concept of time is cyclic, or spiral, in character. The Greeks and Romans of ancient times had their own versions of cyclic time; however, Hindu tradition holds that there is an "infinite repetition of the same phenomenon (creation- destruction-new creation)"[109] in each unit of time, whether that unit be a *yuga* (an "age" of so many thousand years of duration), or a *mahayuga* (four "ages" of unequal duration).

> From this cycle without beginning or end, man can wrest himself only by an act of spiritual freedom (for all Indian soteriological solutions can be reduced to preliminary liberation from the cosmic illusion and to spiritual freedom).[110]

Islamic Prayer

Every Muslim must pray five times daily: between dawn and sunrise, at noon, during the afternoon, at sunset, and after nightfall. The *muezzin*, or prayer caller, sings from the minaret: "Allah is great; I testify that there is no god but Allah." Upon hearing this call, the worshipper first performs ablutions, washing the face, the hands up to the elbows, and the feet to the ankles. The worshipper then goes through a regulated series of body movements, standing, bowing, kneeling, and prostrating, and repeats, at least mentally, a prescribed set of religious formulae, always in Arabic and always facing Mecca.[111] The worshipper must be in a state of ritual purity as the *fatihah*, a prayer from the Koran, is recited. On almost every religious occasion, these words are prayed:

> In the name of God, Lord of the worlds, the merciful, the compassionate, the ruler of the Judgement day! You we serve and You we ask for aid. Guide us in the right path, the path of those with whom You are gracious; not of those with whom You are wroth; nor of those who err.[112]

At noon the service is accompanied with recitations from the Koran.

Judaic Prayer

In Solomon's Temple the sacrifices were offered at stated hours of the day: at dawn, at noon, in late afternoon or evening. During these ceremonies prayer was offered to coincide with the sacrifice. In Psalm 141 there is mention of both sacrifice-offering and prayer:

> May my prayer be like incense in your presence,
>   my uplifted hands like the evening sacrifice
>   (Ps 141:2).

It was common for an Israelite to pray at the Temple facing the sanctuary. Those living in places distant from

Jerusalem always turned to the direction of the Temple, for God was believed to reside there in a special way.

The exact times of prayer are difficult to pin down accurately, for the Temple, the synagogue, indeed, the whole Jewish culture, underwent great development. But there are certain indications in the Scriptures: many see Psalm 4 as an evening prayer and Psalm 6 as one that belongs to the morning. Judith 9:1 shows that Judith prayed at the same time as the Temple evening offering of incense. Daniel 6:11 indicates that the prophet prayed three times a day. This time is also attested to in Psalm 55:18. Private prayer seems to have been timed.[113] An organization call *Anshei Ma'amad* was instituted to enable the people to participate in the cult of the Temple, even though they might live a great distance from it. The country was divided into twenty-four sections, and each section was to send delegates to Jerusalem twice a year for one week. The duty of these representatives was to attend the daily services. They would pray and fast four days of the week, from Monday to Thursday. At home, the people of their district would congregate in the synagogue. They would read the first chapter of Genesis, which was divided into six portions, and they would perform the same devotional exercises as their representatives in Jerusalem.[114]

After the destruction of the Temple by the Romans in 70 C.E., all local public prayer was celebrated in the synagogue. By the time of Christ, a certain basic liturgy of the synagogue had come about. The service began with the *Shema Yisrael,* which is a credal recitation of Deuteronomy 6:4-9; the readings of the Scriptures followed. The Torah, the first five books of the Bible, which was divided into about 154 parts, took about three years of consecutive sabbaths to complete. Then came the reading of the *Haftara,* which is the books of the Prophets, and a homily expounded on the readings. Psalms were sung at intervals. The liturgy ended with a benediction:

> May Yahweh bless you and keep you,
> May Yahweh let his face shine upon you and be
>   gracious to you.
> May Yahweh uncover his face to you and bring you
>   peace (Num 6:24-25).

Modern Judaism celebrates prayer in the evening, in the morning, and in the afternoon.

Christian Prayer

Saint Paul reminds Christians to "...pray constantly; and for all things give thanks to God because this is what God expects you to do in Christ Jesus" (1 Th 5:17-18). And this is what Christians have endeavored to do throughout the centuries since Jesus first offered the prayer of his whole life. Traditionally, all Christian groups have gathered for special set prayers at times other than celebrations of the Eucharist. Organized prayer has been a time-honoured institution in the Church. Scheduled prayer has been given a number of names in the past: the Choir Offices, the Book of Hours, the Daily Services, the Divine Office, the Breviary. Nowadays it is called the Liturgy of Hours. It is the prayer that the liturgical churches offer to God as a community through Christ and in union with him. Praise and adoration are its chief purposes.

God's saving work may be celebrated "at all times and in all places" eucharistically, in public prayer, or in private prayer. A brief description of the main elements of the Liturgy of the Hours has been given by a fourth-century noblewoman named Egeria. She once visited the Holy Land and recorded what she saw and heard.[115]

Saint Bernard, the patriarch of Western monasticism, helped to order the daily prayer for his monks. He distributed the psalter over the course of the week and arranged for the entire Scriptures to be read over the course of the year. He included certain scriptural commentaries and sermons by some of the Fathers. In his scheme the night office consisted of at least twelve psalms and it was the same for the daily office—three psalms at each hour. The ancient *lucernarium (licinicon)*, time for lighting the lamps mentioned by Egeria, was split into the two offices of Vespers and Compline.[116]

Byzantine Christians call the Liturgy of the Hours the *horologion*. Their ecclesiastical day begins at sunset in accord with Genesis 1:5: "Evening came and morning came: the first day." According to Byzantine tradition, the daily prayer comprised only evening and dawn services. Later the monks came together on the first, third, sixth, and ninth hours to perform their psalmody together. "Prime" corresponds to the early morning, "tierce" to the forenoon when the market-place begins to fill, "sext" to the heat of noon, and "none" to the late afternoon.[117]

All the weeks of the liturgical year are divided into groups of eight weeks according to the eight Byzantine musical tones (the Cycle of the Octo-Echos), and each week is called by the tone in which the Office of Sunday is chanted.[118]

"Each day is made holy through liturgical celebration of God's people, especially the eucharistic sacrifice and the divine office..."[119] The Roman Catholic Church has an ancient tradition of sanctifying the day by means of ordered times of prayer in common and in private. Such prayer

> takes its unity from the heart of Christ, for our Redeemer desired "that the life he had entered upon in his mortal body with supplications and with his sacrifice should continue without interruption through the ages in his mystical body, which is the Church." Because of this, the prayer of the Church is at the same time "the prayer of Christ and his body to the Father." We must recognize, therefore, as we celebrate the Office, our own voices echoing in Christ, his voice echoing in ours.[120]

The Liturgy of the Hours has traditionally been seen as a way of complementing the Church's eucharistic worship. The Mysteries of the Lord's Table flow into all the hours of our daily life.[121] But over the generations, many changes entered into the structure of the hours so that its basic arrangements became over-complicated and confusing. In order to reform and restore the Divine Office to its fullness, Pope Paul VI, in November 1970, affixed his signature to the Apostolic Constitution, which promulgated the new Liturgy of the Hours. The document says:

> It is the venerable tradition of the universal Church that Lauds as Morning Prayer and Vespers as Evening Prayer are the two hinges on which the day's Office pivots; they are therefore to be considered as the chief hours, and they are to be celebrated as such.[122]

An Office of Readings may be recited at any hour of the day or in conjunction with Morning or Evening Prayer. Those who lead a contemplative life are free to celebrate Midmorning, Midday, and Midafternoon Prayer. Night Prayer is the final prayer of the day.[123]

Set prayer of the Reformed churches is not always easy to discuss because sometimes it is organized for certain hours, as it is in the Roman Catholic and Eastern Traditions, and sometimes it is spontaneous or is part of the Sunday or midweek service. Fundamentalist churches, such as the Baptists and the Pentecostals, have no "liturgical prayer" other than their usual pattern of worship on Sunday. But the Reformation churches run the gamut of a regular Liturgy of the Hours to mere traces of it in their tradition. They too, are still going through liturgical renewal; it is not fair to predict what they will do, but their interest in the liturgical renewal of Roman Catholics seems to have had some influence on their own traditions.

Presbyterians have orders of worship for mornings and evening services; they are usually extended liturgies of the Word. Sometimes the Lord's Supper is included on Sundays. Methodists have an order for Morning Prayer. Lutherans celebrate Matins and Vespers. Of all the Reformed churches, it would seem that Episcopalians have the greatest sense of a Liturgy of the Hours. Though they are still in the process of liturgical restoration, they now have new orders for prayer in the morning, at noon, and at night. These rites are similar to the present Roman Catholic revision of the Liturgy of the Hours. Some ecumenical monastic communities, like the one at Taize, France, draw from Roman Catholic, Orthodox, and Protestant traditions for their daily prayer (see Appendix B).

The structure for prayer in the different churches is regular, but because Christians have all of the Scriptures as their resource, the readings and the psalms and the hymns change, as do the prayers, according to the theme of the liturgical season. They reflect this spirit of the liturgical season, and often, though not always, mirror an aspect of kenosis or plerosis that is present in the natural season.[124]

By dividing the day into sections in which prayers of praise and adoration and thanksgiving and petition are said, the individual day is made holy; daily celebration of prayer makes the week and the year holy as well. All time becomes sacred because of this continual prayer-response to the saving actions of Jesus Christ. It is by means of rhythmical and ordered prayer that time is sanctified and dedicated to God, and through this process people encounter God and enter into communion with God.

4

Worship and the Material Creation

Introduction

Saint John's Gospel prologue tells us: "In the beginning was the Word: the Word was with God and the Word was God" (Jn 1:1). At Creation a reality other than God came to be. This reality of life has its origin in God. It is difficult to imagine nothing or non-existence. In order to speak of it, one must refer to something that exists and then negate that existence. The problem is that non-being, nothing, or non-existence, refers outside of our space and time reality. "In the beginning" God created and being then came to be. God's loving presence was infused into that which was created so that Creation could continue its own distinct existence. God sent Creation into being, and it continues to exist in itself dependent on God and yet distinct from God. The action of God on the world is in two moments. God's prime action is the setting forth of reality itself: Creation. God is its creator; this means that everything is a result of God's action. Evolution is God's second action on the world: God allows it to continue to exist in time and space categories. God is a sustainer. One may suppose that with Creation time and space began, and with evolution time and space continue. Creation and evolution are terms used to describe the beginning of existence and its continuance.

When one is thinking of God as Creator, one might ponder the scripture of Genesis: "In the beginning God created..." (Gn 1:1). When one is meditating on the mystery of God's continuing sustaining influence in Creation, one can marvel as it evolves back to God. By this creative act, God flings the world into existence. By evolution it finds its way back to God. Creation has a center; our Christian tradition says that Jesus Christ is the organic center of the entire universe,

> that is to say, the center not only of the earth and mankind, but of Sirius and Andromeda, of the angels, of all the realities on which we are physically dependent, whether in a close or distant relationship (and that, in all probability, means the center of all participated being).[125]

If this is so, then by means of Creation, God in Christ offers life to people. When people realize their creaturehood, they make attempts to recognize the Creator. This is what we call worship. Then as the poets of Creation, we chant to God words similar to those of Saint Augustine: "...our hearts are restless until they begin to find rest in You."[126] Most peoples, Christian and other, have taken a mystic approach to Creation by using it as a stepping-stone to union with the Creator.

Pantheism

Prayer is offered by all religious peoples with and through matter. Some religions would have it that God and the universe are two forms of the same thing as they constantly change into one another. Pantheism seems to express this idea. Judaeo-Christianity and some other religious systems would hold that God and the universe are distinct. God, however, can be present in and through Creation. It is one thing to worship God with and through matter, and it is quite another thing to call matter God.

Pantheism, or as it is called in philosophy, monism, holds the view that all that is, insofar as it is at all, is identical with God. The pantheist would say that creatures are made, not out of matter, but are made out of God, for creaturely existence is a manifestation of the divine.[127]

Taoism seems to put forth a religious system that is "Godless" in the usual sense of the word. Nature seems to be "worshipped." One is asked to return to "the un- carved block" to flow with "what is." The *Tao Teh Ching* says:

> Tao is all-pervading, and its use is inexhaustible!
> Fathomless!
> Like the fountain-head of all things.
> Its sharp edges rounded off,
> Its tangles untied,
> Its light tempered,
> Its turmoil submerged,
> Yet crystal clear like still water it seems to remain,
> I do not know whose Son it is,
> An image of what existed before God.[128]

Hinduism, in its most rudimentary form, seems to identify God with matter. Matter is considered to be eternal, a form of God—external clothing, so to speak. Yet since Deity, or Brahma, is so vast a concept, popular deities are conceived of and worshipped because they are easier to approach than the Ultimate Cosmic Force. And so numerous temples dedicated to Krishna, Vishnu, Shiva, and the other gods are found.

Nature Religions

Many religions find God through nature. Sun gods, moon gods, spirits in the trees and in the waters, and a whole host of other deities have been worshipped for thousands of years. The personification of nature itself as a deity is common to many religions. These religions are called fertility religions. Fertility religions call for symbolic male and female deities. Usually the symbolism is the same: man represents God, woman represents earth and Creation. Almost without exception, a female deity rules over the kingdom of animals and plants. This agricultural goddess has total sway over nature. She appears as mistress of life and as virgin and mother. In Mesopotamia male deities were superior to her, while in Cretan religion and its Roman and Greek descendants she definitely was not subordinate. The cult of the Great Mother, *Magna Mater*, has a long history.[129]

The rites symbolized the influence of the Great Mother on the annual death and resurrection of vegetation. It was believed that there was a mystical connection between the fertility of the soil and the creative force of a woman. The Romans borrowed from many of the Greek rites of Demeter and elaborated on them. A part of the ceremonies was the ritual marriage, or hierogamy, of the priest and priestess. It was a symbol of the marriage of heaven and earth. At times the sacred orgy was performed by special cult personnel to ensure growth of the crops. Even today in some cultures the orgy has an important ritual function. It sets flowing the sacred energy of life; an unbounded sexual frenzy on earth corresponds to the union of the mystical divine couple, the god of creation and the goddess of the earth. In nature religions it was thought, and sometimes is thought today, that whatever holy actions are done by the most people together will be the most effective. Female fertility was thought to affect crop fertility, while it was also understood at the same time that the energy within the crops was an aid to human conception.[130]

Celebrations in the fields were held because of belief in a particular kind of reciprocity: if the celebrants engaged in rituals of fertility on the land where seeds had been planted, then the gods would share their divine life-giving power and allow the crops of believers to grow. In engaging in sexual rites of fertility, they were acting out their religious mythology in sacred time. During the holy moments of these rites, heavenly power would be put into the earth so that the crops would grow. Therefore,

> ...any rite or drama aiming at the regeneration of a "force" is itself the repetition of a primal creative act, which took place *ab initio*. A regeneration sacrifice is a ritual "repetition" of the creation...The ritual makes creation over again; the force at work in plants is reborn by suspending time and returning to the first moment of the fullness of creation.[131]

Native American religion is usually Earth-Mother oriented. In the 1860s Smohalla of the Wanapum People called upon his people to abandon White teachings and return to native concepts. One time he declared to some Whites:

> You ask me to plow the ground. Shall I take a knife and tear my mother's breast? Then when I die she will not take me to her bosom to rest. You ask me to dig for stone. Shall I dig under her skin for her bones? Then when I die I cannot enter her body to be born again. You ask me to cut grass and make hay and sell it and be rich like white men. But how dare I cut off my mother's hair?[132]

Modern men and women in North America find it difficult to relate to nature on so intimate a level as Smohalla. Unlike Native Americans, we tend to de-personalize and "thing-ify" nature. Native Americans have the greatest of respect for Mother Earth and all of nature. An appreciation for the sacred in nature demands proper use of nature and her bounty.[133]

Fertility rites and rites of the earth have roots in Paleolithic times. Hunting most usually was the task of the man, but the role of the woman was all important because she was the repository of tradition, the guardian of the home around the fire and the symbol of sexual fecundity.[134] It seems quite easy for some people to believe that a female deity should be in charge of nature. Religious studies have indicated that the earliest matriarchal societies celebrated a mother goddess. Such societies probably are older than those that highly regarded totemic male gods.[135] Witchcraft is a version of fertility religion with male and female counterparts who interact ritually in order to keep the life balance in proper order.

Hebrew Religion

Ancient Israel celebrated the wonderful deeds of God as Lord of history, but she also sang of this lordship over the world and the cosmic forces. Psalm 29 praises Yahweh as Lord of the storm: the frightful power of the storm was considered to be a manifestation of divine force and an invitation to join with the heavenly worship of Yahweh:[136]

> Yahweh's voice over the waters,
>   the God of glory thunders;
>   Yahweh over the countless waters!
> Yahweh's voice in power,
>   Yahweh's voice in splendour;
> Yahweh's voice shatters cedars of Lebanon...
> Yahweh's voice carves out lightning-shafts.
>   Yahweh's voice convulses the desert,
>   Yahweh's voice convulses the desert of Kadesh,
> Yahweh's voice convulses the terebinths, strips
>   forests bare.
> In his palace all cry, "Glory!" (Ps 29:3-5,7,9).

Psalm 19 considers the stars as witnesses of God's sovereignty and signs of God's power. Unlike the pagans, who divinized the heavenly bodies, the Israelites considered them to be models of authentic praise of God by their obedience to an eternal law:[137]

> The heavens declare the glory of God,
>   the vault of heaven proclaims his handiwork;
> day discourses of it to day,
>   night to night hands on the knowledge,
> No utterance at all, no speech,
>   not a sound to be heard,
> but from the entire earth the design stands out,
>   this message reaches the whole world.

High above, he pitched his tent for the sun,
    who comes forth from his pavilion like a
    bridegroom,
    delights like a champion in the course to be run.
Rising on the one horizon,
    he runs his circuit to the other,
    and nothing can escape his heat.

The Law of Yahweh is perfect,
    refreshment to the soul;
the decree of Yahweh is trustworthy
    wisdom for the simple (Ps 19:1-7).

Psalm 148 exhorts the whole cosmos to praise Yahweh because he has made all creatures, and because his works declare his name, his power, his wisdom, and his grace:

Alleluia!
Praise Yahweh from the heavens,
    praise him in the heights.
Praise him, all his angels,
    praise him, all his host!
Praise him, sun and moon,
    praise him, all shining stars,
praise him, highest heavens,
    praise him, waters above the heavens.
Let them praise the name of Yahweh
    at whose command they were made;
he established them for ever and ever
    by an unchanging decree.

Praise Yahweh from the earth,
    sea-monsters and all the depths,
fire and hail, snow and mist,
    storm-winds that obey his word,
mountains and every hill,
    orchards and every cedar,

wild animals and all cattle,
  reptiles and winged birds,

kings of the earth and all nations
  princes and all judges on earth,
young men and girls,
  old people and children together,
Let them praise the name of Yahweh,
  for his name alone is sublime,
his splendour transcends earth and heaven.
  For he heightens the strength of his people,
to the praise of all his faithful,
  the children of Israel, the people close to him
  (Ps 148).

It would seem that the psalmist is a mystic. The psalm-ist definitely perceives both God's transcendence and God's immanence. This sacred writer knows that Yah-weh is above and beyond his Creation, and yet Yahweh is very much a part of it. Creation experiences God's *shekinah*, God's presence, God's "indwellingness." The writer of the psalms possesses a deep consciousness of the activity of Yahweh within the dimensions of God's Creation. The psalmist knows, too, that human beings have a very comfortable place in God's scheme of things:

...you have made him little less than a god, you have crowned him with glory and beauty, made him lord of the work of your hands, put all things under his feet... (Ps 8:5-6).

Just as the Christian is asked to look beyond the bread which is eaten and the wine which is drunk to see the Saviour and the Lord, so the psalmist scans the heavens and the earth and sees the work of the one who so beautifully brings everything into existence and who so marvelously renews the Creation daily. The psalmist reflects not only personal experience, but also the experience of others (Israel) who perceive God's presence:

Our God is in heaven,
    he creates whatever he chooses... (Ps 115:3).

and of still others (the nations) who do not:

They have idols of silver and gold,
    made by human hands.
These have mouths but say nothing,
    have eyes but see nothing,
have ears but hear nothing,
    have noses but smell nothing.
They have hands but cannot feel,
    have feet but cannot walk,
    no sound comes from their throats.
Their makers will end up like them,
    everyone who relies on them (Ps 115:4-8).

It would seem that minds

are conditioned by such factors as heredity, history, and environment...so the clear but undifferentiated and formless vision, seen at the Primary level of awareness, as it passes through the medium of the mind, is distorted and colored. The result is...that we find different schools of thought, different theological and philosophical systems, different value-judgements, and different art forms.[138]

The psalmist's mind was most certainly conditioned by the perception of Yahweh's Creation. The mind of the Christian is shaped by a similar perception of sheer wonderment at the redemptive work of Jesus in the universe.

Christian Religion

Christians have usually avoided the thorny problem of excessively identifying with nature so that worship becomes adoration of the forces within nature. Devotees of the fertility religions, the initiates of the Greek and Roman mysteries

> were eminently amenable to the allurements of a doctrine that deified the whole of physical and tangible reality. The gods were everywhere, and they mingled in every act of life; the fire that cooked the food and warmed the bodies of the faithful, the water that allayed their thirst and cleansed their persons, the very air that they breathed, and the light that illumined their paths were the objects of their adoration.[139]

Instead, Christ himself has been worshipped by Christians through, with, and in nature. His presence is in nature, but one might safely say in the same breath that his presence is also in heaven. In other words, he is immanently present in Creation, yet he transcends the limits of the cosmos. The Christian doctrines of the incarnation and the resurrection speak of his powers of immanence and transcendence. Nature religions might preach immortality, the lastingness of the soul, but Christianity preaches the resurrection of Christ and his brothers and sisters:

> ...the resurrection of Christ is not one instance of resurrection in general...rather it is the unique event flowing from Christ's nature and death that...provides the foundation for the resurrection of those whom he has redeemed.[140]

The rites of the Easter Vigil most profoundly speak of
the plan and execution of God's action of saving people
from everlasting death in order to bestow on them an
everlasting and most exalted life in Jesus. Jesus, the Son
of Mary, the one who first rose from the dead, is greeted
in the new light and thanks are given to him through
the paschal candle. The universe and the whole Church
are called upon to rejoice. The work of God is
proclaimed so that the faithful can see how God has
been Saviour down through the ages. Praises are sung
to Jesus the hero of the human race, the victor over
death. Then the faithful commune with him and with
each other, and in the act of communing the victory is
shared.

At this festal time, matter is used as sign and symbol.
Matter is not deified, but is used in such a manner that
the faithful can look beyond it to the mysteries that it
describes. The Easter Vigil with its mood of waiting and
watching gives way to a mood of deep joy. The believers
are asked to take light from the Light who never fades,
to listen to words as the Word becomes apparent to the
hearers, to bestow on others the Life that has been
given already to the believers, and to eat the bread and
drink the wine of the Lord's own Passover from death to
life, to share at that holy time Jesus' victory over sin. In
all of this, matter is utilized.

God's life is like a field of power into which we are
transplanted by the death and resurrection of Jesus.[141]
This field of power, an effect of the paschal mystery, surrounds individuals and it flows through Creation because it is the power of Jesus; it has no limitation for it
is the life-giving power of divinity. The power of Jesus,
to use the words of the Easter Proclamation, "dispels all
evil, washes guilt away, restores lost innocence, brings
mourners joy; it casts out hatred, brings us peace, and

humbles earthly pride." The power of Jesus to save and to raise up is extended in time and in space. He is, as the hymn says, "joy for all ages."[142] Jesus extends this power to his brothers and sisters by revealing himself to them. He does this in a variety of ways.

Jesus, the Lord of life, permeates the world. By his incarnation, he became a part of the universe. In taking on human flesh, he grafted himself to the universe forever. Pierre Teilhard deChardin puts it this way:

> The Redeemer could penetrate the stuff of the cosmos, could pour himself into the life-blood of the universe, only by first dissolving himself in matter, later to be reborn from it...It is because Christ was "inoculated" in matter that he can no longer be dissociated from the growth of Spirit; that he could henceforth be torn away from it only by rocking the foundations of the universe.[143]

By means of his resurrection from the dead, Christ comes to radiate over the whole universe as consciousness and power and activity. The Church, as the brothers and sisters of the Risen Lord, is the sign of this power and the mediator of this power. Therefore, he also fills the Church with his presence. The Second Vatican Council's *Constitution on the Sacred Liturgy* says:

> ...Christ is always present in his Church, especially in her liturgical celebrations. He is present in the sacrifice of the Mass, not only in the person of the minister, "the same one now offering, through the ministry of priests, who formerly offered himself on the cross," but especially under the Eucharistic species. By His power He is present in the sacraments, so that when a man baptizes it is really Christ Himself who baptizes. He is present in His

word, since it is He Himself who speaks when the holy Scriptures are read in the Church. He is present, finally, when the Church prays and sings, for He promised: "Where two or three are gathered together for my sake, there am I in the midst of them" (Mt 18:20).

Christ indeed always associates the Church with himself in the truly great work of giving perfect praise to God and making men and women holy.[144]

Christ and Matter

Christ has fundamentally taken up his dwelling in matter in order to communicate with his kin the love of the Father. He is brother to the earth and to the trees and the rain and every other inhabitant of the universe. He has most assuredly pitched his tent among his people who are born of both the earth and the Spirit. The sacred rites of Christian people celebrate his two-fold presence.

The New Testament authors knew that something new was happening to the heavens and to the earth because of Christ. He was known as Redeemer; thus from apostolic days it was understood that he had a hand in Creation and the renewing of Creation. There exists what might be termed creation-imagery in the New Testament Scriptures, a few examples of which are mentioned here:

> The one who so freely provides seed for the sower and food to eat will provide you with ample store of seed for sowing and make the harvest of your uprightness a bigger one (2 Cor 9:10).

> You have put on a new self which will progress
> toward true knowledge the more it is renewed in
> the image of its creator (Col 3:10).

> We are God's work of art, created in Christ Jesus...
> (Eph 2:10).

> By his own choice he gave birth to us by the mes-
> sage of the truth so that we should be a sort of first
> fruits of all his creation (Jas 1:18).

The writers of the New Testament were grounded in a
rich Hebrew heritage, which recognized God as Creator.
In speaking of Christ, they were handing on the tradition that had been given them. To speak of Jesus is also
to speak of the Creator.[145]

When the first people were created, blessings came
forth from the Creator, blessings of life and abundance:

> God blessed them saying to them, "Be fruitful, mul-
> tiply, fill the earth and subdue it. Be masters of the
> fish of the sea, the birds of heaven and all the living
> creatures that move (Gn 1:28).

Now, in Christ, new blessings come forth:

> Blessed be God the Father of our Lord Jesus Christ,
> who has blessed us with all the spiritual blessings
> of heaven in Christ (Eph 1:3).

The spiritual blessings of Christ do not end at death
but continue eternally. The blessings are not only
material and temporal blessings, blessings of this earth,
but they are blessings that begin on earth and last
forever. The blessings have to do with redemption from
sin and the new life that comes from redemption. Jesus
Christ, the new Adam, has been entrusted with the mis-

sion of bringing the universe into a state of unity and harmony. He brings the whole created cosmos into a state of blessedness, of wholeness.

The Jesus of the Gospels carries out God's work of blessing. He heals and restores to life what God has created by helping the sick, by feeding the hungry, and by curing the spiritually dying in the forgiveness of their sins. At his ascension Jesus continued the Hebrew Scriptures tradition of blessing.[146] This was his last act on earth:

> Then he took them out as far as the outskirts of Bethany, and raising up his hands he blessed them. Now as he blessed them, he withdrew from them and was carried up to heaven (Lk 24:50-52).

Saint Paul speaks of Creation and the need for the redemption of the cosmos, but he does so from the point of view of humankind as the new creature in Christ.[147] Here are a few passages suggesting the change in Creation due to Christ.

> It is God who said, "Let light shine out of darkness," that has shone into our hearts to enlighten them with knowledge of God's glory, the glory of the face of Christ (2 Cor 4:6).

> It is not being circumcised or uncircumcised that matters; but what matters is a new creation (Gal 6:15).

> So for anyone who is in Christ, there is a new creation; the old order is gone, and a new being is there to see. It is all God's work (2 Cor 5:17-18).

Jesus Christ and his redeemed people and the redeemed cosmos are the new second creation of God, highly exalted because of the love of God's son. Redemption includes the physical Creation by virtue of the fact that it is the locus of humankind.[148]

As the Good News of Jesus Christ was brought from the Semitic world to the world of Hellenistic thought, new understandings of the nature of Christ and his bond with Creation came about. The heresies that had to do with the nature of Christ brought new questions to the minds of Christians. Perhaps it would be well to mention briefly what some of the Fathers had to say about Christ and Creation.

Justin the Martyr discusses Christ as the Logos; he is regarded as God's agent in Creation and revelation. Justin quotes Socrates as saying, "It is not an easy matter to find the father and creator of all things, nor when he is found, is it safe to announce him to all men"; he then immediately responds by saying that Christ made him known through his own power.[149]

Irenaeus of Lyons says in his work *Against Heresies* that Christ is the head of both the visible and invisible realms.[150]

Athanasius, the champion against the Arians of the fourth century, stresses that the flesh of Christ sends forth his saving power to all the universe.[151]

Another fighter of the Arian heresy, Cyril of Jerusalem, once said of Jesus: "He is Maker first and Lord second. First he made all things by the Father's will, and thereafter is Lord of all he made."[152]

John Damascene probably best proclaims the fact of Jesus' reigning over matter. He says:

> I honor all matter and venerate it. Through it, filled, as it were, with a divine power and grace, my salvation has come to me. Was not the thrice happy and thrice blessed wood of the cross matter? Was not the sacred and holy mountain of Calvary matter?

What of the life-giving rock, the holy sepulchre, the Source of our resurrection: was it not matter? Is not the blessed table matter which gives us the bread of life? Are not the gold and silver matter, out of which crosses and altarplates and chalices are made? And before all these things, is not the body and blood of our Lord matter?...Do not despise matter, for it is not despicable.[153]

The Fathers of the Church cherished matter because it mediated the power of the Risen Lord to them. Matter was used in the liturgy; matter was carried about; Christians moved around in matter; matter was everywhere, and they understood that Christ was everywhere as well.

Rogation Days

Christians have always been good at adapting to the elements within a culture. The ancient Romans had annual processions which served as supplications either for blessings from the gods on the fruits of the earth or to avert calamities.[154] During these processions sacrifices were made to the god Robigius. Since the ceremony was for halting of blight, *robigo*, from the crops, this day was called *Robigalia*. Christians took over this custom and baptized it. Our Rogation Days are a form of the ancient times of litanies of supplication. These litanies were instituted to implore the blessings of God on the fruits of the earth. The custom was to recite them in the Spring, the season of the late frosts. There was a propitiatory sacrifice offered on the cultivated lands, which gave promise of the future harvest. The faithful would process around the fields, chanting and invoking the protection of God, the angels, and the saints.[155] Christian Rome celebrated this time on April

25, the day when the pagan Romans used to celebrate the *Robigalia*. The Christian procession even followed the basic pagan route.[156] Rogation Days were

> a time to see God again in things visible like the new leaves on the trees and the new green grass, and in the promise of what is invisible, like the seed buried in the brown earth or the bulb in the flower pot's drab little womb.[157]

In keeping with an orthodox understanding that the things of the earth are good because Christ is Lord of Creation, the Church developed special seasons of prayer for the increase of the earth. The Roman Rite used to observe a week of solemn prayer and fasting four times a year: the Wednesday, Friday, and Saturday of the third week of Advent; the first week of Lent; the week after Pentecost; the middle week in September. The origin of these four penitential seasons is obscure, but they seem to have been connected with the rhythms of agricultural life.[158]

> These ember days represent the Christian transformation of the pagan seasons of prayers for the fruits of the earth which took place three times a year: once at the beginning of summer (the wheat harvest); one towards the end of summer (the wine harvest); and the most important of all in the week before the winter solstice, the *feriae sementinae*, or festival of sowing. It is true that now there are four sets of Ember days, but originally there were three and these at the approximate time that the pagans celebrated their days. The Lenten Ember days are a late addition.[159]

Special days for crop blessings were important for the medieval times because of the peoples' major dependence upon agriculture.

One of the chief characteristics of the Middle Ages is the fact that it was marked by the Christian faith, which gave order to the spiritual beliefs of all its members.[160] In the 13th century, Saint Thomas Aquinas taught about the great order in Creation. For him, things in this universe related to one another and all things in this universe related to God. In Thomas' scheme the end, or goal, of all things is their perfection in God. God is the one who makes sense of the universe. This great theologian says that God is related to the universe much the same way as the body is to the spirit.[161]

Saint Francis of Assisi, a man of his times, spoke of the joys to be found in nature and the need for people to live as brothers and sisters of the earth and of the Lord Jesus. His "Song of the Sun" blessed the beauties of God's Creation.[162] This saint saw Jesus Christ in the ordered beauty of the Creation.

Rites of Blessing

When the Israelites blessed, they were primarily giving praise and thanks to God. God blesses humans with his gifts, and his children bless him by recognizing where all gifts ultimately come from. There were different types of Old Testament blessings. The patriarchs were given a special blessing of fecundity: "Be fruitful, multiply, fill the earth and subdue it" (Gn 1:28); God blessed Noah and his sons and said to them, "Breed, multiply, and fill the earth" (Gn 9:1), and they passed this blessing down to their offspring. Priests blessed the people:

Yahweh spoke to Moses and said, "Speak to Aaron
and his sons and say: This is how you must bless
the Israelites. You will say to them:

May Yahweh bless you and keep you.
May Yahweh let his face shine on you and be
    gracious to you.
May Yahweh show you his face and bring you
    peace."

This is how they must call down my name on the Israelites, and then I shall bless them"
(Num 6:22-27).

The Church pronounces blessings upon people and
things. Any blessings, whether of fields or of religious
images, if they are to be relevantly Christian should
bring out the fact that God's act of redemption is with
and through matter. Therefore, Christians should come
to understand that the objects blessed are a reminder,
or sign, that the work of the kingdom is going on and
that the ones participating in the blessing should be
sharing actively in this work of redeeming the whole
universe.

Sacred Space

Religious people always try to center themselves:

If the world is to be lived in, it must be founded
and no world can come to birth in the chaos of
homogeneity and relativity of profane space. The
discovery of a fixed point—the center—is
equivalent to the creation of the world.[163]

In traditional societies a sacred place constitutes a break in the sameness of space. The break is symbolized by an opening by which passage from one cosmic region to another is made possible. For instance, one might have to go from earth to heaven or from earth to the underworld.

Communication with heaven is expressed by certain images, all of which refer to the center of the world: the *axis mundi*, the pillar or universal column, the ladder (Jacob's Ladder in Gn 28:12-13), the mountain (Zion, Gerizim), the tree, the vine. Around the cosmic axis lies the world.[164]

Every spatial hierophany, or consecration of a place, is equivalent to a cosmogony. Religious people have the desire to live in a pure and holy cosmos, as it was in the beginning, as it was when it came from the hands of the Creator.[165]

A temple is an image of the sanctified cosmos; it is an earthly copy of what exists in heaven. Solomon built his Temple after the celestial model:

> You have bidden me build a temple on your holy mountain, and an altar in the city where you have pitched your tent, a copy of the holy Tent which you prepared at the beginning (Wis 9:8).

In Catholicism the basilica and the cathedral continue this symbolism: The four sides of the building, especially if it is cruciform, symbolize the four cardinal directions. The interior of it is the universe; the sanctuary is heaven.

Architecture determines the boundaries of sacred space, but nature itself can be used to set the limits of holy ground outdoors. A grove of pine trees, an oasis, a cave, a circle of tipis, a grouping of monolithic stones like those at Stonehenge in England, a riverbank, or a mountaintop can be the specific setting for a holy site after appropriate ritual attention has been given. On the symbolic level, a holy site can be male or female; it can be phallic or womblike. Freudian symbolism, as applied to the religious use of objects, would say that trees, mountaintops, and spired churches are phallic and represent a people's reaching toward their deity who has his abode in the heavens. Caves, groves of trees, low places, and circular places of worship are more uteric and represent a people's communication with the female deity whose abode is the earth.

In Australia the Achilpa People carry a sacred pole with them as they travel. They choose the direction they are to take by seeing which way the pole slants. In mythical times Numbakula, their deity, cosmicized their future territory, created their Ancestor, and established their ways of doing things. He fashioned the sacred pole from the trunk of a gum tree and, after anointing it with blood, climbed it and disappeared into the sky. As the people move about, their sacred pole becomes their cosmic axis, with the result that the territory around it becomes a part of their sacred world and is therefore, "livable." This allows them to always be in "their world" while at the same time being in contact with the sky into which their god vanished.[166]

It is important to prepare an area for worship. Our religious nature seems to demand that ordinary space be somehow sanctified. Sacred ground plays an essential role in Australian initiation ceremonies because it represents the image of the primordial world as it was when the god was on earth. As prepared by the Kamilaroi, the ground consists of two circles. The larger one is seventy feet in diameter and has a nine foot central pole crested with emu feathers. In the smaller circle there are two young trees fixed in the ground with their roots in the air. Two older men climb them and chant the traditions of the ceremony. These trees are anointed with blood, a symbol of life. The two circles are connected by a path, and on either side of the path are a number of figures which are either drawn on the ground or are modeled in clay. The larger one, fifteen feet in height, represents the supreme being, Baiamai; a couple represents the mythical ancestors, and a group of twelve human figures stands for the young men who were with the god in his first camp. Other figures represent animals and nests. The ground represents his first camp, the ones who were with him while there, and the gifts which he presented to them.

The Bushongo tribe of Africa also prepare the ground for puberty rites. A long ditch is dug, in which there are four niches. Four men hide in there, disguised respectively as a leopard, a warrior, a smith, and a monkey. The novices are made to walk through the ditch, which represents the path of life: at a certain moment they fall into a pool of water, which represents the death of their old selves.

Another ceremony, the *Ganda*, is still more terrifying. A man disappears into a tunnel and shakes several poles whose tops can be seen from a great distance. The novices believe that he has been attacked by the spirits in the tunnel and is fighting for his life. After secretly rubbing his body with goat's blood, the man comes out of the tunnel as if he were severely wounded and exhausted. He collapses on the ground, and the other men immediately carry him far away from the spot. The novices are then ordered to enter the tunnel, one after the other. In their great fear, they ask to be dispensed. The master of the initiation consents in return for the payment of a certain sum.[167]

For the Sun Dance of the Cheyenne People the ground must be prepared. The ceremony itself is a way of renewing the world. The dance lodge is built according to the mythical tradition. The lodge, a sixteen-sided polyhedron, is about fifty feet in diameter and consists of a central pole and sixteen posts with projecting beams touching the central pole. All the poles are crotched at the top (see Appendix C). Untrimmed saplings laid against the poles provide shade for the participants.[168]

The four days in this "lone tipi" are filled with symbolic imagery and actions portraying earth renewal and continuance. Five separate "earths" are successively smoothed out on the ground. A buffalo skull is ritually consecrated by the insertion of balls of water-grass in the eye sockets and nostrils. Many special pipe cleaners, sticks with wads of buffalo hair, represent the life-sustaining buffalo, and must be changed after the rituals at each "earth" because they would lose some of the earth's power of growth if moved from one to the other.[169] Symbolically speaking, the central crotched pole represents our reflection of the oneness in the universe as it is brought about by the Great Spirit. The other poles represent all the people who, in their own way, have come to dance the dance of life's harmony.[170]

It would seem that Christianity has limited the use of sacred space outdoors. Crop blessings, blessings of the fishing fleets, "living rosaries," city flower festivals, and May processions seem to account for Western Christianity's limited use of God's outdoors.

"Things of the earth" sign forth their Maker. When we Christians begin to really recognize this, our worship will be much enhanced. Brave Buffalo, a Sioux, speaks well of certain forms of what might be called "holy matter":

...I looked at the land and the rivers, the sky above, and the animals around me and could not fail to realize that they were made by some great power. I was so anxious to understand this power...I looked at the moss-covered stones; some of them seemed to have the features of a man, but they could not answer me. Then I had a dream, and in my dream one of these small round stones appeared to me and told me that the maker of all was Wakan tanka, and that in order to honor him I must honor his works in nature...

In all my life I have been faithful to the sacred stones. I have lived according to their requirements and they have helped me in all my troubles.[171]

There should be a change in our attitude toward nature so that we make sure that we praise God with "everything that has breath" (Ps 150). Joyful use of created matter should make for joyful living in abundance. The hills and the valleys are most suitable for celebrating the Lord's death and resurrection; in fact, all places can and should be utilized in the proclamation and celebration of the message of the Living Lord.

Not just the language but the place of worship may need reorienting. Prayer offered in a gigantic nuclear laboratory or on a launching-pad, or under the shadow of a gargantuan cyclotron...may speak in the new language. In offices and clubs, on ski slopes or in basketball courts, not the clerical figure performing his liturgical role, but the whole group of laymen lifting their allegiance in vernacular phrases right where they work or play, can be a worthy relating to the modern milieu.[172]

Sacred Dance

Worship requires physical, verbal, and mental effort. The physical effort is concerned with the proper condition, posture, and use of the body, as well as with the proper arrangement and use of the materials involved in worship. By acting out one's inner experiences, one is able to gain clarity about the nature of images generated in one's own psyche, through which one is able to relate to outward creation.[173]

Ritual drama is acted out in sacred dance, and it is addressed to the deity always. It may be a ritual of praise and thanksgiving, or it may be secular, even for sheer fun; but the relation to the spiritual is always present.[174] The elements of sacred dance include musical rhythm, usually the drum, song, body ornamentation, and the legends. Dance, a part of the whole ceremonial liturgy in a culture, helps to re-present the reality of the spirit dimension.

Just as the body was understood to possess certain religious reference, so did space outside the body come to have referential ability.

> The continuous coming face to face with the divine center was celebrated in a ritual encircling of sacred sites, objects or persons, as well as in round dances around a holy center. To circumscribe the center was to be in constant relationship with the source of being. Thereby geography was transformed into symbolic cosmology, and man at its center became the cosmocrator.[175]

The three dimensions of space (length, breadth, and depth) are zones where the sacred may be worshipped (see Appendix D). Human anatomy, with its points of orientation in space, sanctifies the space around it.

There are a good number of possible combinations of foot, arm, head, and body positions within spatial coordinates. Raised arms can indicate praise and adoration; lowered arms can symbolize death. Arms reaching out horizontally can mean communication; a bowed head can symbolize sorrow. Posture can indeed speak truth:

> Preparation for the sacred dance was often marked by a period of prayer, when the worshipper either lies on the ground in prostration before his god or kneels in a foetal position invoking power; the divine is as yet unmanifest, has not yet been born in him. Only with the entry of the "spirit" into man does he become fully human; and he is then called upon to relate himself to the space-time in action. By virtue of being centered, thereby having both a focus and a direction, man's actions become sacred.[176]

Sacred dance was not foreign to ancient Israel. Here are some scriptural references:

> So they told the Benjaminites to do as follows, "Put yourself in ambush in the vineyards. Keep watch: when the girls of Shiloh come out in groups to dance, you then come out of the vineyards..."
> (Jg 21:20-21).

> And David danced whirling round before Yahweh with all his might, wearing a linen loincloth
> (2 Sm 6:14).

> Israel shall rejoice in its Maker, and children of Zion delight in their king; they shall dance in praise of his name, play to him on tambourines and harp!
> (Ps 149:2-3).

...praise him with tambourines and dancing
(Ps 150:4).

Gregory of Nazienz says in his *Theological Opinions*:
"Dance the dance of David before the ark of the
covenant, for I believe that such a dance holds the
mystery of walking in the sight of God."[177] Saint Basil of
Caesarea said: "Could there be anything more blessed
than to imitate on earth the ring- dance of the angels,
and at dawn to raise our voices in prayer and by hymns
and songs to glorify the rising Creator?"[178] Saint
Ambrose spoke of the dance on two levels:

And just as he who dances with his body, rushes
through the rotating movements of the limbs, acquires a right to share in the round dance, in the
same way, he who dances the spiritual dance, always moving in the ecstasy of faith, acquires a right
to dance in the ring of creation.[179]

Protestant theologian Harvey Cox has something very
important to say about the use of sacred dance:

What eventually happens to the Church or to liturgical dancing is not a matter of urgent concern in itself. What happens to our stifled, sensually-numbed
culture is important. To reclaim the body, with all
its earthly exquisiteness in worship is a hopeful
sign only if it means we are ready to put away our
deodorants and prickliness and welcome the body's
smell and feel back into our ascetic cultural consciousness. Only when that happens will we know
that our civilization has left behind the gnostics and
their wan successors and has moved to a period
when once again we can talk about the redemption
of the body without embarrassment.[180]

The dance helps the body fill sacred space. The dance is one means of elevating to God not only oneself, but also the area where one dances.

5

Creation, Christ, and Today

Introduction

There are different ways of looking at the reality of existence. A scientist would take note of the material world; a sociologist would regard reality as socially constructed; while a Christian would consider the universe and all of its inhabitants from the point of view of redemption. A Christian would recognize that Jesus is the one who heals the universe by blessing it with his presence.

There exists a great need to revitalize Christian worship. If cultures did not change, there would be little need to change worship patterns. But the fact of the matter is that Christians find themselves in the midst of great societal change in all areas of world civilization. The Fathers of the Second Vatican Council said that today's spiritual agitation and the changing conditions of life are part of a broader and deeper revolution.[181] The whole cosmos, and humanity within it, is caught up in the process of being transformed into "what we are waiting for...: the new heavens and new earth" (2 Pet

3:13). Obviously, this has not happened yet; it is still in process. And so until the kingdom comes, there will necessarily have to be adjustments to new ways of living and changes and variation in the patterns of worship according to the cultural context. The signs and symbols of one culture may or may not have meaning for another culture. Therefore, liturgists, both professional and non-professional, clergy and laity, must constantly strive to speak the language of worship in relevant symbols.

Creation

The one primary symbol that all human beings possess is Creation itself, a mighty symbol of God's great action of sharing love. It is the "stuff" of which all religious peoples speak in their rites. Creation is wondrous to behold and still more wondrous to be a part of. It is the occasion and locus of creaturely existence and worship.

As may be seen from earlier sections of this book, most religions have myths about Creation, a fall of some kind, and a plan by the deity to redeem the Creation in a certain manner. Rites of kenosis and plerosis act out these ideas. Christianity is not lacking either in myth or ritual. Indeed it possesses a rich tradition, which is contained in the Scriptures and in the life of the Church since New Testament times.

The faith of Christians, as it has been handed on throughout the centuries, speaks of the cosmos as being both elevated and lapsed. God's constant desire to save has been extended to all ages. God's never-ending love has been offered, but it has not always been well received. In this way humankind is elevated: only men and women, above all other creatures, know that they are able to transcend this world in order to experience God; they also know that they can discern God present in the world. Paleontology and archeology and other sciences that are concerned with times past show that men and women not only have reasoned and have made free choices when they made and used tools and weapons, but also that they have always tried to keep in close contact with God, or the gods, however the Infinite was understood. Early cave drawings attest to this. Humankind's elevation consists in the fact that it has always realized that somehow it is in relationship to the Creator.

In the evolutionary process, people have always had God's favor. First through Creation, then mainly through revelation, people have experienced God. In this acquaintance with God there is elevation. Whether they can "name the Whirlwind" or not, people still realize that they participate in something greater than themselves. As beings in the world, men and women experience in differing degrees and in a veiled manner what traditionally has been called by Christians the Beatific Vision. Some religions call it *satori*, some evolution, others nature, and still others God.

People, too, are lapsed; they are not totally at one with God, with the cosmos, or with each other. The reason for this is called sin. Sin obscures the path to God. Evil is present in the world, and it is not from God, because God saw to it that everything that was done was very good. Evil comes from the world of people who try to "re-create" God's world in their own image. Through choosing not to cooperate with God, selfishness was allowed to set in and to lead to divisions that began to frustrate the unity which God had given to Creation in the beginning.

All men and women are related by virtue of their birth into a common world. The gifts of Creation which come from God are present. From each other they receive the gift of a sin-filled world: the creation has been turned in on itself. From the moment that a baby comes forth from the mother's womb it cries; it cries because it does not know who or where it is. It is in a human world. The child is extremely uncomfortable because it does not know itself or its surroundings or God. Throughout life the growing person tries to become integrated with the world and with God. This task cannot be accomplished alone because one is hemmed in on all sides by the milieu of sin. Someone is needed to show the way. For the Christian, Jesus is that Way. Jesus brings wholeness to a world broken by sin. Therefore, he is the person of liturgical celebration.

Technological Advances

Humankind, in its over-involvement with technology, has already alienated itself from the realm of nature and in so doing has alienated itself from the knowledge of the presence of God. Some would opine that this particular alienation coming from technological advance is merely a manifestation of our general alienation due to the effects of sin. Others would hail technological advance and accept destruction due to technology as "mistakes in planning" rather than part of a tendency toward evil and failure due to what has traditionally been called "original sin." Nevertheless, it would seem that many men and women of today find it difficult to pray and worship. When people were closer to the earth, when the soil was tilled and prayers were said for the increase of the earth, before the rise of modern technology, it was easier to experience and to worship God. God was the one who caused all life to come forth. God was the Creator, the Sustainer, the Provider. With the advent of the technological age, many people tend to depend on themselves solely. They consider themselves to be in total control and feel that they should give thanks only to themselves for a job well done. They seem to have built a world in their own image within the dimensions of Creation itself.

Most people are aware that technology has transformed planet earth and already is pushing into outer space.[182] The reason for this is the desire for human betterment and fulfillment. Not only do human beings attempt to be masters over the animals and the fish and the trees, but also they extend their mastery over nearly the whole of nature and continue to do so.[183] Technology, like any advance of knowledge, might be called both a blessing and a curse. It is a blessing in that a new environment has been created and the old one seems to have been surpassed. Technological advances have allowed the senses and nervous system to be extended in a global embrace.[184] Technology, in allowing a certain amount of transcendence over the limitedness of time and space, helps one to see that *todo el mundo* is actually *un mundo*.

But, at the same time, technology has set in motion new problems. New machines have taken more and more men and women away from the land and have brought them to the cities. Flight from the fields to the cities of cement, asphalt, and wood has resulted in numerous complicated difficulties. It seems that "too much happens too soon." As soon as one problem is solved then more loom forward. Perhaps the words of a Beatles' song asks a poignant question that should be directed to today's technologically-advanced civilization:

"All the lonely people—where do they all come from?"[185] There are probably many answers to this question. Perhaps one remedy for the current malaise might call for a deeper appreciation of the "Mystery of Life."

Life by its very nature cannot be totally figured out. Life is something more than mere human calculations and vain manipulations. Life is not simply a problem; rather it is a mystery, a mystery related to the very mystery of God. Much is being done to promote scientific and technical knowledge. But this is not enough. Human nature also calls for development of poetic and spiritual feelings which sometimes are the best way to relate to and to describe what is actually happening. Human beings are not alone in the cosmos. God is with them. Gerard Manley Hopkins, an English poet of the 19th century, gently reminds those who would listen that

> The world is charged with the grandeur of God,
>   It will flame out, like shining from shook foil;
>   It gathers to a greatness, like the ooze of oil
> Crushed. Why do men then now not reck his rod?
> Generations have trod, have trod, have trod;
>   And all is seared with trade; bleared, smeared
>   with toil;
>   And wears man's smudge and shares man's
>   smell: the soil
> Is bare now, nor can foot feel, being shod.
>
> And for all this, nature is never spent;
>   There lives the dearest freshness deep down
>   things;
> And though the last lights off the black West went
>   Oh, morning, at the brown brink eastward,
>   springs—

> Because the Holy Ghost over the bent
> World broods with warm breast and with ah!
> bright wings.[186]

For the Christian believer, the Holy Spirit indeed creatively broods over her continuing work.

Need for Fresh Appreciation of Nature

It behooves the contemporary world to reroot itself in the world of nature so that the spiritual side of human nature might be revitalized. Nowadays it is very easy to become harried and perplexed and vexed and anxious after working eight or more hours a day in an artificial environment of glass, plaster, plastic, and machine noises. A person can become quite brittle in this milieu. It is also very easy to become bored when nothing seems to change: when the canned music becomes stale, when the same four walls stare back, when the temperature is held constant by mechanical means. People need stability and unity, but they also need variety and change in their rhythm of daily existence.

Nature offers four variations in her essential rhythm. The seasons express the unity and multiplicity of life in four basic ways, but each season also manifests its own inner patience and infinite resilience. Nature serves as a very good sign of God's tremendous kaleidoscopic unselfishness. It is an excellent means of spiritual refreshment for any one living in this technologically-wise 20th century.

Human nature means to be a part of nature. God planned it this way. "At once humbled and ennobled by our discoveries, we are gradually coming to see ourselves as a part of vast and continuing processes..."[187]

Spiritually speaking, those processes have to do with the redemption of the whole cosmos by Jesus Christ. In the words of Pierre Teilhard deChardin,

> ...it is in no way metaphorical to say that man finds himself capable of experiencing and discovering his God in the whole length, breadth and depth of the world in movement.[188]

The whole cosmos is in movement, and God is dynamically redeeming the cosmos in Christ, the one who "invests himself organically with the very majesty of his creation."[189] If this be so, and if they speak of movement in time of creation, then the seasons are fitting signs of that redemptive process.

Rites of Kenosis and Plerosis

Though there are numerous ways to view the connection between Jesus and the universe, only one need be spoken of in this book. The notion of kenosis and plerosis can easily illustrate the relationship between Christ and creation. The rhythms of Creation, especially the particular rhythm of the four seasons, tell of the wondrous actions of Jesus. His life was one of emptying himself in order to fill others. Here are some scriptural passages which speak of kenosis and plerosis:

> Who, being in the form of God,
>> did not count equality with God something to be grasped,
>> But he emptied himself,
>> taking the form of a slave,
>> becoming as human beings are;
>> and being in every way like a human being,

> he was humbler yet,
> even to accepting death, death on a cross
> (Phil 2:6-8).

> He has put all things under his feet, and made him
> as he is above all things, the head of the Church;
> which is his Body, the fullness of him who is filled,
> all in all (Eph 1:23).

> The one who went down is none other than the
> one who went up above all the heavens to fill all
> things (Eph 4:10).

> ...so that, knowing the love of Christ, which is
> beyond knowledge, you may be filled with the utter
> fullness of God (Eph 3:19).

The Church has always celebrated rites of kenosis and plerosis, rites of emptying and rites of filling. These rites are based on a basic Christian mythology which speaks of redemption. The kenosis aspect brings out the themes of original sin, the Fall, humankind's lapsed nature. The first human sin is expressed in Scripture this way:

> The woman saw that the tree was good to eat and
> pleasing to the eye, and that it was enticing for the
> wisdom that it could give. So she took some of its
> fruit and ate it. She also gave some to her hus-
> band...Then the eyes of both of them were opened
> and they realized that they were naked (Gn 3:6-7).

Because of this sin the cosmos, so to speak, was "emptied" of God's friendship and grace. The kenosis aspect also applies to the death of Christ, which is the culmination of a life-long process of emptying himself. The Gospel of Matthew dramatically reports:

But Jesus, again crying out in a loud voice, yielded up his spirit (Mt 27:50).

The plerosis aspect contained in Christian mythology brings out the fact of the original Creation as it came fresh from the hands of God when it was filled with goodness and power:

God saw all he had made and indeed it was very good (Gn 1:31).

It also expresses the redemption of the fallen Creation as it is achieved by Jesus' life, death, resurrection, and ascension:

The Word became flesh,
    he lived among us,
    and we saw his glory,
    the glory that he has from the Father as the only
    Son of the Father,
    full of grace and truth (Jn 1:14).

...He was made visible in the flesh,
    justified in the Spirit,
    seen by angels,
    proclaimed to the gentiles,
    believed in throughout the world,
    taken up in glory (1 Tim 3:16).

Thanks to Jesus the new Creation is filled with life:

Indeed, from his fullness we have, all of us, received—one gift replacing another, for the Law was given through Moses, grace and truth have come through Jesus Christ (Jn 1:16-17).

If death came to many through the offence of one man, how much greater an effect the grace of God

has had, coming to so many and so plentifully as a
free gift through the one man Jesus Christ!
(Rm 5:15).

Kenosis and plerosis fit into the cycle of the four
seasons. Spring and Summer illustrate the action of filling, of vitalizing, or increasing, whereas Autumn and
Winter display the process of emptying and the gradual
fading of life. Any casual observer of nature is able to
perceive this. In this part of the world, Spring technical-
ly runs from March 20 or March 21 to June 20, while
Summer lasts from June 21 until September 22. Autumn
begins September 23 and lasts until December 21 or
December 22, while Winter endures from December 22
or December 23 until March 19 or March 20.

The traditional liturgical seasons express, to one degree or another, the idea of kenosis and plerosis. To a
certain extent they mirror the kenosis-plerosis pattern
of the natural seasons. Liturgical planners and presiders
at liturgies would do well to keep this in mind. It is this
writer's contention that every liturgical feast, for that
matter, has emptying and filling characteristics, either of
which can be brought out according to the expertise of
the liturgist and presider. In every celebration a "holy
exchange" is made; in exchange for our faithfulness God
fills us with life: we who are quite often empty in many
ways are replenished through the mystery of the death
and rising of the Lord as it is celebrated during the year.
The Advent season reveals a certain amount of empti-
ness, a certain measure of "unfilledness," of anticipating
Christ in his second coming. The season of Lent calls for
spiritual renewal, which assumes a certain action of
emptying oneself by penance, prayer, fasting, and
almsgiving, even though the natural season during
which this liturgical season occurs speaks of new life.

The aspect of fullness is indeed present in the celebration of Christmas, the feast which celebrates the Savior's enfleshment in the material world, in spite of the fact that it occurs during a natural season that seems to be empty of life. The Christmas relationship is "...that of contrast between the giver and the receivers; between Him who is himself poor and ourselves who are enriched by his poverty."[190] Easter is the festival *par excellence*, which ritualizes the replenishment and exaltation of the weakened state of the cosmos. Pentecost celebrates the filling up of the cosmos with the new life of Christ's all-permeating Holy Spirit.

It is interesting to note that the major festal times of the Church fit in somewhat with the natural seasons, although not exactly. Lent, which runs from the first part of March until the second week of April, is a Winter-Spring celebration that takes into account the idea of germinating growth. Just as the preparation of the ground allows for the steady growth of crops, so this spiritual preparation period looks forward to a harvest of spiritual maturity. Easter, which is celebrated in April or March, is a Spring celebration that speaks of the new life given to the world by the Risen Jesus. Another Spring festival, Pentecost, is annually celebrated in late May or the first week of June, and it suggests the fundamental unity of the universe and all peoples as the Spirit of Jesus comes to hover over the whole of Creation permanently. Advent is an Autumnal festival period, which extends from late November or early December to late December. It prophesies impending new life just as the remaining dry leaves blow away from the stripped trees. It foretells the new life that is to come into the world in Jesus. His birthday celebration, December 25, occurs just as Winter begins. His coming assures the world of hope in the midst of cold and barrenness. One might say that just as our natural life also grows by means of large cycles of time made up of many days, so does our Christian life. The liturgy takes the natural year, the cycle of human life which is in harmony with the rhythm of the cosmos, and presents the great phases of the mystery which we are to undergo throughout the year's recurring days, while at the same time it transfigures each of these days.[191]

Nature constantly interacts with itself in one great process of filling and emptying. Because the sun's rays reach and warm the earth, living forms are able to flourish. The distance of the earth from the sun affects the chemical cycles which ensure the survival of life and its tremendous variety of species. Evidence for a regular yearly journey around the sun exists in the form of seasonal effects. Because the axis of the earth is inclined to the plane along which it travels, there are specific changes of light, temperature, and precipitation that are repeated. The Seasons are the times of this repetition. These effects have a profound influence on the food supply and growth of plants and animals. Living things grow or decline according to the proximity of the sun, which gives off its energy. Nature uses this energy to regulate itself so that life systems are maintained. The maintenance of life systems speaks of a constant cycle of living and dying, a cycle of emptying and filling.

Perhaps a theology of the new Creation, a "theology of ecology," could be engendered from an appreciation of Nature's operations.[192] Perhaps an intense study of nature as part of the Creation would lead to a much more creative use of the earth's elements in worship. But it is first of all necessary for people to come to know their place in the Creation in relation to matter itself. People are to neither abuse matter by destroying the ecology, nor be ruled by matter. Constantly before us is the question of how much the physical environment should be interfered with. We know only too well what happens to fauna or flora when waste chemicals are dumped into a river by a factory. Also before us is the question having to do with the interference with basic human life of unreigned technology. How easy it is to be conditioned and controlled by the ringing of the telephone! How easy it is to be angered by a "mistake" in a computer's issuance of a much-needed paycheck!

It is the experience of the new Creation in Christ, rather than the technology alone, that can give humankind a changed role in Creation. People are the God-given masters over Creation: "God blessed them saying, 'Be fruitful, multiply, fill the earth and subdue it'" (Gn 1:28); however, it is not easy to be always on top of things, for as God has said:

> Accursed be the soil because of you.
>> Painfully will you get your food from it
>> as long as you live.
> It will yield you brambles and thistles,
>> as you eat the produce of the land.
> By the sweat of your face,
>> will you earn your food,
> until you return to the ground,
>> as you were taken from it (Gn 3:17-19).

The task is to creatively shape the world in which we live so that it will provide a worthwhile future for others. A redeemed humanity and a restored Creation go together. Each needs the other; neither is complete alone. For it is through redeemed people that the restoration of Creation can be achieved.

Holiness and wholeness fit together in a theology that involves ecology. At the risk of being facetious, one might say that one is holy to the extent that one contributes to the wholeness of the new creation that is gradually becoming more beautiful in Christ; this new creation takes into account the redemption of the cosmos and the redemption of the individual. The ultimate redemption of matter depends on humankind's response of faith:

> ...for the whole creation is waiting with eagerness for the children of God to be revealed. It was not for its own purposes that creation had frustration imposed on it, but for the purposes of him who imposed it—with the intention that the whole creation itself might be freed from slavery to corruption and brought into the same glorious freedom as the children of God (Rm 8:19-21).

An ecological theological approach moves from a preoccupation with crops to a concern for all matter. Just as matter is used by God, so can it be used redemptively by people in partnership with God. Psalm 8 speaks clearly about this task:

> Yet you have...made him lord of the works of your hands,
> put all things under his feet... (Ps 8:5-6).

Therefore, the fully developed range of humankind's intelligence and manipulative skills, along with their promise of betterment and their threat of destruction, is the real context for a celebration of Creation. Once this is understood, worthwhile liturgical celebration of the Seasons can result.

The Paschal Mystery Today

Today there is a great need for a fresh celebration of Christ's paschal mystery presence in the world. The Christ who is veiled in space and time is the same one who, in diverse ways, manifests himself in the world by virtue of the medium of nature and redeems it by his suffering, death, resurrection and ascension. One might say that "the cosmos is even more mysterious now than in times past.[193] We live in a world of partial vision: "Now we see only reflections in a mirror" (1 Cor 13:12). By and large we do not possess a heightened awareness of Christ's all-embracing presence. It would seem that nowadays there is a screen hiding divinity from us. Perhaps the screen, which seems to have been so thin in the time of the ancient Hebrews and is almost non-existent among primitive cultures, has been thickened unnecessarily by us. Would not a closer relation to nature help to displace that screen? Perhaps the screen is created by people themselves. Must there necessarily be a screen? It would seem that only deeper and deeper spiritual experiences can rid us of that screen.

Christ's presence in nature will go unnoticed unless people are able to develop a greater sense of primal wonder. Good prayer, both private and liturgical, begins to take shape when people are cognizant of their exalted position in Creation and speak with God of their "joys and hopes, griefs and anxieties."[194] Prayer begins with a reflection of primal wonder and is best expressed by artistic and religious language, not the fact-laden language of scientific terminology.

Prayer that leaves out the cosmic dimension of existence is limited prayer. People live in and with nature. To focus in prayer only on one part of Creation, human existence, is not enough if Christians are to be truly, and biblically, prayerful. Like the psalmist of ages past, the modern Christian should pray through, with, and in the rest of Creation. And prayer should be offered, to quote from a prayer in the East Syrian liturgy, "...at all times and at all seasons."[195] Pierre Teilhard deChardin, in a powerful, moving prayer, includes matter in his praise of Christ. This prayer of his might serve as a paradigm for a new prayer of Creation:

> Glorious Lord Christ: the divine influence secretly diffused and active in the depth of matter, and the dazzling center where all the innumerable fibres of the manifold meet; power as implacable as the world and as warm as life; you whose forehead is of the whiteness of snow, whose eyes are of fire, and whose feet are brighter than molten gold; you whose hands imprison the stars; you who are the first and the last, the living and the dead and the risen again; you who father into your exuberant unity every beauty, every affinity, every energy, every mode of existence; it is you to whom my being cried out with a desire as vast as the universe, "In truth you are my Lord and my God."[196]

An ecological understanding of humankind's dominion in Christ of the Creation would give the Church something vitally important and relevant to say to the modern world in regard to problems of technology, nuclear energy, societal change, Third World development, and environmental problems. The Church must not speak to these problems with pat answers; oftentimes the old answers just will not do. It is the same with the liturgical adaptation.

Liturgical Adaptation

The purpose of the Second Vatican Council was to enable Christ's Church "to bring herself up to date."[197] And this she has been trying to do. But any process of renewal contains a certain element of crisis within it. Nevertheless,

> ...while the Church is living through a period of crisis, we should not over-dramatize this fact inasmuch as this is a condition accompanying any authentic process of renovation.
>
> One of the areas where the crisis is real, if not spectacular, is the prayer life of Christians. They feel ill at ease with the forms bequeathed to them by recent tradition.[198]

Christian liturgical life needs to be a real part of everyday human activity, and yet the daily life of people needs to make communal worship alive and personally significant.[199]

Every liturgical celebration is an action of Christ the priest and of his body the Church.[200] Faith in Jesus as the Lord of all life is not to be limited to one expression only. The Church has a lengthy history of adapting in many and various ways the external expression of her faith to peoples of different cultures. Yet the perennial problem of worship has to do with retaining the vital core of traditional Christian worship while at the same time introducing in some assimilative way certain specific, contemporary, and culturally-relevant forms.

By means of the liturgy, one becomes theologically, liturgically, historically, and scripturally adept. One prays what one believes, *lex orandi lex credendi*. The liturgy is definitely didactic of what the Lord is doing for his people and it is celebrational of that fact and event. But just as the Church in the world and in the local parish is constantly in need of reform and renewal, so too its liturgy. Just as the individual and collective understanding of the faith develops, so do specific expressions of liturgical worship. The Fathers of the Second Vatican Council knew this and so they gave certain guidelines for its reform and adaptation in the *Constitution on the Sacred Liturgy*.

Here are some pertinent sections from this important document:

> Popular devotions of the Christian people are warmly commended, provided they accord with the laws and norms of the Church...Nevertheless these devotions should be so drawn up that they harmonize with the liturgical seasons, accord with the sacred liturgy, are in some way derived from it, and lead the people to it, since the liturgy by its very nature far surpasses any one of them (Section 13).

> ...there must be no innovation unless the good of the Church genuinely and certainly requires them; and care must be taken that any new forms adopted should in some way grow organically from forms already existing (Section 23).

> Even in the liturgy, the Church has no wish to impose a rigid uniformity in matters which do not involve the faith or the good of the whole community. Rather, she respects and fosters the spiritual adornments and gifts of the various races and peoples. Anything in their way of life that is not indissolubly bound up with superstition and error she studies with sympathy and, if possible, preserves intact. Sometimes, in fact, she admits such things into the liturgy itself, as long as they har-

monize with its true and authentic spirit (Section 38).

> Provided that the substantial unity of the Roman rite is maintained, the revision of liturgical books should allow for legitimate variations and adaptations to different groups, regions, and peoples, especially in mission lands. Where opportune, the same rule applies to the structuring of rites and the devising of rubrics (Section 38).

> In some places and circumstances, however, an even more radical adaptation of the liturgy is needed and entails greater difficulties (Section 40).[201]

This first chapter of the *Constitution on the Sacred Liturgy* gives the general principles for the restoration, and adaptation, of liturgical prayer. Since its promulgation in December of 1963, much progress has been made. However, the Church must never be satisfied solely with devotions and ceremonies that have been handed on through the centuries; she must constantly renew and develop them so that they may be helpful to others in the future.

Catholics and other Christians in the Western world, coming from countries which have very much been formed by Roman Rite Christianity, are people familiar with the great marvels of modern science and industry; they are people who nowadays are not as comfortable as some other cultures in worshipping Christ through nature. A principle set forth in the *Constitution on the Sacred Liturgy* says that the unchangeable part of the liturgy established by Christ should be set forth

> according to the religious sense of each group and each culture, for the very purpose of the ritual expression of this divine nucleus is that it become

through their full and active participation something really their own.[202]

The "religious sense" of a group of American business computer salespersons and the liturgical expression of that religious sense would be strikingly different from that of Christian farmers on the Tonga Islands.

The Christian doctrine of Creation is not opposed to technology. A modern liturgical expression of this doctrine should encompass the experiences and values of contemporary living as long as they harmonize with the liturgy's true and authentic spirit. But right now it seems that technology is going its separate way, leaving behind a healthy appreciation for nature. Before there can be any genuine liturgical expression of a technological society, there must exist a greater respect for the realm of nature. What good is it to go head over heels with technological research if that research ends up in the destruction of the natural world? And on the other hand, what good is there in decrying technology and humankind's genius if nature's great potential is not fully developed?

Perhaps it is time to return to nature for a while in order to regain the ability to sanctify, to make holy, and to make whole, the milieu of technological existence. If one has the ability to worship God in, with, and through the natural Creation, then, perchance, one will be able to worship God in, with, and through Creation as it is being cultivated by means of contemporary human ingenuity. For a technological people to meaningfully celebrate God's presence in their world, they should be able to at least celebrate God in nature.

"Christian ritual-making is the art through which we articulate, in terms of the natural rituals of our own culture, the new meaning of life which Jesus awakens in human hearts."[203] Religious rituals begin with people; they proclaim how a people regard mystery. The mystery that Christians living in a technological age experience is the same mystery that Christians of the past have experienced. That is why the basic traditional elements in a sacred ritual will be perennially relevant. However, with its ability to de-emphasize the sense of mystery in life, technology tends to limit the vision; hence the richly symbolic liturgies composed in the pre-technological age have limited meaning for today. What is needed is a new liturgical expression, based on the old, which takes into account the milieu of technology as well as the milieu of nature. This new form of liturgical expression "should grow organically from forms already existing."[204] The substance of the Roman Rite, which includes elements proper to Western culture, elements which have given it its peculiar form and expression, should be adapted to the needs of different peoples,[205] especially to people of a technological society who have lost touch with nature.

Liturgical celebrations that draw together nature and technological life should focus on the Creation context of all worship and its relation to life. They should be a medium of teaching, for in liturgical celebrations the Church says something of importance about itself. The celebrations should also be means of communication because in them the Church proclaims something of importance to the world: "...Jesus Christ as Lord, to the glory of God the Father" (Phil 2:11).

6

Conclusion

It seems that this book travels through history and surveys the religious rituals of a variety of peoples. It speaks of time as being holy, and discusses how the day and the year are used in the celebration of the festivals; it delves into some of the significant moments of peoples' lives as they travel the road of life itself; it studies the liturgical sanctification of time; then it looks at how matter is utilized in worship; and finally, it emphasizes the need for a fresh celebration of the paschal mystery, which would take into account the physical Creation.

People being people in the action of saying and doing and using things are the raw material of liturgy. Their tools are words and actions and environments. They work with Scripture and try to understand what God is saying; they confess, praise, and intercede together and separately. Liturgy is not to be simply a spectacle to watch, but an action to share. A celebration of Creation calls for participation in a shareable experience.

Matter matters. It matters both to God and to people. God made matter, gave it to people for dominion, and used it in revelation and redemption. Therefore, it should neither be neglected nor refused but accepted. It is important to people because it is the sphere of their dominion. Therefore, any liturgical celebration must take matter seriously. If the power in the universe is perceived as malevolent, and matter is thought of as evil, then propitiation will be preached. But if the power in the universe is understood to be benevolent, then worshipful affirmation and thanksgiving will result. Matter is object, not subject. It must never be allowed to be considered as ultimate reality. Therefore any liturgical celebration must be a recall to the reality of matter as object. This will result in penitence and absolution for the misuse of matter. Matter is also manageable: it responds to the actions of people. Adam, the first steward, misused it; Christ uses it in a beautiful way as he redeems his people. Any liturgical celebration must offer the hope of new possibilities as men and women share with each other the work of the new creation.[206]

The worship experience should express the worshipper himself or herself rather than the cabbage or the hybrid wheatsheaf being held up to God. It must also be released from a concern merely with crops and be allowed to move into a total creation context. If it starts with sowing and reaping, it must no longer be allowed to stop there but move out into the whole life. It must speak of humankind's responsibility for its fellow-creatures and for the natural world. The bring-the-offering-into-church stance must lead directly into a send-the-person-out-of-church-into-the-world thrust.[207]

This book does not call for the abandonment of traditional liturgical rituals of rogation or harvest celebrations, which are celebrated in the context of the four seasons. Rather, it calls for a re-appraisal that will bring about a combining of traditional ideas with contemporary concerns in a commitment of renewal and responsibility. The world *is* different today than it was in pre-technological ages. Now more than ever, besides nature, we depend on the modern gadgets that allow for more leisure time than our ancestors were allowed. These same modern tools enhance the production of food and other commodities that can be shared on a global scale. We really do have the future of the world in our hands. It is all up to us.

The Scriptures show us that the Israelites in the centuries before Jesus gave offerings to God which clearly linked together their life and their salvation and their hopes and dreams for the future. Though their offerings of wheat and barley and grapes were placed in woven baskets that were definitely different from today's plastic container of technological items, still, the act of offering to God is the same. But those living in a technological society, those who experience nature only indirectly, those who seek to worship God as inheritors of a rich liturgical tradition that used to rely more directly on nature, need to ask themselves some important questions:

What nowadays are we really offering to the Lord?

What needs to be said to the Lord as we place our offering?

What must we do and be after we have shared in this particular liturgical experience?[208]

Today the basket is both people-shaped and world-shaped. Christians bring themselves in surrender and availability and come as representatives of humankind as a whole. They bring with them the matter that they touch and control and use in their own lives; representatively they bring all of matter and all of their experiences in the token offering at any liturgical celebration. They are to say "Thank you," "Sorry," and "Please," but most of all they are to say "Yes!" as they affirm themselves in surrender and identify themselves in penitence, faith, and commitment to God and other people. They are to take their place in the divine purpose: they are to accept the partnership offered to them along with others in Christ, and they are to set out obediently as agents of the kingdom in specific local and global actions as time permits.[209]

The seasons should no longer be considered as merely "profane time" for they are indeed "sacred time"; they are marvelous times for communion with cosmos and Creator. They are times for recognizing the activity of God in the process of renewing the world. In short, they are times which speak of the coming of the Kingdom. As the *Constitution on the Church* says,

> Then the human race as well as the entire world, which is intimately related to man and achieves its purpose through him, will be perfectly reestablished in Christ...In the Church...we learn through faith the meaning, too, of our temporal life, as we perform, with hope of good things to come, the task committed to us in this world...The final age of the world has already come upon us. The renovation of the world has been irrevocably decreed and in this age is already anticipated in some real way.[210]

We realize nowadays that we do not live in the static three-leveled universe which includes the realm of time and matter, the angelic realm, and the realm of God. Rather, contemporary theology emphasizes that the universe is in the dynamic process of being prepared to become the Kingdom of God. The cosmos is no longer conceived of in terms of endless sameness, but as a unified developmental evolutionary historical process which had a beginning and will have an end, in which new things are constantly happening with ever-accelerating speed and which seems to be going someplace even though it is quite beyond the possibility of empirical, scientific prediction to say where.[211]

Celebrations of the seasons, celebrations of Christ's profound presence in the world, should utilize matter as fully as possible. The review of religious cultures in this book definitely shows how matter is able to be used. Roman Catholicism has a rich tradition of praising God through matter; prior to the age of technology, people understood easily the connection between matter and God. But now there is need for a general restoration of such an attitude. The *aggiornamento* called for by Pope John XXIII is something that should be continuous and sought after by Christians of all the churches.

This book urges a greater theological respect for physical Creation. It asks that matter be used as fully as possible in liturgical celebrations—both living matter and the products that come forth from the hands of men and women. The Church should actively witness to times of planting and reaping in the fields; it should bless the handiwork of its people who live with technology; it should celebrate outside whenever possible; it should be aware of the rhythm of modern living as well as the rhythms of nature; it should put matter into motion; it should move around in it and dance in it, touch it, taste it, listen to the sounds of life, play with its colors. In short, it should celebrate the goodness of the world as it comes from the Creator-Redeemer.

PART TWO

1

A Springtime Eucharist (*Plerosis*)

This liturgy could be celebrated in a clearing in the forest or on top of a hill.

Procession to Holy Site

With singing and dancing; a cross is placed in the center of the holy site, and flowers are placed around it by the worshippers; the people encircle the cross.

Rite of the Word

Psalm 147
(Recited antiphonally.)

> Alleluia!

> Praise Yahweh—it is good to sing psalms to our
>   God—how pleasant to praise him.
> Yahweh, Builder of Jerusalem!
>   He gathers together the exiles of Israel

healing the broken-hearted
   and binding up their wounds;
he counts out the number of the stars,
   and gives each one of them a name.
Our Lord is great, all-powerful,
   his wisdom beyond all telling.
Yahweh sustains the poor,
   and humbles the wicked to the ground.

Sing to Yahweh in thanksgiving,
   play the harp for our God:
He veils the sky with clouds,
   and provides the earth with rain,
makes grass grow on the hills
   and plants for people to use,
gives fodder to cattle
   and to young ravens when they cry.
He takes no delight in the power of horses,
   no pleasure in human sturdiness;
his pleasure is in those who fear him,
   in those who hope in his faithful love.

Praise Yahweh, Jerusalem,
   Zion, praise your God.
For he gives strength to the bars of your gates,
   he blesses your children within you,
he maintains the peace of your frontiers,
   gives you your fill of finest wheat.
He sends his word to earth,
   his command runs quickly,
he spreads the snow like flax,
   strews hoarfrost like ashes,
he sends ice-crystals like bread crumbs,
   and who can withstand that cold?
When he sends his word it thaws them,
   when he makes the wind blow, the waters are
   unstopped.

He reveals his word to Jacob,
  his statutes and judgements to Israel.
For no other nation has he done this,
  no other has known his judgements.

Holy Silence

The Magic of Spring
(Canon Sheen, Dublin: Mercier Press, 1973, 9-10)

Matthew 6:25-34

Homily on the Meaning of the Season
(the new birth and the freshness and the fullness that is
before us)

Rite of the Eucharist

Preparation of the Site

Water is blessed and offered to the four directions and given to each person to bless himself or herself—a symbol of the Spring rains and a symbol of baptismal rebirth; incensation of the four directions. Incense is brought to each worshipper, who then wafts some "holy smoke" to the nose and prays silently; four fires are lit. The fires are carried around the circle of worshippers and each person places the hands over the flames and immediately cups the hands over the eyes—a symbol of Christ the light of the world illuminating our eyes and warming our hearts. The four fires are then placed around the cross. Technological items (tools and the like) are brought forward, blessed, and laid at the foot of the cross. Four items, including bread and wine, are placed next to the four fires. Some of the bread and wine is separated for the Eucharist, the rest is left at the cross. The bread and wine is passed around for the people to bless—a symbolic gesture signifying the priesthood of the people of God; then it is offered by the priest. The cross of our salvation is symbolized by the four directions, the four fires, and the four items.

Eucharistic Prayer for Springtime
(based on Psalm 104. This may be chanted.)

Priest: The Lord be with you.

Assembly: And also with you.

Priest: Lift up your hearts.

Assembly: We lift them up unto the Lord.

Priest: Let us give thanks to the Lord our God.

Assembly: It is right to give him thanks and praise.

Priest: It is good for us at all times and in all places to give thanks to You, O Lord, holy Father, almighty Creator and loving Saviour. But especially this Spring when You renew the earth with your loving care and You renew our hearts as we call to mind all that You do for us. Blessed are You, O God; how great You are! Clothed in majesty and splendour, wearing the light as a robe! Therefore, we praise You with angels and all of Your Creation:

All: Holy, holy, holy... (Sung and round danced.)

Priest: O Lord our Creator, You stretch out the heavens like a tent, You build your palace on the waters above; making the clouds your chariot, gliding on the wings of the wind; appointing the winds your messengers, flames of fire your servants.

Assembly: You fixed the earth on its foundations, forever and ever it shall not be shaken; you

covered it with the deep like a garment, the waters overtopping the mountains.

Priest: At your reproof the waters fled, at the voice of your thunder they sped away, flowing over mountains, down valleys, to the place you had fixed for them; you made a limit they were not to cross, they were not to return and cover the earth.

Assembly: **In the ravines you opened up springs, running down between the mountains, supplying water for all the wild beasts; the wild asses quench their thirst, on their banks the birds of the air make their nests, they sing among the leaves.**

Priest: From your high walls you water the mountains, satisfying the earth with the fruit of your works: for cattle you make the grass grow and for people the plants they need, to bring forth food from the earth, and wine to cheer people's hearts, oil to make their faces glow, food to make them sturdy of heart.

Assembly: **The trees of Yahweh drink their fill, the cedars of Lebanon which he sowed; there the birds build their nests, on the highest branches the stork makes its home, for the wild goats there are the mountains, in the crags rock badgers find refuge.**

Priest: You made the moon to mark the seasons, the sun knows when to set: You bring on darkness, and night falls when all the forest beasts roam around; young lions roar for their prey, asking God for their food.

Assembly: **The sun rises and away they steal, back to their lairs to lie down, and we go out to work, to labour until evening falls. How countless are your works, Yahweh, all of them made so wisely! The earth is full of your creatures.**

Priest: Then there is the sea, with its vast expanses teeming with countless creatures, creatures both great and small, there ships pass to and fro and Leviathan whom you made to sport with.

Assembly: They all depend on you to feed them when they need it. You provide the food they gather, your open hand gives them their fill.

Priest: Turn away your face and they panic; take back their breath and they die and revert to dust. Send out your breath and life begins; you renew the face of the earth.

But God, we are a sinful people. We hurt each other and do not love. We destroy your land and disturb the rivers and the skies with pollution of our own doing. We kill without reason. We do not always know how to love as we should.

O God, in your mighty wisdom You chose to cleanse and renew our world. When the time was ripe you sent us Jesus, your own Son. He loved your world and delighted to wander in the desert, to climb the mountains, to bathe in the cool water of the rivers. He taught us to love and to share his love.

With a love born of heaven and earth, Jesus gathered his friends together the night before he died. He shared with them a meal of bread and wine, fruits of your earth. He took bread, blessed it, broke it, and gave it to them saying, "This is my body which will be given up for you."

He took a cup of wine, blessed it and gave it to them, saying, "This is the cup of my blood, the blood of the new and eternal covenant. It will be shed for you and for all so that sins may be forgiven. Do this in my memory."

All: Lord, by your cross and resurrection you have set us free. You are the saviour of the world.

Priest: O Giver of life, present in all your creation, transform this bread and wine into the living presence of Jesus. Transform us into his holy people. Give us wisdom to create a new world where all may share the fruits of the land. Give us knowledge to develop what is lying fallow, to bring forth what is as yet only a seed in our minds. Fill up what is lacking in our lives. May we learn to respect life wherever we find it.

We give you praise, O Creator.

We give you thanks, O Redeemer.

Through Christ, and with Christ, and in Christ, in the unity of the Holy Spirit all glory and honour is yours, loving Father, forever and ever. Amen!

Our Father
(sung with raised hands)

Sharing of Communion

Silent Meditation or Music

Rite of Bestowal

The bestowal of technological gifts to others or for others and giving of seeds or plants and passing out of flowers and surplus bread and wine from the base of the cross.

Rite of Blessing

Blessing over people and sending them back into the world to transform it with the power of Jesus' love.

Closing Song

2

A Summertime Midday Liturgy
(Plerosis)

Call to Worship

The minister calls (or chants) to the people words of invitation to worship, such as, "Now is the time. Praise the Lord! Stop what you are doing and praise his holy name!"

Opening Song:
"He's Got the Whole World in His Hands," (Anonymous)
"A Song of Blessing" (Ron Ellis, 1979, NALR)
"The Spirit is A-Movin' " (Carey Landry, 1969, NALR)

The worshippers, wherever they are on the beach, bend down to take up a handful of sand, which they bring with them. While the opening song is sung, the minister directs each one to pour his or her handful of sand into a little pile near the cooking fire. The minister then fashions a large cross with this sand in the middle of the circle of people. An abalone shell filled with ocean water is then placed on the middle of the cross.

Then an opening prayer is offered by the minister in these or similar words: "O Lord, your sun is high in the sky; your Son is reigning in high heaven. May we who enjoy your creation come to be where he is forever and ever."

Rite of Praise

Psalm 46
(Recited antiphonally)

> God is our shelter, our strength,
>> ever ready to help in time of trouble,
> so we shall not be afraid when the earth gives way,
>> when mountains tumble into the depths of the sea,
> and its waters roar and seethe,
>> the mountains tottering as it heaves.
> Yahweh Sabaoth is on our side.
>> our citadel, the God of Jacob!
>
> There is a river whose streams refresh the city of God,
>> and it sanctifies the dwelling of the Most High.
> God is in the city, it cannot fall,
>> at break of day God comes to its rescue.
> Nations are in an uproar, kingdoms are tumbling,
>> when he raises his voice the earth crumbles away.
> Yahweh Sabaoth is with us,
>> our citadel, the God of Jacob!

Canticle of the Sun
(Francis of Assisi)

This canticle may be found in endnote 162 in the "Notes" section of this book.

A holy silence is maintained as worshippers, from where they are seated, explore with their eyes, listen with their ears, and feel with their bodies the beauties of God's Creation.

Psalm 145
(Recited antiphonally)

I shall praise you to the heights, God my King,
    I shall bless your name for ever and ever.
Day after day I shall bless you,
    I shall praise your name for ever and ever.
Great is Yahweh and worthy of all praise,
    his greatness beyond all reckoning.
Each age will praise your deeds to the next,
    proclaiming your mighty works.

Your renown is the splendour of your glory.
    I will ponder the story of your wonders.
They will speak of your awesome power,
    and I shall recount your greatness.
They will bring out the memory of your great
    generosity,
    and joyfully acclaim your saving justice.
Yahweh is tenderness and pity,
    slow to anger, full of faithful love.
Yahweh is generous to all,
    his tenderness embraces all his creatures.

All your creatures shall thank you, Yahweh,
    and your faithful shall bless you.
They shall speak of the glory of your kingship
    and tell of your might,
making known your mighty deeds to the children
    of Adam,
    the glory and majesty of your kingship.
Your kingship is a kingship for ever,
    your reign lasts from age to age.

Yahweh is trustworthy in all his words,
  and upright in all his deeds.
Yahweh supports all who stumble,
  lifts up those who are bowed down.
All look to you in hope
  and you feed them with the food of the season,
and, with a generous hand,
  you satisfy the desires of every living creature.

Upright in all that he does,
  Yahweh acts only in faithful love.
He is close to all who call upon him,
  all who call on him from the heart.
He fulfills the desires of all who fear him,
  he hears their cry and he saves them.
Yahweh guards all who love him,
  but all the wicked he destroys.

My mouth shall always praise Yahweh,
  let every creature bless his holy name for ever
  and ever.

Holy Silence

Reading:
"Beauty" (LeBlanc and Talbot, How Green is Green?)

The beauty in the world lies in its love. If there
were no love there would be no beauty. God is
love, therefore the universe is beautiful. Think of a
clear crisp night after a sudden rainfall. Feel the
cool breeze on your warm cheeks. Taste the freshness of the night in your lungs, and look with your
eyes at the marvels above. The sky so dark, the stars
so bright, and the moon with its mystic radiance
glows. And think of the one who created all this.
How magnificent He must be, beyond our comprehension.

The waves roll and smash themselves into nothing as they crawl upon the beach. Yet sea and sky seem to fuse into one at the farthest point; wherever that may be. The bright sun reflecting across the glassy water, splitting the blue into two converging masses. The loud but pleasing thunder as the waves collide among the smooth time-worn rocks. The foam bubbling over like a giant sea monster emerging from beneath the surface and spreading out to swish between your toes. And think of the one who created all this. How magnificent He must be, beyond all comprehension.

In the straw lay a babe, a weak and tender bundle of love—the creation must be beautiful; looking so simple yet so complete, so perfect. And God chose to reveal Himself in the manger. He came so humble, so common, so simple, yet he came to die that we might know true beauty. And this beauty was His love for us, and think of the one who did this for us. How magnificent He must be, beyond our comprehension, but our friend.

Meditation:

Now there is time to feel the presence of God and to meditate on it. For two or three minutes the worshippers may go into the water, lie in the sun, or just smell the good food cooking on the fire.

The worshippers then come back and gather into the circle once more while a guitarist plays soft music and then leads the worshippers in a round-song like "Love, Love, Love, Love" or all sing together the Sanctus.

Psalm 93
(Recited antiphonally)

Yahweh is king, robed in majesty,
  robed is Yahweh and girded with power.
The world is indeed set firm, it can never be
  shaken;
your throne is set firm from of old;
  from all eternity you exist.

The rivers lift up, Yahweh,
  the rivers lift up their voices,
  the rivers lift up their thunder.
Greater than the voice of many waters,
  more majestic than the breakers of the sea,
  Yahweh is majestic in the heights.

Your decrees stand firm, unshakable:
  Holiness is the beauty of your house,
  Yahweh, for all time to come.

and/or Psalm 111

Alleluia!

I give thanks to Yahweh with all my heart
  in the meeting place of honest people, in the
  assembly.
Great are the deeds of Yahweh,
  to be pondered by all who delight in them.
Full of splendour and majesty his work, his saving
  justice stands firm for ever.
He gives us a memorial of his great deeds;
  Yahweh is mercy and tenderness.
He gives food to those who fear him;
  he keeps his covenant ever in mind.
His works show his people his power
  in giving them the birthright of the nations.
The works of his hands are fidelity and justice
  all his precepts are trustworthy,
established for ever and ever,
  accomplished in fidelity and honesty.

Deliverance he sends to his people,
  his covenant he imposes for ever;
  holy and awesome is his name.
The root of wisdom is fear of Yahweh;
  those who attain it are wise.
  His praise will continue for ever.

Reading:
"The Spirit of Pluralism" (Greeley, 7)

The God who Creates is the principle of unity in
the universe; the God who Calls is the principle of
variety and diversity. The more unique and special
each one of us becomes when we respond to that
which is most authentically us, the more different
we become from others. And as more human
beings respond to the Spirit which speaks to that
which is most creative in themselves, the greater
the variety and heterogeneity in the world. The
Spirit of This World tells us not to be different, to
stay in line, to go along, to avoid the deadly sanc-
tions which envy can impose, to flee from the risks
of self revelation and the shame of having that
which is most secret in us seen by all. The Spirit of
This World wants to keep the world a neat, orderly,
gray, dull place.

The Holy Spirit, the Spirit of and beyond this
world, wants the human world to abound with the
same wild profligate diversity which can be seen in
the world of rocks, the world of plants, the world
of animals. Only among humankind is it possible to
resist the impulse of the variety-crazed Spirit.
Bluebirds do not decide to be blue, the Grand
Canyon cannot give up its many hues, the petunia
cannot refuse to blossom, the fish darting among
the corals cannot decide that its beauty is irrelevant.
Only we humans can say no to the Spirit as he

wheels and deals through the universe, twirling and whirling, dancing and leaping, spinning and jumping, shooting forth sparks of this divine creativity wherever he goes. We are the only ones who can say, "Holy Spirit, thanks, but no thanks."

Homily and Sharing Time

Offering of Personal Petitions and Thanksgivings

Rite of Blessing

The people are blessed by the minister placing his or her hands on the hands or head of each one.

A final prayer is offered. The minister then exhorts the worshippers to enjoy God's life-giving presence whenever possible, but also to work that others might enjoy the goodness of our world. The service ends with a song sung while the worshippers go to the abalone shell filled with water and make the sign of the cross and then depart to build up a good appetite for the barbecue that is to follow in the afternoon.

3

An Autumnal Harvest Liturgy (*Kenosis*)

Preparation of the Holy Site

At a certain time of the day the worshippers from a farming area gather at a particular farm. There is a joyful procession to the center of a field from the farmhouse. The farm would ideally be one that includes agriculture as well as the raising of livestock. In the procession the people bear first-fruits of the harvest; they also bring such animals as can be managed easily (horses, cows, sheep, etc.). Already a tractor and plough are in the field near the center. When all are gathered, the tractor starts up at a signal from the priest. It ploughs a large circle around the worshippers so that they are contained within it. The area within the circle is sprinkled with blessed water, which is dispersed by means of a small leafy branch. A fire is lit in a brazier that is placed in the middle of the circle. Harvest gifts are placed at four places around the fire so that a cross is formed by means of them. There is music and singing and possibly a round-dance. Then all are seated.

Rite of the Word

Psalm 65
(Recited antiphonally)

> Praise is rightfully yours,
>   God in Zion.
> Vows to you shall be fulfilled,
>   for you answer prayer.
> All humanity must come to you
>   with its sinful deeds.
> Our faults overwhelm us,
>   but you blot them out.
> How blessed are those whom you choose
>   and invite to dwell in your courts.
> We shall be filled with the good things of your
>   house,
>   of your holy temple.
>
> You respond to us with the marvels of your saving
>   justice,
>   God our Saviour,
> hope of the whole wide world,
>   even the distant islands.
> By your strength you hold the mountains steady,
>   being clothed in power,
> you calm the turmoil of the seas,
>   the turmoil of the waves.
> The nations are in an uproar,
>   in panic those who live at the ends of the earth;
>   your miracles bring shouts of joy to the gateways
>   of morning and evening.
>
> You visit the earth and make it fruitful,
>   you fill it with riches;
> the river of God brims over with water,
>   you provide the grain.

To that end you water its furrows abundantly,
    level its ridges,
soften it with showers
    and bless its shoots.
You crown the year with generosity,
    richness seeps from your tracks,
the pastures of the desert grow moist,
    the hillsides are wrapped in joy,
the meadows are covered with flocks,
    the valleys clothed with wheat;
    they shout and sing for joy.

Holy Silence

Genesis 1:26-29

God said, "Let us make man in our own image, in the likeness of ourselves, and let them be masters of the fish of the sea, the birds of heaven, the cattle, all the wild animals and all the creatures that creep along the ground."

God created man in the image of himself,
    in the image of God he created him,
    male and female he created them.

God blessed them, saying to them, "Be fruitful, multiply, fill the earth and subdue it. Be masters of the fish of the sea, the birds of heaven and all the living creatures that move on earth." God also said, "Look, to you I give all the seed-bearing plants everywhere on the surface of the earth, and all the trees with seed-bearing fruit; this will be your food. And to all the wild animals, all the birds of heaven and all the living creatures that creep along the ground, I give all the foliage of the plants as their food." And so it was. God saw all he had made, and indeed it was very good.

Holy Silence

The Church in the Modern World
(Section 69; Abbott, Documents, 278)

> God intended the earth and all that it contains for the use of every human being and people. Thus, as all men follow justice and unite in charity, created goods should abound for them on a reasonable basis...A man should regard his lawful possessions not merely as his own but also as common property in the sense that they should accrue to the benefit of not only himself but of others...The right to have a share of earthly goods sufficient for oneself and one's family belongs to everyone...If a person is in extreme necessity, he has the right to take from the riches of others what he himself needs.

Holy Silence

The Radical Bible
(Haug and Rump, 119)

> The present population of Earth is estimated at 3,500 million people and calculations based on success of present population control programmes, put it at 6,500 million by the year 2000...As many as two-thirds of the world's present population are suffering from malnutrition and the threat of large-scale famine is still with us despite some nutritional advances...It has been estimated that a child born in the United States today will consume during his lifetime at least twenty times as much as one born in India, and contribute about fifty times as much pollution to the environment.

Holy Silence

Rite of Commitment

Paper and pencils are passed about. Worshippers are asked by the priest to commit themselves to do something of their own choosing to alleviate world hunger, and then to write their commitment on the paper. While all are pondering and writing, a soloist sings a song, such as "The Harvest is Gathered" (Hayward Osborne *Lord of the Harvest* [London: Joseph Weinberger, Ltd., 1974], 7):

> The harvest is gathered, the crops are all in,
> And now will our glad celebrations begin,
> With vegetables, fruit and the corn to make bread
> To feed everyone in the long months ahead.
>
> There's plenty for everyone, be well assured,
> We just couldn't eat all the food that is stored.
> The produce not needed at once, we'll preserve,
> So we shall have thousands of tons in reserve.
>
> For God has been kind to his people again,
> And so many gifts has he given to men.
> We'll drink till we're tipsy, and eat till we're fat;
> We know we're all right—let us leave it at that.
>
> But people are hungry in faraway lands,
> While we have so much surplus food on our
> hands.
> Our barns are all bulging, our stockpiles are high,
> While God's people starve, and while God's
> people die.
>
> Who cares if they're Christians? Who cares if
> they're not?
> If we have the foodstuff that they haven't got.
> But they are our brothers, and so we must give
> A share of our food so that they too may live.

So give to the hungry, and give to the poor,
  And give to the needy, and then give some more;
For all are God's children, and so we must share
  The gifts we are given with men everywhere.

The priest then throws some incense into the fire, then a few grains of the new wheat, a few drops of freshly squeezed grape juice, a few drops of fresh milk, some more incense, and then the worshippers come forward individually and place their folded pieces of paper in the fire, the burning of which is a symbol that God is accepting their offering. A short hymn, such as "Of My Hands" by Ray Repp (1966, FEL) may be sung.

Rite of Blessing

The priest gives a spontaneous blessing of the fruits of the field, the animals present, farm tools and other kinds of tools, the raised hands of the worshippers.

Rites of Sending Forth

The priest exhorts the worshippers to use well the gifts that God has given, to work for the Kingdom when all men and women will be able to share in the Lord's bounty.

Closing Song:
"We Are the Light of the World" (Jean Anthony Greif, 1966, OCP)
"Follow Christ" (Sebastian Temple, 1967, Franciscan Communications)

Then all share a meal made with harvest foods.

4

Wintertime Eucharistic Liturgy of Forgiveness (*Kenosis*)

Preparation of the Holy Site

The worshippers, singing a penitential song such as "Keep in Mind" by Lucien Deiss, proceed to a river's edge on a day when the snow is all around. They carry a large cross made from an old dead tree. All gather in a semi-circle around the cross. The priest takes the cross and marks a semi-circle in the snow with its base so that the worshippers are positioned between it and the river. The cross is then placed by assistants in a hole in the edge of the river so that it is within the water, yet firmly grounded and accessible to the worshippers.

Rite of the Word

Genesis 1:1-25
(Creation before the coming of men and women)

Holy Silence

Genesis 3:1-13,16-24
(The Fall)

Holy Silence

Genesis 8:15-22
(Noah and his family and the animals leave the ark and God promises to sustain life forever)

Holy Silence

Jeremiah 2:1-13
(God's people have exchanged their glory for what has no power in it)

Holy Silence

Proverbs 21:13

> The one who shuts an ear to the poor one's cry
>   shall plead and not be heard.

Holy Silence

Isaiah 5:8-9

> Woe to those who add house to house
>   and join field to field
> until there is nowhere left
>   and they are the sole inhabitants of the country.
> Yahweh Sabaoth has sworn this in my hearing,
>   "Many houses will be brought to ruin,
>   great and fine ones left untenanted;
> for ten acres of vineyard
>   will yield only one barrel,
> and ten bushel of seed
>   will yield only one bushel!"

Holy Silence

Ezekiel 34:17-22

> As for you, my sheep, the Lord Yahweh says this: I shall judge between sheep and sheep, between rams and he-goats. Not content to drink the clearest water, you foul the rest with your feet. And my sheep must graze on what your feet have trampled and drink what your feet have fouled. Very well, the Lord Yahweh says this: I myself shall judge between the fat sheep and the thin sheep. Since you have jostled with flank and shoulder and butted all the ailing sheep with your horns, until you have scattered them out-side, I shall come and save my sheep and stop them from being victimised. I shall judge between sheep and sheep.

Holy Silence

Isaiah 65:17-18,20-25
(The new Creation and messianic times)

Homily

There could be a homily about sin, especially sins against the Creation (pollution, raping the land, etc.), and personal sin and God's mercy. The worshippers might add their own comments and solutions.

Rite of Reconciliation

Litany of Sorrow

For polluting rivers and fields: forgive us, O God.

For strip-mining the land and leaving it ravaged: forgive us, O God.

For not sharing this world's goods: forgive us, O God.

For limiting the use of the many kinds of natural energies you give us: forgive us, O God.

For...(*similar litanic prayers offered by worshippers*): forgive us, O God.

The priest goes from person to person and speaks words of comfort such as:

> Yahweh is good,
>> his faithful love is everlasting,
>> his constancy from age to age (Ps 100:5).

At this time individuals may feel the need to mention their own sinfulness; or they might simply wish to receive a special blessing.

When the priest has gone to everyone, he or she gives a group penance—something that is constructive and positive for the person that relates to ecology and the progress of humankind.

Absolution

Penance

A fire is lighted in a brazier that is placed in the center. The worshippers each collect a handful of snow, or if there is none, some river water. This is placed in a pot and heated. As it is warming up, it is blessed by the priest and all are invited to make the sign of the cross with this water. At the end of the liturgy this water is poured into the river. This action ties in the sacrament of reconciliation with the flowing waters of baptismal forgiveness. A song such as "The Circle Game" by Joni Mitchell (1966, Siquomb Publishing Co.) is appropriate at this time.

Yesterday a child came out to wonder

Caught a dragonfly inside a jar
  Fearful when the sky was full of thunder
And tearful at the falling of a star
  Then the child moved ten times round the
  seasons
Skated over ten clear frozen streams
  Words like, when you're older, must appease him
And promises of someday make his dreams

Refrain

And the seasons they go round and round
  And the painted ponies go up and down
We're captive on the carousel of time
  We can't return, we can only look behind
From where we came
  And go round and round
In the circle game.

Sixteen springs and sixteen summers gone now
  Cartwheels turn to car wheels thru the town
And they tell him, take your time, it won't be long
  now
Till you drag your feet to slow the circles down

(Refrain)

So the years spin by and now the boy is twenty
Though his dreams have lost some grandeur
  coming true
There'll be new dreams, maybe better dreams and
  plenty
Before the last revolving year is through.

(Refrain)

Rite of the Eucharist

The cross is then decorated with evergreen branches and the like that show signs of life even in the midst of Winter death. Bread and wine are brought forward and the Eucharist begins. The Eucharistic Prayer can be spontaneous, as it was in very ancient times, depending on the ability of the presider; otherwise one of the fine Eucharist Prayers available from different sources might be used (for example, there is one dealing with the theme of water in *Bread Blessed and Broken* edited by John Mossi, S.J.) or perhaps a Eucharistic Prayer of Reconciliation from the Roman Sacramentary might be most appropriate at this time. The celebration might continue with a hike along the river with singing at intermittent intervals.

PART THREE

1

Cosmic Prayer of Praise and Connectedness with All Beings

For Christians, the Holy Eucharist (Holy Communion) is a special time of oneness—a "oneness with" Jesus, other living and deceased Christians, all other people, and also with the very fabric of the universe. All too often, though, Christians have concentrated only on their oneness with Jesus and his Church, to the exclusion of everyone and everything else that inhabits our universe. The more we wonder at something, the more opportunity we have for knowledge and wisdom. Wondering at the mystery of God's abiding oneness with us in Jesus is a many-faceted jewel; we need to take the time to ponder its meanings for us. The Holy Communion is one special way of celebrating this oneness, but there are others that we may contemplate. The following meditation may be of help.

An outdoor natural setting is best, but a city skyline at night or a fine view from a tall building might also serve well. If we are truly contemplative, we can be open to the mystery of God's loving presence "at all times and in all places" in our lives. It is important only that we be open and expectant.

An accepted creed (Nicene, Apostles, or contemporary composition) is the nexus of this particular meditation, although other ancient or modern prayers would also be helpful. Even a painting or a piece of music might help one to prayerfully express both praise and connectedness with the cosmos.

Song:
"Canticle of Creation" (Marty Haugen, 1980, GIA)

Prayer

> O Creator,
>   O You who make all life holy,
> this universe is alive with your goodness.
>   Help me (us) to more fully share in this life.
> Open up my (our) mind(s) and all of my/our
>   senses so that I (we) might give voice to what
>   You have given us.
> I (we) await You here and now. Amen.

Scriptures
(A holy silence is kept between the readings.)

> Alleluia!

> Praise Yahweh from the heavens,
>   praise him in the heights.
> Praise him, all his angels,
>   praise him, all his host!
> Praise him, sun and moon,
>   praise him, all shining stars,
> praise him, highest heavens,
>   praise him, waters above the heavens.
> Let them praise the name of Yahweh
>   at whose command they were made;

he established them for ever and ever
　　by an unchanging decree.

Praise Yahweh from the earth,
　　sea-monsters and all the depths,
fire and hail, snow and mist,
　　storm-winds that obey his word,
mountains and every hill,
　　orchards and every cedar,
wild animals and all cattle,
　　reptiles and winged birds,

kings of the earth and all nations,
　　princes and all judges on earth,
young men and girls,
　　old people and children together.
Let them praise the name of Yahweh,
　　for his name alone is sublime,
his splendour transcends earth and heaven.
　　For he heightens the strength of his people,
to the praise of all his faithful,
　　the children of Israel, the people close to him
　　(Ps 148).

...I shall remind you of the works of the Lord,
　　and tell of what I have seen.
By the words of the Lord his works come into
　　being
　　and all creation obeys his will.
The shining sun looks down on all things,
　　and the work of the Lord is full of his glory.
The Lord has not granted the Holy Ones the power
　　to tell of all his marvels
which the Almighty Lord has solidly constructed
　　for the universe to stand firm in his glory.
He has fathomed both the abyss and the human
　　heart
　　and seen into their devious ways;

for the Most High knows all there is to know
and sees the signs of the times.
He declares what is past and what will be,
and reveals the trend of hidden things.
Not a thought escapes him,
not a single word is hidden from him.
He has embellished the magnificent works of his
wisdom,
he is from everlasting to everlasting,
nothing can be added to him, nothing taken away,
he needs no one's advice.
How lovely, all his works,
how dazzling to the eye!
They all live and last for ever,
and, whatever the circumstances, all obey.
All things go in pairs, by opposites,
he has not made anything imperfect:
one thing complements the excellence of another.
Who could ever grow tired of gazing at his glory?
(Si 42:15-25).

Look, I am making the whole of creation
new...What I am saying is trustworthy and will
come true...It has already happened. I am the Alpha
and the Omega, the Beginning and the End
(Rv 21:5-6).

Meditation on an Affirmation of Faith

As an example, the Nicene Creed is offered because of
its significant meaning historically for Christians. At each
line or juncture of the text, time might be spent on its
meaning nowadays regarding union with God and different dimensions of the creation: things visible and invisible (animals, plants, minerals, spirit beings, possible
creations of God beyond our planet, human beings, and
so on).

If a more inclusive-language translation is available,
that one would be preferable.

> We believe in one God,
>   the Father, the Almighty
>   maker of heaven and earth,
>   of all that is seen and unseen.
>
> We believe in one Lord, Jesus Christ,
>   the only Son of God,
>   eternally begotten of the Father,
>   God from God, Light from Light
>   true God from true God,
>   begotten, not made, one in being with the Father.
>   Through him all things were made.
>   For us men and for our salvation he came down
>   from heaven:
>   by the power of the Holy Spirit he was born of
>   the Virgin Mary, and became man.
>   For our sake he was crucified under Pontius
>   Pilate;
>   he suffered, died, and was buried.
>   On the third day he rose again in fulfillment of
>   the Scriptures;
>   he ascended into heaven and is seated at the
>   right hand of the Father.
>   He will come again in glory to judge the living
>   and the dead,
>   and his kingdom will have no end.
>
> We believe in the Holy Spirit, the Lord, the giver of
>   life,
>   who proceeds from the Father (and the Son).
>   With the Father and the Son he is worshipped
>   and glorified.
>   He has spoken through the prophets.

We believe in one holy catholic and apostolic
church.
We acknowledge one baptism for the forgiveness
of sins.
We look for the resurrection of the dead,
and the life of the world to come. Amen.

(Excerpted from *Prayers We Have In Common:
Agreed Liturgical Texts Proposed by the
International Consultation on English Texts*,
Philadelphia: Fortress Press, 1970, 11).

Homily

The homilist might speak about the relatedness of
everything, the wonderful unity that God has put into
everything, our ability to disturb that unity, and what we
might now do to restore the original unity, the original
blessing of God.

Holy Action

The prayer participants are now invited to look
around the area so that they might gather items from
Nature that could help to illustrate their faith. They
especially might be invited to symbolize by their finds
the various "orders" of creation: spirit beings (angels,
"spirit powers"), other possible planetary inhabitants,
humans (the "two- leggeds"), animals (the "four-leg-
geds"), birds (the "winged ones"), and all other creatures that swim, fly, or run, as well as plants and
minerals. It is important that those praying come to realize more deeply that everything is alive to God and
should be to us also. They could talk about the relationship of their finds.

Song:
"I Want to Praise Your Name" (Bob Hurd, 1984, OCP)

Blessing

Those praying could be invited by the leader to encircle the items that were found. As a drum or other instrument is played, all could round dance to words such as these: "God is our Creator; we are blessed by God. The earth is our mother; we will take care of her; we belong to one another; let love always join us." As the blessing words are danced, the ones praying may make the sign of the cross over themselves and each other.

Song:
"Jesus is Life" (Carey Landry, 1977, NALR)
"It's a Brand New Day" (Paul Quinlan, 1971, NALR)

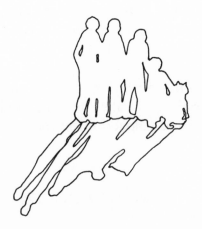

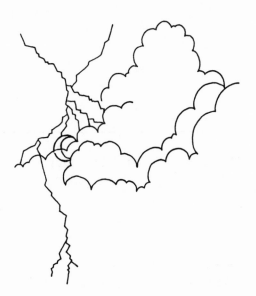

2

Blessing of the Sky

Song:
"The Children of Sunlight" (Ed Gutfreund, 1975, NALR)

Welcome

Prayer

> O God,
>> your power and majesty are manifested in the
>> great sky above us.
>
> Our eyes take in this special part of your splendour.
> May the eyes of our mind and spirit also be open
>> to You.
>
> Help us to see and understand the signs of our
>> own times
>> that we might speak clearly of You to this
>> generation and all those who follow.
>
> May the vast array that is before us remind us to
>> always look to You as our strength.
>
> We praise You now and forever. Amen.

Scriptures

When you raise your eyes to heaven, when you see the sun, the moon, the stars—the entire array of heaven—do not be tempted to worship and serve them (Dt 4:19).

David addressed the words of this song to Yahweh, when Yahweh had delivered him from the clutches of all his enemies and from the clutches of Saul. He said:

Yahweh is my rock and fortress,
    my deliverer is my God.
I take refuge in him, my rock,
    my stronghold, my refuge.
My Saviour, you have saved me from violence;
I call to Yahweh, who is worthy of praise,
    and I am saved from my foes...

I called to Yahweh in my anguish,
    I cried for help to my God,
from his Temple he heard my voice,
    my cry came to his ears!

Then the earth quaked and rocked,
    the heavens' foundations shuddered,
    they quaked at his blazing anger.
Smoke rose from his nostrils,
    from his mouth devouring fire
    (coals were kindled at it).
He parted the heavens and came down,
    a storm-cloud underneath his feet;
riding one of the winged creatures, he flew,
    soaring on the wings of the wind.
He wrapped himself in darkness,
    his pavilion dark waters and dense cloud.
A brightness lit up before him,
    hail and blazing fire.

Yahweh thundered from the heavens,
 the Most High made his voice heard.
He shot his arrows and scattered them,
 his lightning flashed and routed them.
The very springs of ocean were exposed,
 the world's foundations were laid bare,
at the roaring of Yahweh,
 at the blast of breath from his nostrils!

He reached out from on high, from above,
 snatched me up,
 pulled me from the watery depths,
rescued me from my mighty foe,
 from my enemies who were stronger than I
 (2 Sm 22:1-4,7-18).

Rain down, you heavens, from above,
 and let the clouds pour down saving justice,
let the earth open up and blossom with salvation,
 and let justice sprout up with it;
 I, Yahweh, have created it! (Is 45:8).

After Jesus had been born at Bethlehem in Judaea
during the reign of King Herod, suddenly some
wise men came to Jerusalem from the east asking,
"Where is the infant king of the Jews? We saw his
star as it rose and have come to do him homage..."
Then Herod summoned the wise men to see him
privately. He asked them the exact date on which
the star had appeared and sent them on to Bethlehem with the words, "Go and find out about the
child, and when you have found him, let me know,
so that I too may go and do him homage." Having
listened to what the king had to say, they set out.
And suddenly the star they had seen rising went forward and halted over the place where the child
was. The sight of the star filled them with delight,
and going into the house they saw the child with

his mother Mary, and falling to their knees they did him homage (Mt 2:1-2,7-11).

The Pharisees and Sadducees came, and to put him to the test they asked if he would show them a sign from heaven. He replied, "In the evening you say, 'It will be fine; there's a red sky,' and in the morning, 'Stormy weather today; the sky is red and overcast.' You know how to read the face of the sky, but you cannot read the signs of the times" (Mt 16:1-3).

It was by faith that Abraham obeyed the call to set out for a country that was the inheritance given to him and his descendants, and that he set out without knowing where he was going...It was equally by faith that Sarah, in spite of being past the age, was made able to conceive, because she believed that he who had made the promise could fulfill it. Because of this, there came from one man, and one who already had the mark of death on him, descendants as numerous as the stars of heaven and the grains of sand on the seashore which cannot be counted (Heb 11:8,11-12).

So we have confirmation of the words of the prophets; and you will be right to pay attention to it as to a lamp for lighting a way through the dark, until the dawn comes and the morning star rises in your minds (2 Pet 1:19).

Homily

A homilist might speak to those gathered about the beauty and goodness of God's creation, especially highlighting our responsibilities in keeping the skies clear of pollution. Concerns about promoting peace in outer space might also be touched upon. All are given a chance to share their thoughts.

Sky Meditation

Everyone is invited by a leader to lie down on the ground facing the sky. All may spend some time enjoying the intricate changing patterns of the clouds, sunlight, warmth, etc. Music may accompany this action.

Spontaneous Prayers

A leader begins praying and invites those gathered to respond with words such as: "Let your love shine upon us" or "Touch our earth with your love." All may share in the prayer with acclamations, praises, petitions, and so on.

Blessing

As all raise their hands toward the sky, a leader offers a blessing, with smoking incense or other sweet-smelling herbs and plants. Then she or he moves among the people gathered and, as the smoke wafts skyward, each person may symbolically wash with the incense smoke.

Song:
"Rainbow" (Daryll Ducote, 1978 Damean Music)

3

Blessing of the Earth

Song:
"I Want to Praise Your Name" (Bob Hurd, 1984, OCP)

Prayer

> Great Spirit,
>   fill us with light.
> Give us strength to understand and eyes to see.
> Teach us to walk the soft earth as relatives to all
>   that live. Amen (a Lakota prayer).

Rite of Signing

All gather in a circle. Each person receives from a leader (or from the person to the left) the sign of the cross or other marking on the forehead or hands. Moist earth is used. Special words or the following might be said during the signing: "Dust you are and to dust you shall return" (Gn 3:19).

Scriptures

Some Scriptures are shared. A holy silence is kept between the readings.

> Yahweh God shaped man from the soil of the ground and blew the breath of life into his nostrils, and man became a living being (Gn 2:7).

> God also said, "Look, to you I give all the seedbearing plants everywhere on the surface of the earth, and all the trees with seedbearing fruit; this will be your food" (Gn 1:29).

> If you live according to my laws, if you keep my commandments and put them into practice, I shall give you the rain you need at the right time; the soil will yield its produce and the trees of the countryside their fruit; you will thresh until vintage time and gather grapes until sowing time. You will eat your fill of bread and live secure in your land (Lv 26:3-5).

> As for you, my sheep, the Lord Yahweh says this: I shall judge between sheep and sheep, between rams and he-goats. Not content to drink the clearest of water, you foul the rest with your feet. And my sheep must graze on what your feet have trampled and drink what your feet have fouled. Very well, the Lord Yahweh says this: I myself shall judge between the fat sheep and the thin sheep. Since you have jostled with flank and shoulder and butted all the ailing sheep with your horns, until you have scattered them outside, I shall come and save my sheep and stop them from being victimised. I shall judge between sheep and sheep. I shall raise up one shepherd, my servant David, and put him in charge of them to pasture them; he will pasture them and be their shepherd. I, Yahweh, shall be their God, and my servant David will be

ruler among them. I, Yahweh, have spoken. I shall make a covenant of peace with them; I shall rid the country of wild animals. They will be able to live secure in the desert and go to sleep in the woods. I shall settle them round my hill; I shall send rain at the proper time; it will be a rain of blessings. The trees of the countryside will yield their fruit and the soil will yield its produce; they will be secure on their soil. And they will know that I am Yahweh when I break the bars of their yoke and rescue them from the clutches of their slave- masters. No more will they be a prey to the nations, no more will the wild animals of the country devour them. They will live secure, with no one to frighten them. I shall make splendid vegetation grow for them; no more will they suffer from famine in the country; no more will they have to bear the insults of other nations. So they will know that I, their God, am with them and that they, the House of Israel, are my people—declares the Lord Yahweh. And you, my sheep, are the flock of my human pasture, and I am your God—declares the Lord Yahweh
(Ez 34:17-31).

To Yahweh belong the earth and all it contains,
     the world and all who live there (Ps 24:1).

Israel, come back to Yahweh your God;
     your guilt was the cause of your downfall.
Prove yourself with words
     and come back to Yahweh.
Say to him, "Take all guilt away
     and give us what is good,
          instead of bulls we will dedicate to you our lips.
Assyria cannot save us,
     we will not ride horses any more,

or say, "Our God!" to our own handiwork,
    for you are the one in whom orphans find
    compassion."

I shall cure them of their disloyalty,
    I shall love them with all my heart,
    for my anger has turned away from them.
I shall fall like dew on Israel,
    he will bloom like the lily
and thrust out roots like the cedar of Lebanon;
    he will put out new shoots,
he will have the beauty of the olive tree
    and the fragrance of Lebanon.
They will come back to live in my shade;
    they will grow wheat again,
they will make the vine flourish,
    their wine will be as famous as Lebanon's.

What has Ephraim to do with idols any more
    when I hear him and watch over him?
I am like an evergreen cypress,
    you owe your fruitfulness to me (Hos 14:2-9).

You have already been told what is right
    and what Yahweh wants of you.
Only this, to do what is right, to love loyalty
    and to walk humbly with your God (Mic 6:8).

How does it help, my brothers, when someone who
has never done a single good act claims to have
faith? Will that faith bring salvation? If one of the
brothers or one of the sisters is in need of clothes
and has not enough food to live on, and one of you
says to them, "I wish you well; keep yourself warm
and eat plenty," without giving them these bare
necessities of life, then what good it that? In the
same way faith: if good deeds do not go with it, it is
quite dead...

Well now, you rich! Lament, weep for the miseries that are coming to you. Your wealth is rotting, your clothes are all moth-eaten. All your gold and silver are corroding away, and the same corrosion will be a witness against you and eat into your body. It is like a fire which you have stored up for the final days. Can you hear crying out against you the wages which you kept back from the labourers mowing your fields? The cries of the reapers have reached the ears of the Lord Sabaoth. On earth you have had a life of comfort and luxury; in the time of slaughter you went on eating to your heart's content. It was you who condemned the upright and killed them; they offered you no resistance.

Now be patient, brothers, until the Lord's coming. Think of a farmer: how patiently he waits for the precious fruit of the ground until it has had the autumn rains and the spring rains! You too must be patient; do not lose heart, because the Lord's coming will be soon (Jm 2:14-17,5:1-8).

More, as you are rich in everything—faith, eloquence, understanding, concern for everything, and love for us too—then make sure that you excel in this work of generosity too. I am not saying this as an order, but testing the genuineness of your love against the concern of others. You are well aware of the generosity which our Lord Jesus Christ had, that, although he was rich, he became very poor for your sake, so that you should become rich through his poverty. I will give you my considered opinion in the matter; this will be the right course for you as you were the first, a year ago, not only to take any action but also even to conceive the project. Now, then, complete the action as well, so that the fulfillment may—so far as your resources permit—be proportionate to your enthusiasm for the project. As long as the enthusiasm is there, the basis on which it is acceptable is what someone has, not what someone does not have. It is not that you ought to relieve other people's needs and leave yourselves in hardship; but there should be a fair balance—your surplus at present may fill their deficit, and another time their surplus may fill your deficit. So there may be a fair balance; as scripture says:

No one who had collected more had too much,
   no one who collected less had too little
   (2 Cor 8:7-15).

If anyone is well off in worldly possessions and sees his brother in need but closes his heart to him, how can the love of God be remaining in him?
(1 Jn 3:17).

"And so the kingdom of Heaven may be compared to a king who decided to settle his accounts with his servants. When the reckoning began, they brought him a man who owed ten thousand talents; he had no means of paying, so his master gave orders that he should be sold, together with his wife and children and all his possessions, to meet the debt. At this, the servant threw himself down at his master's feet, with the words, 'Be patient with me and I will pay the whole sum.' And the servant's master felt so sorry for him that he let him go and cancelled the debt. Now as this servant went out, he happened to meet a fellow- servant who owed him one hundred denarii; and he seized him by the throat and began to throttle him, saying, 'Pay what you owe me.' His fellow-servant fell at his feet and appealed to him, saying 'Be patient with me and I will pay you.' But the other would not agree; on the contrary, he had him thrown into prison till he should pay the debt. His fellow-servants were deeply distressed when they saw what happened, and they went to their master and reported the whole affair to him. Then the master sent for the man and said to him, 'You wicked servant, I cancelled all that debt of yours when you appealed to me. Were you not bound, then, to have pity on your fellow-servant just as I had pity on you?' And in his anger the master handed him over to the torturers till he should pay all his debt. And that is how my heavenly Father will deal with you unless you each forgive your brother from your heart" (Mt 18:23-35).

Rite of Viewing

Slides are shown (or a video or movie) that majestically describe the earth that we live on. Music should accompany the viewing. It is recommended that only earth scenes be shown at first. Toward the end of the viewing, there could be scenes of human beings interacting with the earth (rock climbing, planting, reaping, picnicking).

Homily

A leader shares a few words and begins a discussion about our own human participation in the fate of the earth. Special attention may be given to local or regional efforts at ecology or soil conservation.

Offering

People are invited to share their monetary wealth to help a particular project which supports a good earth-human relationship.

Song:
"Mountains and Hills" (Dan Schutte, 1971, NALR)

Rite of Blessing

The people could be blessed with a bowl of seeds that they can later plant; a bowl of earth or sand that contains smoking incense or other blessed herbs; or a natural wooden cross that has been daubed with moist earth or clay of different colors or one that is decorated with vines or flowers.

Rite of Sending Forth

Those gathered are sent forth to plant seeds or trees in a nearby plot of land.

Song:
"Ashes" (Tom Conry, 1978, OCP)

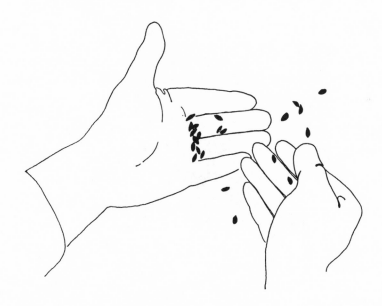

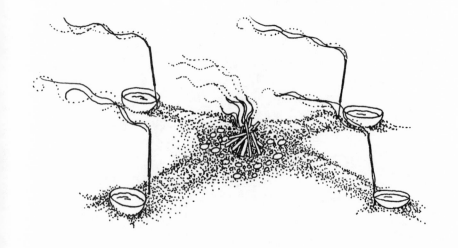

4

Personal or Group Meditation Concerning the Four Elements

This meditation can help us to understand more deeply our interrelatedness with everything around us. The four elements of earth, air, fire, and water have been honored among many Peoples of the earth from time immemorial as particular ways of being in special contact with the Creator. For everyone they are a given; they do not have to be invented or dreamed up. Peoples in traditional or technological societies can play and pray with the elements because they are so universal. Because of our own unique time and place in God's continuous creation (evolution in its various aspects), now more than ever we must consider the effects of all our decisions on the next seven generations. We do not live only in the present. As human inhabitants of Mother Earth, we must consider those who come after us: now we are the ancestors of those who as yet are unborn. We must consider also all the other life forms of our planet and, if we are to reach out further into outer space, even those of our vast universe.

As each element is prayed with, attention should be given to what it is in contrast to the other elements: its special power and properties, and its use (both beneficial and destructive) by us in the past and nowadays. Special consideration needs to be given to what we must do, both individually and collectively, to ensure its proper use in the future.

It is important that symbols of the four elements be present, even in simple or abbreviated form. If the meditation is outdoors, natural phenomena are most suitable (a hill, a breeze, the sun, a river or lake). If the setting is in a room or a church or other religious building, ceramic trays of earth, candles, bowls of water, balloons, etc. may be utilized.

If more than one person is meditating, then the symbols of the four elements could be in the center of them.

A cross (or other special religious symbol) could creatively be made up of the elements. For instance, a cross formed from natural earth with small bowls of water at each of its points, incense sticks or pots of incense also at the four points, and a small fire or flame in the middle of the cross.

Song:
"All You Works of God" (Marty Haugen, 1989, GIA)

Welcome
(if others are present)

Prayer
(voiced or silent)

Scriptures

Yahweh created me,
  first-fruits of his fashioning,
From everlasting, I was firmly set,
  from the beginning, before the earth came into
  being.
The deep was not, when I was born,
  nor were there springs with their abounding
  waters.
Before the mountains were settled,
  before the hills, I came to birth;
before he had made the earth, the countryside,
  and the first elements of the world.

When he fixed the heavens firm, I was there,
  when he drew a circle on the surface of the deep,
when he thickened the clouds above,
  when the sources of the deep began to swell,
when he assigned the sea its boundaries—
  and the waters will not encroach on the shore—
when he traced the foundations of the earth, I was
  beside the master craftsman
  delighting him day after day,
ever at play in his presence,
  at play everywhere on his earth,
  delighting to be with the children of men
  (Prv 8:22-31).

Other Reading Source

A Speech of 1854 given to Governor Isaac Stevens of Washington Territory by Chief Sealth (Seattle), dramatically and poetically speaking of our earthly environment by the Creator (*How Can One Sell the Air?*, 1980)

Consideration of Each Element

The Gift of Earth

Symbol of Meditation: a mountain, an ant hill, a field, a meadow, a bowl of earth or sand, etc.

Scripture

> Yahweh said to Abram after Lot had parted from him, "Look all round from where you are, to north and south, to east and west, for all the land within sight I shall give you and your descendants for ever. I shall make your descendants like the dust on the ground; when people succeed in counting the specks of dust on the ground, then they will be able to count your descendants too! On your feet! Travel the length and width of the country, for I mean to give it to you (Gn 13:14-17).

Other Reading Source:
Thinking Like a Mountain: Toward a Council of All Beings *(John Seed, 1988).*

Prayer
(voiced or silent)

Action Question

What can I (we) do to use the earth more responsibly?

Song:
"In Defense of Creation" (Jim Strathdee, 1987, Desert Flower Music)
"Sing to the Mountains" (Bob Dufford, 1975, NALR)
"God Whose Farm is All Creation" (John Arlott, 1980, CBW)

The Gift of Air

Symbol of Meditation: moving clouds, or slides of clouds, or a balloon, a flute, etc.

Scripture

> You stretch out the heavens like a tent,
>> build your palace on the waters above,
> making the clouds your chariot,
>> gliding on the wings of the wind,
> appointing the winds your messengers,
>> flames of fire your servants (Ps 104:3-4).

Other Reading Source:
Breath of the Invisible *(John Redtail Freesoul, 1986)*

Prayer
(voiced or silent)

Action Question

What can I (we) do to ensure purer air now and in the years ahead?

Song:
"All You Works of God" (Marty Haugen, 1989, GIA)
"There's A Song in My Heart (Don Neumann and Tim Tlucek, 1975, NALR)
Audiotape of birds calling, wolves singing, etc.

The Gift of Fire

Symbol of Meditation: the sun, or a campfire, or a candle, or a gas stove, etc.

Scripture

> When Pentecost day came round, they had all met together, when suddenly there came from heaven a sound of a violent wind which filled the entire house in which they were sitting; and there appeared to them tongues of fire; these separated and came to rest on the head of each of them. They were all filled with the Holy Spirit and began to speak different languages as the Spirit gave them power to express themselves (Acts 2:1-4).

Other Reading Source:
Being of the Sun *(Ramon Sender and Alicia Bay Laurel, 1973)*

Prayer
(voiced or silent)

Action Question

What can I (we) do to use fire more wisely?

Song:
"The Fire of Love" (Sebastian Temple, 1967, GIA)

The Gift of Water

Symbol of Meditation: ocean, lake, river, rainstorm, melting ice cubes, etc.

Scripture

> When a Samaritan woman came to draw water, Jesus said to her, "Give me something to drink." ...The Samaritan woman said to him, "You are a Jew. How is it that you ask me, a Samaritan, for something to drink?" ...Jesus replied to her: "If you only knew what God is offering and who it is that is saying to you, 'Give me something to drink,' you would have been the one to ask, and he would have given you living water...no one who drinks the water I shall give him will ever be thirsty again: the water I shall give him will become in him a spring of water, welling up for eternal life" (Jn 4:7-10,14).

Other Reading Source:
Earth Wisdom *(Dolores La Chapelle, 1978)*

Prayer
  (voiced or silent)

Action Question

What can I (we) do to use water in such a way that it is not wasted?

Song:
  "Come to the Water" (John Foley, 1978, NALR)
  "Sprinkling Rite" (Donald Reagan, 1979, NALR)
  Audiotape of the sounds of a river or a storm

Blessing

Each person blesses herself or himself and departs in silence.

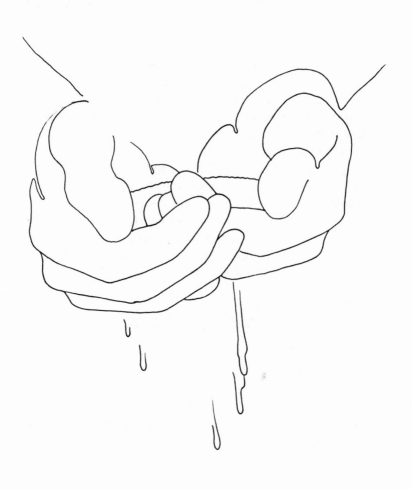

5

Giving Thanks for the Gift of Water

Water, in one form or another, is everywhere on the earth. Some people have plenty of it and use it wisely, while others definitely waste it. Pitifully, there are other inhabitants of areas of the world who pray for it constantly and are slow in receiving it. Some governments, national and area-wide, hoard it from those around them.

Water affects us in so many ways. Often we are not conscious of its bounty until we are deprived of it. The following meditation may help some of us to treat water as a manifold gift of the Creator, that needs to be protected so that generations to come may enjoy it to its fullest capacity.

For optimum benefits from this prayer form, it is important that the one praying is close to a body of water: a river, a pond, an ocean or sea; one can also experience water as rain or as snow or as thundercloud. If one is necessarily confined indoors, even a bowl of ice cubes floating in water may suffice as the focused object of meditation.

After a person or group has properly become disposed to praying, the scriptures are read. Silence is kept between the readings. Other non-scriptural reading sources may be helpful: a poem, a story, etc. After the time of scripture reading, a holy action may include drawing or painting or simply experiencing the various modes of water's existence: swimming, walking in the rain or snow, using the hands or other parts of the body to sense the water, etc. Such joyous water experiences should lead the one praying to some kind of positive action in regard to good water stewardship. The possibilities for this are myriad. The meditation ends with a blessing with water and perhaps a song.

Location of Holy Site

The worshipper goes to a place which is at the same time comfortable and conducive to prayerful meditation.

Prayer

> O God,
>   as I (we) sit here (as I (we) walk in your
>   creation),
> touch me (us) with gentle drops of mercy;
>   wash me (us) with your loving kindness again
>   and again;
> cover me (us) with your goodness;
>   surround me (us) with good friends;
> may I (we) be a powerful but gentle channel of
>   your love to everyone and everything I (we) see
>   today. Amen.

Scriptures

> The flood lasted forty days on earth. The waters swelled, lifting the ark until it floated off the ground. The waters rose, swelling higher above the

ground, and the ark drifted away over the waters. The waters rose higher and higher above the ground until all the highest mountains under the whole of heaven were submerged. The waters reached a peak of fifteen cubits above the submerged mountains. And all the living things that stirred on earth perished; birds, cattle, wild animals, all the creatures swarming over the earth, and all human beings. Everything with the least breath of life in its nostrils, everything on dry land, died. Every living thing on the face of the earth was wiped out, people, animals, creeping things and birds; they were wiped off the earth and only Noah was left, and those with him in the ark. The waters maintained their level on earth for a hundred and fifty days (Gn 7:17-24).

Moses led Israel away from the Sea of Reeds, and they entered the desert of Shur. Then they travelled through the desert for three days without finding water. When they reached Marah, they could not drink the Marah water because it was bitter; this is why the place was named Marah. The people complained to Moses saying, "What are we to drink?" Moses appealed to Yahweh for help, and Yahweh showed him a piece of wood. When Moses threw it into the water, the water became sweet. There he laid down a statute and law for them and there he put them to the test.

Then he said, "If you listen carefully to the voice of Yahweh your God and do what he regards as right, if you pay attention to his commandments and keep all his laws, I shall never inflict on you any of the diseases that I inflicted on the Egyptians, for I am Yahweh your Healer."

So they came to Elim where there were twelve springs and seventy palm trees; and there they pitched camp beside the water (Ex 15:22-27).

The whole community of Israelites left the desert of Sin, travelling by stages as Yahweh ordered. They pitched camp at Rephidim where there was no water for the people to drink. The people took issue with Moses...Yahweh then said to Moses, "Go ahead of the people, taking some of the elders of Israel with you. In your hand take the staff with which you struck the River, and go. I shall be waiting for you there on the rock (at Horeb). Strike the rock, and water will come out for the people to drink." This was what Moses did, with the elders of Israel looking on (Ex 17:1-2,5-7).

But Yahweh your God is bringing you into a fine country, a land of streams and springs, of waters that well up from the deep in valleys and hills... (Dt 8:7).

Yahweh, your faithful love is in the heavens,
　　your constancy reaches to the clouds,
your saving justice is like towering mountains,
　　your judgments like the mighty deep.
　　Yahweh, you support both man and beast;
how precious, God, is your faithful love.
　　So the children of Adam take refuge in the
　　shadow of your wings.
They feast on the bounty of your house,
　　you let them drink from your delicious streams;
in you is the source of life... (Ps 36:5-9).

You fixed the earth on its foundations,
　　at the voice of your thunder they sped away,
flowing over mountains, down valleys,
　　to the place you had fixed for them;
you made a limit they were not to cross,
　　they were not to return and cover the earth.

In the ravines you opened up springs,
　　running down between the mountains,

supplying water for all the wild beasts;
   the wild asses quench their thirst,
on their banks the birds of the air make their nests,
   they sing among the leaves.
From your high halls you water the mountains,
   satisfying the earth with the fruit of your works:
for cattle you make the grass grow,
   and for people the plants they need,
to bring forth food from the earth,
   and wine to cheer people's hearts,
oil to make their faces glow,
   food to make them sturdy of heart.
The trees of Yahweh drink their fill,
   the cedars of Lebanon which he sowed;...
   (Ps 104:5-16).

Into the sea go all the rivers,
   and yet the sea is never filled,
and still to their goal the rivers go (Eccl 1:7).

Can the papyrus flourish except in marshes?
   Without water can the rushes grow?
Even when green and before being cut,
   fastest of all plants they wither.
Such is the fate of all who forget God;...
   (Job 8:11- 12).

...my people have committed two crimes:
   they have abandoned me, the fountain of living
   water,
and dug water-tanks for themselves,
   cracked water- tanks that hold no water
   (Jer 2:13).

"If anyone gives so much as a cup of cold water to
one of these little ones because he is a disciple,
then in truth I tell you, he will most certainly not go
without reward" (Mt 10:42).

"If only you knew what God is offering and who it is that is saying to you, 'Give me something to drink,' you would have been the one to ask, and he would have given you living water...Whoever drinks this water will be thirsty again; but no one who drinks the water that I shall give him will ever be thirsty again: the water that I shall give him will become in him a spring of water welling up for eternal life (Jn 4:10,14).

Then the angel showed me the river of life, rising from the throne of God and of the Lamb and flowing crystal-clear. Down the middle of the city street, on either bank of the river were the trees of life, which bear twelve crops of fruit in a year, one in each month, and the leaves of which are the cure for the nations (Rv 22:1-1).

Holy Action

This is a good time to swim or wade in the water or take a short hike in the snow. One should let all the senses be open to the experience.

Blessing

The worshipper blesses herself/himself with the water or snow in the sign of the cross. Some water may also be taken away in a container for later spiritual use. This should be a reminder of baptismal commitment or a dedication to work for a sound world and local ecology in regard to water.

Song:
"Baptism" (Lou Fortunate, 1976, J. S. Paluch Co.)

6

Giving Thanks for the Gift of All Minerals

Song:
"Mountains and Hills" (Dan Schutte, 1970, NALR)

Welcome and Instruction

A leader welcomes those who have gathered at the mountainside or a river area or other place where minerals are in great abundance. Beforehand, they have been invited to bring along any jewels or precious stones that are special to them. All take some time now to explore the area, picking up any rocks or colored stones that appeal to them. These are brought back to the gathering place and put in a circle around an equal-sided central cross that has been made up of loose stones. Each person puts them down and takes a seat in a circle around the cross.

Prayer

O God, the Rock that supports us all,
  we bless and thank You for gathering us here at
  this time.
May we feel your constant strength and see the
  beauty that sparkles all around.
Help us to know more and more the preciousness
  of our environment,
  the preciousness of one another,
for we are your children, O God, forever and ever.
  Amen.

Scriptures

He (Moses) then said, "Please show me your glory."
Yahweh said, "I shall make all my goodness pass
before you, and before you I shall pronounce the
name Yahweh; and I am gracious to those to whom
I am gracious and I take pity on those on whom I
take pity. But my face," he said, "you cannot see, for
no human being can see me and survive." Then
Yahweh said, "Here is a place near me. You will
stand on the rock, and when my glory passes by, I
shall put you in a cleft of the rock and shield you
with my hand until I have gone past. Then I shall
take my hand away and you will see my back; but
my face will not be seen" (Ex 33:18-23).

The Israelites, the whole community, arrived in the
first month at the desert of Zin. The people settled
at Kadesh. There Miriam died and was buried.
There was no water for the community, so they
banded together against Moses and Aaron. The
people laid the blame on Moses. "We would rather
have died," they said, "as our brother died before
Yahweh! Why have you brought Yahweh's community into this desert, for us and our livestock to

die here? Why did you lead us out of Egypt, only to bring us to this wretched place? It is a place unfit for sowing, it has no figs, no vines, no pomegranates, and there is not even water to drink!" Leaving the assembly, Moses and Aaron went to the entrance of the Tent of Meeting. They threw themselves on their faces, and the glory of Yahweh appeared to them. Yahweh then spoke to Moses and said, "Take the branch and call the community together, you and your brother Aaron. Then, in full view of them order this rock to release its water. You will release water from the rock for them and provide drink for the community and their livestock." Moses took up the branch from before Yahweh, as he had directed him. Moses and Aaron then called the assembly together in front of the rock. He then said to them, "Listen now, you rebels. Shall we make water gush from this rock for you?" Moses then raised his hand and struck the rock twice with the branch; water gushed out in abundance, and the community and their livestock drank (Num 20:1-11).

He is the Rock, his work is perfect,
    for all his ways are equitable.
A trustworthy God who does no wrong,
    he is the Honest, the Upright One! (Dt 32:4).

Hannah then prayed as follows:

My heart exults in Yahweh,
    in my God is my strength lifted up,
my mouth derides my foes,
    for I rejoice in your deliverance.
There is no Holy One like Yahweh,
    (indeed, there is none but you)
    no Rock like our God (1 Sm 2:1-2).

David addressed the words of this song to Yahweh,
when Yahweh had delivered him from the clutches
of all his enemies and from the clutches of Saul. He
said:

Yahweh is my rock and my fortress,
    my deliverer is my God.
I take refuge in him, my rock,
    my shield, my saving strength,
    my stronghold, my place of refuge...
...For who is God but Yahweh,
    who is a rock but our God...
Life to Yahweh! Blessed be my rock!
    Exalted be the God of my salvation...
    (2 Sm 1-3,32,47).

May the words of my mouth always find favour,
    and the whispering of my heart,
    in your presence, Yahweh,
my rock, my redeemer (Ps 19:14).

In you, Yahweh, I have taken refuge,
    let me never be put to shame,
in your saving justice deliver me, rescue me,
    turn your ear to me,
    make haste!
Be for me a rock-fastness,
    a fortified citadel to save me.
You are my rock, my rampart;
    true to your name, lead me and guide me!
    (Ps 31:1-3).

God, hear my cry,
    listen to my prayer.
From the end of the earth I call to you
    with fainting heart.
Lead me to the high rock that stands far out of my
    reach (Ps 61:1-2).

In you, Yahweh, I take refuge,
  I shall never be put to shame.
In your saving justice rescue me, deliver me,
  listen to me and save me.
Be a sheltering rock for me,
  always accessible;
you have determined to save me,
  for you are my rock, my fortress (Ps 71:1-3).

Trust in Yahweh for ever,
  for Yahweh is a rock for ever (Is 26:4).

Listen to me, you who pursue justice,
  you who seek Yahweh.
Consider the rock from which you were hewn,
  the quarry from which you were dug (Is 51:1).

"Therefore, everyone who listens to these words of
mine and acts on them will be like a sensible man
who built his house on rock. Rain came down,
floods rose, gales blew and hurled themselves
against that house, and it did not fall: it was
founded on rock. But everyone who listens to these
words of mine and does not act on them will be
like a stupid man who built his house on sand. Rain
came down, floods rose, gales blew and struck that
house, and it fell; and what a fall it had!"
(Mt 7:24-27).

When Jesus came to the region of Caesarea Philippi
he put this question to his disciples, "Who do
people say the Son of Man is?" And they said, "Some
say John the Baptist, some Elijah, and others
Jeremiah or one of the prophets." "But you," he
said, "who do you say I am?" Then Simon Peter
spoke up and said, "You are the Christ, the Son of
the living God." Jesus replied, "Simon son of Jonah,
you are a blessed man! Because it was no human
agency that revealed this to you but my Father in

heaven. So I now say to you: You are Peter and on
this rock I will build my community. And the gates
of the underworld can never overpower it"
(Mt 16:13-18).

It was now evening, and since it was Preparation
Day—that is, the day before the Sabbath—there
came Joseph of Arimathaea, a prominent member
of the Council, who himself lived in the hope of
seeing the kingdom of God, and he boldly went to
Pilate and asked for the body of Jesus. Pilate,
astonished that he should have died so soon, summoned the centurion and enquired if he had been
dead for some time. Having been assured of this by
the centurion, he granted the corpse to Joseph who
laid him in a tomb which had been hewn out of the
rock. He then rolled a stone against the entrance to
the tomb. Mary of Magdala and Mary the mother of
Joset took note of where he was laid (Mk 15:42-47).

I want you to be quite certain, brothers, that our
ancestors all had the cloud over them and all
passed through the sea. In the cloud and in the sea
they were all baptised into Moses: all ate the same
spiritual food and all drank the same spiritual
drink, since they drank from the spiritual rock
which followed them, and that rock was Christ
(1 Cor 10:1-4).

In the spirit, he carried me tó the top of a very high
mountain, and showed me Jerusalem, the holy city,
coming down out of heaven from God. It had all
the glory of God and glittered like some precious
jewel of crystal-clear diamond. Its wall was of great
height and had twelve gates; at each of the twelve
gates there was an angel, and over the gates were
written the names of the twelve tribes of Israel; on
the east there were three gates, on the north three
gates, on the south three gates, and on the west

three gates. The city walls stood on twelve foundation stones, each one of which bore the name of one of the twelve apostles of the Lamb. The angel that was speaking to me was carrying a gold measuring rod to measure the city and its gates and wall. The plan of the city is perfectly square, its length the same as its breadth. He measured the city with his rod and it was twelve thousand furlongs, equal in length and in breadth, and equal in height. He measured its wall, and this was a hundred and forty-four cubits high—by human measurements. The wall was built of diamond, and the city of pure gold, like clear glass. The foundations of the city wall were faced with all kinds of precious stone: the first with diamond, the second lapis lazuli, the third turquoise, the fourth crystal, the fifth agate, the sixth ruby, the seventh gold quartz, the eighth malachite, the ninth topaz, the tenth emerald, the eleventh sapphire and the twelfth amethyst. The twelve gates were twelve pearls, each gate being made of single pearl, and the main street of the city was pure gold, transparent as glass. I could not see any temple in the city since the Lord God Almighty and the Lamb were themselves in the temple, and the city did not need the sun or the moon light, since it was lit by the radiant glory of God, and the Lamb was a lighted torch for it. The nations will come to its light and the kings of the earth will bring it their treasure (Rv 21:10-24).

Homily

The homilist might help the people to understand that all minerals are a treasure, that the whole world, indeed, is a precious commodity entrusted into our hands. We are the ones who must choose when and how rocks (mountains or small gems) must be cut and polished, and for what purpose this should be done. Dangers of strip-mining, etc., could also be touched upon, as well as our over-dependence on gold, silver, or precious gems.

Poem

A reading of a nature poem such as "Oh, Lovely Rock" by Robinson Jeffers (*Selected Poetry*, 1959) would be appropriate at this time.

Exchange of Found Stones and Accompanying Sign of Peace

All are invited by a leader to give a stone or other pretty mineral to someone else as a gift. Music could accompany this exchange. At the same time, an embrace or kiss as a sign of God's love is fitting.

Blessing

All are invited by the leader to approach the central cross, touch it with a hand, and immediately make the sign of the cross on one another.

Song:
"All Things Bright and Beautiful" (Cecil F. Alexander, 1959, Songdex)

○

7

Giving Thanks for the Gift of Trees and All Plant Life

This ceremony should be held outdoors, perhaps to celebrate the first day of Spring or Arbor Day or Conservation Week. If not, small trees or shrubs and other plants could be artistically placed in a church, chapel, or room. A home patio might also serve quite well as the location.

Song:
"Wood Hath Hope" (John Foley, 1978, NALR).

Opening Prayer

As a prayer is offered, blessed cedar or sweetgrass or sage or other incense is burned and those present waft the smoke over themselves. Holy silence is kept between the readings that follow.

Scriptures

> Let the heavens rejoice and earth be glad!
> Let the sea thunder, and all it holds!

Let the countryside exult, and all that is in it,
    and all the trees of the forest cry out for joy...
    (Ps 96:11-12).

The trees of Yahweh drink their fill,
    the cedars of Lebanon which he sowed;
there the birds build their nests,
    on the highest branches the stork makes its
    home... (Ps 104:16-17).

He (Jotham) went and stood on the top of Mount
Gerizim and shouted at the top of his voice: "Hear
me, leaders of Shechem, so that God may also hear
you! One day the trees went out to anoint a king to
rule them. They said to the olive tree, 'Be our king!'
The olive tree replied, 'Must I forgo my oil which
gives honour to god and men, to stand and sway
over the trees?' Then the trees said to the fig tree,
'You come and be our king!' The fig tree replied,
'Must I forgo my sweetness, forgo my excellent
fruit, to go and sway over the trees?' Then the trees
said to the vine, 'You come and be our king!' The
vine replied, 'Must I forgo my wine which cheers
gods and men, to go and sway over the trees?' Then
the trees all said to the thorn bush, 'You come and
be our king!' And the thorn bush replied to the
trees, 'If you are anointing me in good faith to be
your king, come and shelter in my shade. But, if
not, fire will come out of the thorn bush and
devour the cedars of Lebanon' (Jgs 9:7-15).

Yes, you will go out with joy
    and be led away in safety.
Mountains and hills will break into joyful cries
    before you
    and all the trees of the countryside clap their
    hands.
Cypress will grow instead of thorns,
    myrtle instead of nettles.

And this will be fame for Yahweh,
an eternal monument never to be effaced
(Is 55:12-13).

The next day the great crowd of people who had come up for the festival heard that Jesus was on his way to Jerusalem. They took branches of palm and went out to receive him, shouting, "Hosanna! Hosanna! Blessed is he who is coming in the name of the Lord, the king of Israel" (Jn 12:12-13).

This, in fact, is what you were called to do, because Christ suffered for you and left an example for you to follow in his steps. He had done nothing wrong, and had spoken no deceit. He was insulted and did not retaliate with insults; when he was suffering he made no threats but put his trust in the upright judge. He was bearing our sins in his own body on the cross, so that we might die to our sins and live for uprightness; through his bruises you have been healed (1 Pet 2:21-24).

Rite of Sprinkling

Lots of blessed water is then sprinkled over the plants or poured into the earth around the roots. A reading from the book *Thinking Like a Mountain: Towards a Council of All Beings*, or something similar, would be appropriate at this time.

Homily

A leader might share some words about the preciousness of trees; problems concerning the threatened tropical rain forests and their disappearance might be touched upon. Those present could be asked to share their commitments to promote the growth and conservation of trees locally.

Song of Celebration:
"Bloom Where You're Planted" (Carey Landry, 1970, NALR)

Rite of Blessing

A cross made from green or flowered branches could be used to bless those gathered.

Song:
"Sow a Seed" (Wendy Vickers, 1975, NALR)

8

Giving Thanks for the Gift of Animals

This ceremony helps us humans to offer prayerful voice on behalf of the animals. We come before the Creator with them, in thanksgiving for them, in prayer for them. Elements of the service can be adapted to rest homes for the elderly or for groups of children; with some minor adaptation it could become an annual parish liturgy.

Song:
"All Creatures of Our God and King" (attributed to Saint Francis of Assisi, translated by William H. Draper, 1926, OCP).

Prayer

> Loving Creator,
>> we share your Earth with animals and all other
>> life forms.
> As they help us in so many ways, help us to care for
> them,
>> to enjoy their presence,

to help them and one another follow the ways
You have made for us.
Give us the love and compassion of Jesus. Amen.

Scriptures

The Bible and other reading sources (spiritual or non-religious) are placed on an animal pelt or tanned animal skin in the center of those gathered.

Yahweh God shaped man from the soil of the ground and blew the breath of life into his nostrils, and man became a living being...Yahweh God said, "It is not right that the man should be alone"...So from the soil Yahweh God fashioned all the wild animals and all the birds of heaven. These he brought to the man to see what he would call them; each one was to bear the name the man would give. The man gave names to all the cattle, all the birds of heaven and all the wild animals (Gn 2:7,18-20).

How countless are your works, Yahweh,
all of them made so wisely!
The earth is full of your creatures (Ps 104:24).

The upright has compassion on his animals,
but the heart of the wicked is ruthless
(Prv 12:10).

I think to myself: where human beings are concerned, this is so that God can test them and show them that they are animals. For the fate of human and the fate of animal is the same: as one dies, so the other dies; both have the selfsame breath. Human is in no way better off than animal—since all is futile. Everything goes to the same place, everything comes from the dust, everything returns to the dust. Who knows if the human spirit mounts

upward or if the animal spirit goes downward to
the earth? (Eccl 3:18-22).

The wolf will live with the lamb,
    the panther lie down with the kid,
calf, lion and fat-stock beast together,
    with a little boy to lead them.
The cow and the bear will graze
    their young will lie down together.
    The lion will eat hay like an ox.
The infant will play over the den of the adder;
    the baby will put his hand into the viper's lair.
No hurt, no harm will be done on all my holy
    mountain,
    for the country will be full of the knowledge of
    Yahweh
    as the waters cover the sea (Is 11:6-9).

He gives strength to the weary,
    he strengthens the powerless.
Youths grow tired and weary,
    the young stumble and fall,
but those who hope in Yahweh will regain their
    strength,
    they will sprout wings like eagles,
though they run they will not grow weary,
    through they walk they will never tire
    (Is 40:29-31).

Loudly the cattle groan!
    The herds of oxen are bewildered
because they have no pasture.
    The flocks of sheep bear the punishment too...
Land, do not be afraid;
    be glad and rejoice,
    for Yahweh has done great things.
Wild animals, do not be afraid;
    the desert pastures are green again,

the trees bear fruit,
>vine and fig tree yield their richness
>(Jl 1:18,2:21-22).

When that day comes I shall make a treaty for them with the wild animals, with the birds of heaven and the creeping things of the earth;... (Hos 6:25-27).

"That is why I am telling you not to worry about your life and what you are to eat, nor about your body and what you are to wear. Surely life is more than food, and the body more than clothing! Look at the birds in the sky. They do not sow or reap or gather into barns; yet your heavenly Father feeds them. Are you not worth much more than they are?" (Mt 6:25-27).

And at once the Spirit drove him into the desert and he remained there for forty days, and was put to the test by Satan. He was with wild animals... (Mk 1:12-13).

One of the scribes then came up and said to him, "Master, I will follow wherever you go." Jesus said, "Foxes have holes and the birds of the air have nests, but the Son of Man has nowhere to lay his head" (Mt 8:19-20).

"I am the good shepherd: the good shepherd lays down his life for his sheep" (Jn 10:11).

Rite of Touching and Caressing and Communicating with Animals

Now is the special time for individuals to take an animal into their arms to be petted. Children especially should enjoy this time, though not only children! If a "holy commotion" occurs, this is good and can be rejoiced in. The worshippers should particularly be cognizant of the uniqueness, not only of each species, but also of each individual animal or pet. The Creator of all is to be silently thanked at this time.

A shared homily may follow, with the interrelationship of the insects, the swimming creatures, the winged creatures, the four-footed creatures, the two-footed creatures, and all life forms being pointed out.

Song:
"Like the Deer in Winter" (Paul Quinlan, 1971, NALR)

Litany

A litany is prayed. Various animals are mentioned along with their special traits, and the Creator is thanked. Children should be encouraged to voice the litany. Each time the response could be a hearty "Alleluia!" Here is an example:

With the friendship of dogs and cats, we bless you...Alleluia!

With the strength of bears, we bless you...Alleluia!

With the speed of cheetahs, we bless you...Alleluia!

With the graceful bigness of whales, we bless you...Alleluia!

With the happy songs of birds, we bless you...Alleluia!

With (*make up your own*), we bless you...Alleluia!

Blessing

A small animal is held up before the people by a leader and all are blessed with this animal in the sign of the cross, much the same way that a priest or other church leader would traditionally bless with a cross or crucifix.

Song:
"On Eagle's Wings" (Mike Joncas, 1979, NALR)

9

Giving Thanks for the Gift of All
Human Beings

Our Creator/Redeemer did not just begin to be inter-
ested in human beings with the enfleshment of the Son
at Bethlehem, or with the spiritual heroes of Judaism.
God was already with the Peoples of the world from the
first moment that human consciousness was a special
presence on the earth. God has been working through
all the cultural expressions of the Peoples of the earth.
This saving love has been at work from even before the
dawn of human history, preparing the Peoples of the
world to recognize their own features in the image of
Jesus. Nowadays, if we are open to it in faith, we can see
this happening.

Song:
"Just Begun" (John Foley, 1977, NALR)

Procession

A good time for this ceremony is as the sun is setting
and casting the shadows of the worshippers on the
ground. A fire is built on the ground in the shape of an

equal-sided cross (the earth being dug out in the shape of a cross with the firewood laid inside the cross). This symbolizes the four directions and becomes the center of the people. At a given signal (bell sound, drum beat, or triumphant alleluia), all the people process forward and form a circle around the fire. Traditional or symbolic clothing may be worn. When they have formed the circle, they are welcomed by the leader.

Welcome

Prayer

> O God of all people, we are gathered here this
>   evening to praise You and to thank You for
>   creating us.
> At times it is hard to be human:
>   we make so many mistakes and we hurt one
>   another.
> Be with us now.
>   Open up your Holy Word to us.
>   Open our ears that we might hear and
>   understand.
> Help us to know who we are and how we might
>   even more deeply love one another as your Son
>   loves us.
> Be with us in our journey as we create together
>   our world.
>
> **All: Amen!**

Scriptures

> God said, "Let us make man in our own image, in
> the likeness of ourselves, and let them be masters
> of the fish of the sea, the birds of heaven, the cattle,
> all the wild animals and all the creatures that creep
> along the ground."

God created man in the image of himself,
 in the image of God he created him,male and
 female he created them (Gn 1:26-27).

God, endow the king with your own fair
 judgement,
 the son of the king with your own saving justice,
that he may rule your people with justice,
 and your poor with fair judgement.
Mountains and hills,
 bring peace to his people!
With justice he will judge the poor of the people,
 he will save the children of the needy...
For he rescues anyone needy who calls to him,
 and the poor who has no one to help.
He has pity on the weak and the needy,
 and saves the needy from death.
From oppression and violence he redeems their
 lives,
 their blood is precious in his sight...
in him shall be blessed every race in the world,
 and all nations call him blessed
 (Ps 72:1-4,12-14,17).

And Mary said,

My soul proclaims the greatness of the Lord
 and my spirit rejoices in God my Saviour;
because he has looked upon the humiliation of his
 servant.
 Yes, from now onwards all generations will call
 me blessed,
for the Almighty has done great things for me.
 Holy is his name,
and his faithful love extends age after age
 to those who fear him.
He has used the power of his arm,
 he has routed the arrogant of heart.

He has pulled down princes from their thrones
  and raised high the lowly.
He has filled the starving with good things,
  sent the rich away empty.
He has come to the help of Israel his servant,
  mindful of his faithful love—
according to the promise he made to our
  ancestors—
  of his mercy to Abraham and to his descendants
  forever (Lk 1:46-55).

He came to Nazara, where he had been brought up, and went to the synagogue on the Sabbath day as he usually did. He stood up to read, and they handed him the scroll of the prophet Isaiah. Unrolling the scroll he found the place where it is written:

The spirit of the Lord is on me,
  for he has anointed me to bring good news to
  the afflicted.
He has sent me to proclaim liberty to captives,
  sight to the blind,
to let the oppressed go free,
  to proclaim a year of favour from the Lord
  (Lk 4:16-19).

..."And who is my neighbour?" In answer Jesus said, "A man was once on his way down from Jerusalem to Jericho and fell into the hands of bandits; they stripped him, beat him and then made off, leaving him half dead. Now a priest happened to be travelling down the same road, but when he saw the man, he passed by on the other side. In the same way a Levite who came to the place saw him, and passed by on the other side. But a Samaritan traveller who came on him was moved with compassion when he saw him. He went up to him and bathed his wounds, pouring oil and wine on them. He then lifted him onto his own mount and took him to an inn and looked after him. Next day he took out two denarii and handed them to the inn keeper and said, 'Look after him, and on my way back I will make good any extra expense you have.' Which of these three, do you think, proved himself a neighbour to the man who fell into the bandits' hands?" He replied, "The one who showed pity towards him." Jesus said to him, "Go, and do the same yourself" (Lk 10:29-37).

With so many witnesses in a great cloud all around us, we too, then should throw off everything that weighs us down and the sin that clings so closely, and with perseverance keep running in the race that lies ahead of us. Let us keep our eyes fixed on Jesus, who leads us in our faith and brings it to perfection... (Heb 12:1-2).

My house will be called
a house of prayer for all peoples (Is 56:7).

Song:
"When From Our Exile" (Huub Oosterhuis and Bernard Huijbers, 1975, NALR)

Homily

A leader comments on the readings in light of this particular gathering and invites those present to share their understanding of solidarity with all peoples and the kinds of barriers that people often set up against others.

Rite of Viewing
(optional)

If possible, slides of different races, cultures, and age groups of people are now shown, indicating the particular features of our common humanity. Music should accompany the slides.

If slides are not possible, show the video *It's In Every One Of Us* (Wernher Krutein and David Pomeranz, San Francisco: New Era Media, 1987).

Or, in place of slides or a video, a discussion concerning the fate of humanity and our world may take place.

Rite of Human Affirmation

Those gathered are invited to pray silently for a while. They may choose to grow in some area of greater human understanding: race relations, local cultures whose origin is geographically farther away, teenage-adult communications, and so on. Paper and pencils may be provided for them to privately write down their commitment for personal growth in a certain area. At a later time their desire may be shared with those who can be helpful in a particular area of human relations. The options are indeed many and varied.

Song:
"Beginning Today" (Darryl Ducote and Mike Balhoff, 1978, Damean Music).

Blessing

Small and inexpensive gifts are passed out to those present. These gifts are representative of many cultures (carvings, beadwork, drawings, other craft handiwork). All who receive them admire them, show them to those near them, and then join arms in solidarity with one another to receive the blessing.

The leader stands in the midst of the encircled people and raises her/his hands in blessing, saying:

May our human goodness which has its origin in
   our God continue to grow in every way in every
   culture around our world.
More and more may we learn to respect one
   another, to learn from one another, to share our
   gifts.
In the power that comes from our God who is
   Creator, Redeemer, and Breathgiver, may we live
   forever!"

All: Amen!

Song:
*"Build up the City" (Gordon Truitt and Carey Landry,
1971, NALR).*

Holy Meal

A meal of cultural and national foods could follow; or
marshmallows or other campfire treats could me toasted
over the central fire.

10

Food Blessing and Holy Meal in Honour of the Native Peoples of the Western Hemisphere (or Other Areas of the Earth)

Around the world all of us have much to be thankful for, especially concerning the subject of food. Over the last few hundred years, the foods contained within the cornucopia of the Western hemisphere have been made available to the peoples of the various continents of the world. Potatoes and maize corn, to name but a couple of foods, are enjoyed around the world. Each culture and nation has worked them into their own diet. But the array of culinary items is vast. Even now, traditional fruits and vegetables of all sorts which have been cultivated for thousands of years by the Native Peoples of the Americas are being "discovered" in our own times. Vegetables like chayotes and fruits like papayas are regularly bought in our stores by those who only recently have come to know of them. Recent population mobility and immigration trends have caused food to be very important indeed. A good supply of strong hybrid strains of ancient North and South American plants has more than once come to the aid of starving populations: Biafra, Sudan, Ethiopia, Turkey, to mention only a few of the more recent beneficiaries.

To share food is to share solidarity. Now, more than ever, all religious people, but especially Christians, have a chance to fellowship with food. As they eat they can share the Good News.

As one glances at the list, one is able to pick and choose foods that can fit a menu for a few people or many. It is hoped that as the foods are enjoyed, they would be eaten both in thanksgiving and in the memory of those innumerable Indigenous Peoples who worked with soil and plants and water so that in our own time we can benefit from their sense of sacred agriculture.

Common Name	Scientific Name	Indigenous Name
Tomato	Lycopersicam esculentum	Tomatl (Nahuatl)
Potato	Solanum tuberosum	Batata (Haitian)
Maize	Zea mays	Mahiz (Taino)
Maple Sugar	Acer saccharum	Sesebahkwud (Ojibway)
Pecan	Carya pecan	Pagan (Ojibway)
Chocolate	Theobroma cacao	Xocoah (Nahuatl)
Chayote	Sechium edule	Chayotli (Nahuatl)
Papaya	Carica papaya	Papai (Otomac)
Acorn	Quercus kelloggii	Sixrxin luks (Costanoan)
Avocado	Persea drymifolia	Ahuacatl (Nahuatl)

Squash	Curcurbita pepo	Askootasquash (Proto-Algonquian)
Buffalo	Bison bison	Pte (Dakotah)
Moose	Alces alces andersoni	Moons (Ojibway)
Peanut	Arachis hypogaea	Oomah (Dakotah)
Sweet Potato	Ipomoea batatas	B'don Sku-yah (Dakotah)
Sturgeon	Acipenser transmontanus	Nes (Patwin)
Clover	Trifolium ciliolatum	Patcuku (Miwok)
Cassava	Manihot	Casabi (Taino)
Yam	Dioscorea trifida	Camotl (Nahuatl)
Turkey	Meleagris gallopave	Mesesa (Ojibway)
Guinea Pig	Cavia porcellanus	Cuye (Aymara)
Pine Nut	Pinus lambertiana	Xiren (Costanoan)
Hickory Nut	Carya cordiformis	Metigwaubauk (Ojibway)
Persimmon	Diospyros virginiana	Pasiminan (Cree)
Indian Turnip	Arisaema triphyllum	Ihe (Crow)
Clam	Tagelus californianus	Tookee (Dakotah)
Cranberry	Vaccinium oxycoccux	Mushkegemin (Ojibway)
Chokecherry	Prunus serotina	Baachuua (Crow)
Manzanita	Arctostaphylos pringlei	Choo-tush (Costanoan)
Madrone	Arbutus menziesii	Iukan (Costanoan)

Prickly Pear Cactus	Opuntia phaeacantha	Bichkiliia (Crow)
Pineapple	Ananas comusus	Baachiiuhpe (Crow)
Yucca	Yucca schidigera	Sowungwa (Hopi)
Buffaloberry	Shepnerdia canadensis	Kapakumish (Ojibway)
Huckleberry	Vaccinium ovatum	Kapiliashte (Crow)
Camas	Camassia quamash	Quamash (Chinook)
Sage	Artemesia tridentata	Cheetilichitche (Crow)
Saguaro Cactus	Cereus giganteus	Saguaro (Piman)
Jalapeno	Exogonium purga	Jalap (Nahuatl)
Nut Grass	Brodiaea laxa	Aabi (Paiute)
Ocotillo	Fouquieria splendens	Ocotl (Nahuatl)
Canada Goose	Branta canadensis	Nagita (Paiute)
Jicama	Exogonium bracteatum	Xicama (Nahuatl)
Springtime Trout	Salmo clarki	Tama agai (Paiute)
Mesquite	Prosopis juliflora	Mizquitl (Nahuatl)
White Mariposa Lily	Calochortus venustus	Issheelooshe (Crow)
Yampa	Carum gairdneri	Ma'ssa (Blackfoot)

Sunflower	Helianthus annuus	Baalahchituua (Crow)
Pumpkin	Cucurbita pepo	Egwissimaun (Ojibway)
Juniper	Juniperus occidentalis	Setekene (Miwok)
Gooseberry	Ribes oxyacanthoides	Shaubomin (Ojibway)
Wild Pea	Lothyrus vestitus	Lulumati (Miwok)
Wild Rice	Zizania aquatica	Waubuhnoomin (Ojibway)
Chili	Capsicum annuum	Chili (Nahuatl)
Yuca	Manihot Esculenta	Yuca (Tukano)
Salmon	Oncorhynchus keta	Nooth (Wintu)
Toyon	Photinia arbutifolia	Koso (Miwok)
Jackrabbit	Lepus californicus	Pot-kil-lis (Wintu)
Blackberry	Rubus vitifolius	Mahmid (Wukchumne)
Wild grape	Vitis girdiana	In-suh naw-tip (Wukchumne)
Paca	Cuniculus paca	Paca (Tupi)
Agouti	Dasyprocta agoutis	Acuti (Guarani)
Cayenne	Capsicum frutescens longum	Kyinha (Tupi)
Indian Potato	Apios tuberosa	Wapatowa (Cree)
Cowish	Lomatium cous	Kowish (Nez Perce)
Water Lily	Nymphaea odorata	Woca (Klamath)

Cattail	Typha latifolia	Toi (Paiute)
Deer	Odocoileus hemionus	Maso (Yaqui)
Black Potato	Solanum turbosum	Ch'unu (Quechua)
Tapioca	Manihot esculenta	Mandioca (Tupi)
Century Plant	Agave utahensis	Mescal (Nahuatl)
Sarsaparilla	Smilax febrifuga	Guayaquil (Maya)
Guava	Psidium guayava	Guayaba (Arawak)
Red Snapper	Lutjanus aya	Huachinango (Nahuatl)
Chirimoya	Annona cherimola	Chirimuya (Quechua)
Guanabana	Annona muricata	Soursop (Taino)

Suggested Meal, Which Offers Native Foods of North and South America

As each course is offered, someone could speak of the food's origin as well as where its recipe is typical. For example, maple syrup has always been popular with the Native People of the Eastern Woodlands of North America and this particular recipe—for instance, Corn Nut Pottage with Maple Syrup—has been popular with the Iroquois Peoples for many centuries. Or, the tamale-like hallaca symbolizes the various cultures of Venezuela (the palm leaf, meat, and maize dough represent the Native Peoples; the chicken, raisins, and green olives are typical foods of the European settlers).

Appetizer	Thimbleberries and salmon eggs (Canadian West Coast)	Dried thimbleberries and partially dried salmon eggs.
Salad	Ceviche (Guatemala)	Raw fish marinated in lemon juice and served with onions and hot peppers.
Soup	1. Plateau Pinon (Southwest U.S.A.)	Turkey, wild carrots, wild onions, wild garlic, shepherd's purse greens, other wild greens, pinon nuts, water.
	2. Chipi-chipi (Venezuela)	Shellfish, water, spices (such as in a bouillabaisse).
Bread	1. Hopi Piki (Southwest U.S.A.)	Juniper ash, water, blue cornmeal, sunflower oil.
	2. Arepas (Venezuela)	Flour, water.
	3. Acorn (California)	Acorn flour, water.
	4. Tortillas (Mexico)	Maize, water, salt.
Stew	1. Menominee Venison and Wild Rice (North Eastern U.S.A.)	Venison, salt, water, wild onions, wild rice.
	2. Viudo de Pescado (Colombia)	Fish cooked in holes in the ground and covered with hot stones.

Roast	Canada Goose (California inner-mountain area)	Goose, cranberries, juniperberries, apples.
Fish	(North America)	Dried salmon or trout
Beans	(North and South America)	Pinto beans or other beans, salt, water.
Rice	(North and South America)	Rice, water, salt, spices, meat or fish or fowl.
Dessert	1. Crow Chokeberry Pudding (Montana)	Chokecherries, water, arrowroot, sugar, cornstarch.
	2. Fruit (North and South America)	Mangos, papayas, guavas, blueberries, nuts.
Drinks	1. Ocotillo Ice (Southwest U.S.A.)	Ocotillo blossoms, water, sugar, lemon.
	2. Sassafras Tea (Northeast U.S.A.)	Sassafras roots, water.
	3. Fruit juice (Central and South America)	Mango, papaya
	4. Chocolate, hot or cold (Central and South America)	Cocoa powder, water or milk, sugar, cinnamon or other spices.

5. Chicha (Colombia)	Fermented maize and fruit.
6. Pulque (Mexico)	Fermented juice of agave.
7. Tepache (Mexico)	Pulque, pineapple, cloves.
8. Tequila (Mexico)	Distilled from agave, water, salt, lime.

Blessing over the Meal

O Creator, O Sustainer, O Lover of all Peoples,
  we ask your blessing on our food.
We thank You for bringing each one of us to this
  moment of enjoying a meal together.
May we be strengthened to live for You and one
  another.
May the sharing of this food help us to remove the
  chains of oppression which still subjugate many
  of our brothers and sisters.

Feed them, feed us,
  with your love.
May we always honor the memory of those who
  have gone before us, especially... (*an extinct
  People or Tribe may be mentioned here*)
...and may we always work together so that we may
  share the abundance that ultimately comes from
  You.
We ask this in Jesus' name. Amen.

Songs may be sung between the courses, or there
could be a continuous variety of musical entertainment.

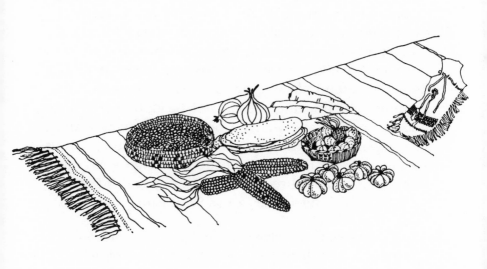

11

Meditation Concerning the Day of My (Our) Salvation

It seems that, except for children and the theatre and women's cosmetics, many people in technological societies have forgotten the importance of ritually painting the body. What a vast opportunity we have in decorating our bodies to express our faith! The Church on a special day of the year, Ash Wednesday, puts palm or other ashes on our heads to remind us of our origin, our present reality, and our future destiny. Holy oils are used at times in celebrating the sacraments, and perhaps once in a while invisible crosses are traced over our bodies at certain blessing times. There is no reason why painting and drawing should not be done on human bodies to celebrate what we believe. The hands, arms, feet, legs, back, chest, and head are a spiritual canvas waiting only for the creative believer to sign forth salvation truths that are lived out in *this* body at *this* time.

There is nothing to fear, for as Saint Paul reminds us,

> I urge you, then, remembering the mercies of God,
> to offer your bodies as a living sacrifice, dedicated

and acceptable to God; that is the kind of worship for you, as sensible people (Rm 12:1).

True, for me everything is permissible, but I am determined not to be dominated by anything...But the body...is for the Lord, and the Lord is for the body...Do you not realize that your bodies are members of Christ's body...? (1 Cor 6:12,14,15).

...we carry with us in our body the death of Jesus so that the life of Jesus, too, may be visible in our body (2 Cor 4:10).

Christ will be glorified in my body, whether by my life or my death (Phil 1:20).

The sun and moon and stars, works of God's creation, along with the cross and other Christian symbols, are fitting objects that can be part of a temporary design on the body. The following meditation can be lived out within the space of twenty-four hours by one person or many. Depending upon the creativity of the artist, the heavenly array, as well as the earth, can be portrayed in such a way that they speak simply and yet profoundly of the salvific work of Jesus. The paintings can be changed at different points in the day. After each painting of the body the scriptures may be meditated with and spontaneous vocal or silent prayer may follow. It is recommended that during this holy time there would occur the singing of short repetitive mantra-like verses of scripture or other spiritual songs.

Sunrise

High above, he pitched a tent for the sun,
who comes forth from his pavilion like a

227

bridegroom,
delights like a champion in the course to be run.
Rising on the horizon
he runs his circuit to the other,
and nothing can escape his heat (Ps 19:5-6).

From the rising of the sun to its setting,
praised be the name of Yahweh! (Ps 113:3).

But from the farthest east to farthest west
my name is great among nations,
and everywhere incense and a pure gift are offered
to my name...
But for you who fear my name,
the Sun of justice will rise with healing in his
rays... (Mal 1:11,3:20).

But I say this to you, love your enemies and pray
for those who persecute you; so that you may be
children of your Father in heaven, for he causes his
sun to rise on the bad as well as the good...
(Mt 5:44-45).

Noon

Commit your destiny to Yahweh,
be confident in him, and he will act,
making your uprightness clear as daylight,
and the justice of your cause as the noon (Ps
37:5-6).

For my part, I appeal to God,
and Yahweh saves me;
evening, morning, noon,
I complain and groan (Ps 55:16-17).

Sundown

> He made the moon to mark the seasons,
>> the sun knows when to set (Ps 104:19).

Night

> On my bed when I think of you,
>> I muse on you in the watches of the night,
> for you have always been my help (Ps 63:6-7).

> It is good to give thanks to Yahweh,
>> to make music for your name, Most High,
> to proclaim your faithful love at daybreak,
>> and your constancy all through the night,
> on the lyre, the ten-stringed lyre,
>> to the murmur of the harp (Ps 92:1-3).

> You bring on darkness, and night falls,
>> when all the forest beasts roam around;
> young lions roar for their prey,
>> asking God for their food (Ps 104:20-21).

> And night will be abolished; they will not need lamplight or sunlight, because the Lord God will be shining on them (Rv 22:5).

12

Meditating on My (Our) Use of Time

"Let's go," "Hurry up," "Time productive," "Time effi-
cient," "Time is money," "Time related,"—these are
phrases that we often hear in our modern world.
Nowadays many of us seem to be so busy with results
that our actions very well can be, to quote Shakespeare,
"much ado about nothing."

Time is also a gift from God; along with the space that
we occupy, it is the locus of how we live out our salvation from moment to moment, minute to minute, hour
to hour, day to day, year to year. Change for good or
bad takes place in time. We often need to stop what we
are doing to see exactly how we are doing with our
time, to notice how well we are using our time for God,
for others, and for ourselves.

Here is a meditation that may be of help to those who
often feel "too busy to pray."

Song:
"If You Want Your Dreams To Be" (Franco Zefferilli,
from the movie Brother Sun, Sister Moon, 1972)

Prayer

O God of all time and historical happenings,
  now and again You break into my (our) life with
  all sorts of special happenings.
Keep me (us) open to daily surprises
  as a little child is.
Help me (us) to fill my (our) time with what is
  good for others,
  for our world and for myself ourselves).
May I (we) become transparent to your actions
  every moment of my (our) life. Amen.

Scripture

...each of your faithful ones pray to you
  in time of distress (Ps 32:6).

The lives of the just are in Yahweh's care,
  their birthright will endure for ever;
they will not be put to shame when bad times
  come,
  in time of famine they will have plenty
  (Ps 37:18-19).

Blessed is anyone who cares for the poor and the
  weak;
  in time of trouble Yahweh rescues him (Ps 41:1).

And so, I pray to you, Yahweh,
  at the time of your favour;
in your faithful love answer me,
  in the constancy of your saving power (Ps 69:13).

Remember me; how long have I left?
  For what pointless end did you create all the
  children of Adam? (Ps 89:47).

There is a season for everything,
  a time for every occupation under heaven:
A time for giving birth,
  a time for dying;
A time for planting,
  a time for uprooting what has been planted.
A time for killing,
  a time for healing;
a time for knocking down,
  a time for building.
A time for tears,
  a time for laughter;
a time for mourning,
  a time for dancing.
A time for throwing stones away,
  a time for gathering them;
a time for embracing,
  a time to refrain from embracing.
A time for searching,
  a time for losing;
a time for keeping,
  a time for discarding.
A time for tearing,
  a time for sewing;
a time for keeping silent,
  a time for speaking.
A time for loving,
  a time for hating;
a time for war,
  a time for peace (Eccl 3:1-8).

"The time is fulfilled, and the kingdom of God is close at hand. Repent, and believe in the gospel" (Mk 1:15).

Besides, you know the time has come; the moment is here for you to stop sleeping and wake up, because by now our salvation is nearer than when we first began to believe. The night is nearly over, daylight is on the way; so let us throw off everything that belongs to the darkness and equip ourselves for the light (Rm 13:11-12).

Make the best of the present time... (Eph 5:16).

...the time is near (Rv 1:3).

Poem:
"God is alive, magic is afoot" (Leonard Cohen, beautiful losers, New York: Viking Press, 1966).

or

Meditation Song:
"Spirits in the Material World" (The Police, Every Breathe You Take - The Singles, 1986)

Action

The one praying might reflect on how he or she normally spends a day (a week, or a weekend), looking for patterns of things that usually occur. A list might be drawn up of these regular life activities. Then questions like the following may be asked:

Where does God fit into my day?

How often do I take time for prayer?

How much quality time do I spend helping others?

How much quality time do I allow for myself?

After some answers have been formulated, the one praying then looks around at something in nature that expresses either slow or rapid growth: a tree, an insect, moving clouds. Many lessons may be learned from observing Nature.

Prayer

O God,
  speak to me (us) of time and eternity.
Show me how I (we) should live.
  Help me (us) to fill my (our) time wisely.
May I (we) become more like Jesus. Amen.

Blessing

May God who took the time to create me (us) bless
  my (our) time here in this place.
May Jesus who took the time to redeem me (us)
  bless my (our) time here in this place.
May the Spirit who takes the time to renew me (us)
  bless my (our) time here in this place.

Song:
"This is the Day" (Marty Haugen, 1980, GIA)

13

Meditation in Honour of Saint Francis of Assisi, Patron Saint of Ecology

Francis of Assisi (1181-1226) was someone who learned to live out what many Native American people would call "walking in balance." He came to understand his own part in the larger, ecological picture, which includes the spirituality of every thing and every one.

This meditation can be prayed alone or with others. Though it honours the love of the Creator manifested in the life of Francis, the real focus concerns the commitment to a balanced and spiritual life of the one praying.

Song:
"Simple Gifts" (Shaker Song)

Prayer

> O loving God,
>   our friend Francis of Assisi reminds us that we
>   and everything around is a gift.

In your love show us how to be good friends of
nature,
good stewards of your Creation. Amen.

Scriptures

God created man in the image of himself,
in the image of God he created him,
male and female he created them.

God blessed them, saying to them, "Be fruitful,
multiply, fill the earth and subdue it. Be masters of
the fish of the sea, the birds of heaven and all the
living creatures that move on the earth." God also
said, "Look, to you I give all the seed-bearing plants
everywhere on the surface of the earth, and all the
trees with seed-bearing fruit; this will be your food.
And to all the wild animals, all the birds of heaven
and all the living creatures that creep along the
ground, I give all the foliage of the plants as their
food" (Gn 1:27-31).

Not all flesh is the same flesh: there is human flesh;
animals have another kind of flesh, birds another
and fish yet another. Then there are heavenly
bodies and earthly bodies; the heavenly have a
splendour of their own, and the earthly a different
splendour. The sun has its own splendour, the
moon another splendour, and the stars yet another
splendour; and the stars differ among themselves in
splendour. It is the same too with the resurrection
of the dead: what is sown is perishable, but what is
raised is imperishable; what is sown is con-
temptible but what is raised is glorious; what is
sown is weak, but what is raised is powerful; what
is sown is a natural body, and what is raised is a
spiritual body.

If there is a natural body, there is a spiritual body too (1 Cor 15:39-45).

Story of Saint Francis' Life

This may be shared orally or read from a book such as *The Little Flowers of St. Francis,* (Raphael Brown, trans., Garden City, New York: Image Books, 1958).

Prayers in the Tradition of Francis: "Canticle of the Sun"

See footnote 162 in this book.

"Pied Beauty"

This is a prayer-poem by Gerald Manley Hopkins about the tremendous varieties of God's Creation.

"Holy Mother Earth, the trees and all nature are witnesses of your thoughts and deeds"

This is a Winnebago People saying from *Touch the Earth* by T. C. McLuhan, page 5.

Holy Silence

Silence is kept for a few minutes.

Act of Commitment

The one praying writes down one or more specific actions that promote ecological balance (planting, helping to teach good soil or water stewardship, promoting animal welfare locally). Later the commitment is shared with others.

Blessing

> May Yahweh bless you (me) and keep you (me).
> May Yahweh let his face shine on you (me) and be
>   gracious to you (me).
> May Yahweh show you (me) his face and bring you
>   (me) peace (Num 6:24-26).

Song:

"Prayer of St. Francis" (Sebastian Temple, Franciscan Communications, 1975).

14

A Circular Blessing Prayer

For many traditional people of the world, a circle is a very important symbol of unity. A circle draws people in; a circle has a center for all to focus on. It is still an ever-important spiritual symbol for Native Peoples of North and South America and many others. Even chapels and churches have been built in a circular pattern, as well as cathedrals (in Ethiopia and in Liverpool, for example).

Among many Native Peoples of this continent, the sacred hoop is manifold in meaning. It represents the universe, the growth patterns of trees, planets and their orbits, the earth, the sun, bird nests, a warrior's shield, a drum, ripples in a pond, and many other naturally beautiful things. Combined with an internal cross, it becomes a powerful wheel symbol, a "medicine wheel," which speaks of both unity and the four directions. This symbol, as should be the case with any religious symbol, needs to be treated with the greatest respect because it reminds us of the sacred relationship of Creator and Creation (including human beings).

The following prayer, though Christian, owes its form to the spiritual legacy of countless generations of Native Peoples of this part of the world. With respect, I offer it.

Preparation

Beforehand, leaders prepare the holy site (outdoors or indoors). The more natural the setting the better. An image of Jesus or a cross is placed on a piece of leather or animal pelt or low basket and surrounded with flowers. Surrounding the image or cross is a paper or other natural material wreath with the following words adopted from Lakota Sundance sacred pole songs (*Teton Sioux Music*, 1918) written on it:

> I am standing
>   In a sacred way
> At the earth's center
>   Beheld by the people
> Seeing the tribe
>   Gathered around me.
> At the places
>   of the four winds

At four points are placed symbols of air (an empty bowl), fire (a candle in a bowl), earth (bowl of earth), and water (bowl of water). People gather in a large circle around these objects and place in front of them flowers or herbs that they have brought. The leaders are also part of this circle.

Song:
"Without Seeing You" (Lucien Deiss, 1970, WLP)
"My Soul is Longing" (Lucien Deiss, 1965, WLP)
"Break Not the Circle" (Fred Kaan, 1975, Agape)
Taize or Gelineau chant

Prayer

O God, like this circle, your love is without end.
Center us on your Son Jesus that we might really
  know what it is to be one with You and all of our
  relations.
In the power of your Spirit may we treat with
  respect all our relatives,
    whether they be human beings or the other
    creatures with which we share this universe.
    Amen.

Scriptures

For who is the greater: the one at table or the one
who serves? The one at table, surely? Yet here I am
among you as one who serves! (Lk 22:27).

For where two or three meet in my name, I am
there among them (Mt 18:20).

They were still talking about all this when he himself stood among them and said to them "Peace be
with you!" (Lk 24:36).

Song Medley

Various kinds of songs are sung, one after the other.
Some are in English, some are in other languages, some
are sung with separate male-female parts, others are
sung alternately only by men or women, some are sung
by children, some by adults, and some all together. Perhaps a special tribal song such as this Arapaho one
might be appropriate:

Ninaa' niahu'na,	I circle around,
Ninaa' niahu'na,	I circle around,
Bi' taa' wu ha' nai' sal,	The boundaries of the earth,

Bi' taa' wu ha' nai' sal,	The boundaries of the earth,
Hi' naa' thi na'	Wearing the long wing
niwu' huna,	feathers as I fly,
Hi' naa' thi na'	Wearing the long wing
niwu' huna,	feathers as I fly.

Blessing

As all stand, a leader weaves in and out of the circle between the worshippers, carrying the image of Jesus or a cross. Spontaneous words of blessing are said by him or her.

Sign of Peace and Exchange of Flowers and Herbs

Song

A cantor, accompanied by drumming, sings as everyone round dances for a while and then leave to go and share a meal together nearby.

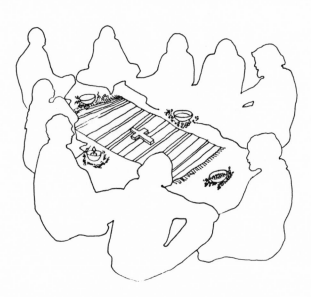

15

Blessing in Thanksgiving for the Gift of Our Bodies

This is a scriptural meditation that can call to mind our Hebrew and Christian traditions of recognizing the body as good because it is a creation of God and the locus of our spirit, our consciousness.

This blessing can be prayed alone, preferably outside on a nice day when the sun's warmth is comfortable on the body. As each body part is mentioned, a section of Holy Scripture is read and silently meditated on. Then that particular part of the body is blessed by a sign of the cross with oil, body paint, earth, water, or simply by touch.

This blessing can also be prayed with others who are assisted in the cross signings by a leader. Music or song may accompany each section or be played throughout.

Body

> Do you not realize that your body is the temple of the Holy Spirit, who is in you and whom you received from God? You are not your own property,

then; you have been bought at a price. So use your body for the glory of God (1 Cor 6:19-20).

Feet

How beautiful on the mountains,
   are the feet of the messenger of good news,
who proclaims salvation and says to Zion,
   "Your God is king!" (Is 52:7).

Jesus knew that the Father had put everything into his hands, and that he had come from God and was returning to God, and he got up from table, removed his outer garments and, taking a towel, wrapped it round his waist; he then poured water into a basin and began to wash the disciples' feet and to wipe them with the towel he was wearing...When he had washed their feet and put on his outer garments again he went back to the table. "Do you understand," he said, "what I have done to you? You call me Master and Lord, and rightly; so I am. If I, then, the Lord and Master, have washed your feet, you must wash each other's feet. I have given you an example so that you may copy what I have done to you" (Jn 13:3-5,12-15).

Thigh

On his thigh a name was written: King of kings and Lord of lords (Rv 19:16).

Legs

His legs are alabaster columns set in sockets of
   pure gold (Song 7:1-2).

Hands

> Up, cry out in the night-time
>   as each watch begins!
> Pour your heart out like water
>   in Yahweh's presence!
> Raise your hands to him
>   for the lives of your children (Lam 2:19).

Arms

> So he sat down, called the Twelve to him and said,
> "If anyone wants to be first, he must make himself
> last of all and servant of all." He then took a little
> child whom he set among them and embraced, and
> he said to them, "Anyone who welcomes a little
> child such as this in my name, welcomes me; and
> anyone who welcomes me, welcomes not me, but
> the one who sent me" (Mk 9:35-37).

Shoulders

> The people who walked in darkness
>   have seen a great light;
> on the inhabitants of a country in shadow dark as
>   death
>   light has blazed forth...
> For the yoke that weighed on it,
>   the bar across its shoulders,
> the rod of its oppressor,
>   these you have broken as on the day of Midian...
> For a son has been born for us, a son has been
>   given to us,
>   and dominion has been laid on his shoulders;
> and this is the name he has been given, "Wonder-
>   Counsellor, Mighty God,
>   Eternal-Father, Prince-of-Peace" (Is 9:1-5).

Breast

He spoke the following parable to some people who prided themselves on being upright and despised everyone else, "Two men went up to the Temple to pray, one a Pharisee, the other a tax collector. The Pharisee stood there and said this prayer to himself, 'I thank you, God, that I am not grasping, unjust, adulterous like everyone else, and particularly that I am not like this tax collector here. I fast twice a week; I pay tithes on all I get.' The tax collector stood some distance away, not daring even to raise his eyes to heaven; but he beat his breast and said, 'God, be merciful to me, a sinner.' This man, I tell you, went home again justified; the other did not. For everyone who raises himself up will be humbled, but anyone who humbles himself will be raised up" (Lk 18:9-14).

Head

"And then they will see the Son of Man coming in a cloud with power and great glory. When these things begin to take place, stand erect, hold your heads high, because your liberation is near at hand" (Lk 21:27-28).

Eyes

The man said to me, "Son of man, look carefully, listen closely and pay attention to everything I show you, since you have been brought here only for me to show it to you. Tell the House of Israel everything that you see" (Ez 40:4).

Ears

> Jesus came to Nazareth, where he had been brought up, and went into the synagogue on the Sabbath day as he usually did. He stood up to read, and they handed him the scroll of the prophet Isaiah. Unrolling the scroll he found the place where it is written:
>
> "The Spirit of the Lord has been given to me,
>   for he has anointed me. He has sent me to bring
>   good news to the poor,
> to proclaim liberty to captives,
>   and to the blind new sight, to set the
>   downtrodden free,
> to proclaim the Lord's year of favour."
>
> He then rolled up the scroll, gave it back to the assistant and sat down. And all eyes in the synagogue were fixed on him. Then he began to speak to them, "This text is being fulfilled today even as you listen" (Lk 3:15-21).

Nose

> As God's dear children, then, take him as your pattern, and follow Christ by loving as he loved you, giving himself up for us as an offering and a sweet-smelling sacrifice to God (Eph 5:1-2).

Mouth

> Better your faithful love than life itself;
>   my lips will praise you.
> Thus I will bless you all my life,
>   in your name lift up my hands.
> All my longings fulfilled as with fat and rich foods,
>   a song of joy on my lips and praise in my mouth
>   (Ps 63:3-5).

Body

Then he took bread, and when he had given thanks, he broke it and gave it to them, saying, "This is my body given for you; do this in remembrance of me" (Lk 22:19).

Now Christ's body is yourselves, each of you with a part to play in the whole! (1 Cor 12:27).

16

Blessing of the Body with
Water and Soap (and Perfume
or Another Fragrant Scent)

This simple rite reminds us that time passes quickly
and the body is always in movement, even more so in
our busy everyday world. Water and washing can mean
rest and renewal. No matter what the time of day or
night, even a few moments apart can be beneficial. We
are reminded of the ceremonial washings of the Jews
and other religious peoples, even of the Native
American sweat huts and Aztec *temescals*.

Scripture

> I will wash my hands in innocence
>   and join the procession round your altar,
>   Yahweh,
> to make heard the sound of thanksgiving,
>   to proclaim all your wonders (Ps 26:6-7).
>
> Have mercy on me, O God, in your faithful love,
>   in your great tenderness wipe away my offence;

wash me thoroughly from my guilt,
   purify me from my sin (Ps 51:1-2).

Purify me with hyssop till I am clean,
   wash me till I am whiter than snow (Ps 51:7).

But when you fast, put scent on your head and
wash your face, so that no one will know you are
fasting except your Father who sees all that is done
in secret; and your Father who sees all that is done
in secret will reward you (Mt 6:16-18).

Holy Silence

Blessing Prayer

You who purify all of us with the love of Jesus,
   continue to wash me in that same love so that I
   might be a blessing to those who enter my life
   each day.
May your goodness and forgiveness flow upon
   them through me.
May the sweet anointing of your Spirit cause me to
   travel with many companions on the path of life.
   Amen.

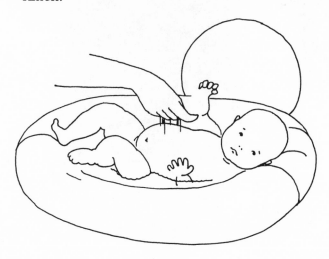

17

Prayer of Darkness and Light

The following two related prayer forms are to be of
help to an individual (or a group of people) on a retreat
of some kind, especially on a backpacking retreat in the
wilderness. They can also be prayed within the confines
of one's home. The Scriptures, especially the Gospel of
John, speaks of a special relationship of night and day,
of light and dark. Dark speaks of the need for salvation;
light becomes the setting to live out that salvation.

The symbols of light in the darkness can be either a
campfire or candle. For the reading of the Scriptures, a
flashlight or candle might be helpful. It is important that
the one praying be conscious of the power of the light
to pierce the darkness. It is then easier to see the powerful effect of the love of Jesus on a darkened world. The
songs should be sung, or at least be listened to from a
tape recording. Some of the actions may be repeated
(stoking of fire with the accompanying words or lighting
of extra candles) as the time passes.

The Prayer of Darkness can be prayed at sundown or
later at night. The Prayer of Light is best prayed just
before dawn and later in the morning.

Darkness

Song:
  "Only a Shadow" (Carey Landry, 1971, NALR)

Prayer

O God, as the sun sets and darkness comes,
  hold me (us) in your love.
Guide me (us) through this night.
  In my (our) silence speak to me (us),
in my (our) doubting, comfort me (us),
  in my (our) fear, strengthen me (us).
Help me (us) to follow Jesus through the difficult
  and painful moments so that I (we) might share
  the joy of his rising up into eternal day. Amen.

Scripture
  *(to be read at sunset with the aid of candlelight
  or flashlight)*

...and light shines in darkness,
  and darkness could not overpower it (Jn 1:5).

That evening the disciples went down to the shore
of the sea and got into a boat to make for Caper-
naum on the other side of the sea. It was getting
dark by now and Jesus had still not rejoined them.
The wind was strong, and the sea was getting
rough. They had rowed three or four miles when
they saw Jesus walking on the sea and coming
towards the boat. They were afraid, but he said,
"It's me. Don't be afraid." They were ready to take
him into the boat, and immediately it reached the
shore at the place they were making for
(Jn 6:16-21).

So we have confirmation of the words of the
prophets; and you will be right to pay attention to

it as to a lamp for lighting a way through the dark, until the dawn comes and the morning star rises in your minds (2 Pet 1:19).

Now we see only reflections in a mirror, mere riddles, but then we shall be seeing face to face (1 Cor 13:12).

Action

The fire can be stoked and kept going. As a poker or stick is pushed into the fire the following words may be said in a rhythm:

I
   keep life

in the fire
   as God's Spirit

keeps
   the love

of Jesus
   in me.

Or, if other candles are lit:

In my darkness
   I add

light to light
   so that

I might
   add

to the brightness
   of those

in my life
    that God

has given
    me.

Blessing

May the goodness of the Creator be with me/us
    now and always.
May the love of Jesus be with me/us now and
    always.
May the comfort of the Spirit be with me/us now
    and always and forever. Amen.

Song:

*"Isaiah 49 (I Will Never Forget You)" (Carey
Landry, 1975, NALR)*

Light

Song:

*"Let There Be Light" (David Hurd, 1985, GIA)
"Those Who See Light" (Nancy Elze, 1978, FEL)
"The Light Has Come" (Ron Ellis, 1973, Raven
Music)*

Prayer

O God,
    O Sun of light and warmth and power and
    healing,
I welcome You this morning.
    Brighten up my life.
Cover my body and my spirit with your warmth.
    Show me how I should live this day. Amen.

Scriptures

(to be read at sunrise with the aid of candlelight or flashlight)

God said, "Let there be light," and there was light. God saw that the light was good, and God divided light from darkness (Gn 1:3-4).

Yahweh is my light and my salvation,
    whom should I fear?
Yahweh is the fortress of my life,
    whom should I dread? (Ps 27:1).

Yours is the day and yours is the night,
    you caused the sun and light to exist... (Ps 74:16).

The people that walked in darkness
    have seen a great light;
on the inhabitants of a country in shadow dark as
    death
    light has blazed forth (Is 9:1).

"You are light for the world. A city built on a hilltop cannot be hidden. No one lights a lamp to put it under a tub; they put it on the lamp-stand where it shines for everyone in the house. In the same way your light must shine in people's sight so that, seeing your good works, they may give praise to your Father in heaven" (Mt 5:14-16).

You were darkness once, but now are light in the Lord; behave as children of light... (Eph 5:8).

Action

As the fire or candles are being put out, the following may be recited:

Though I put out this fire (quench this wick), may
    God never take away the love that lights my
    way—
love that lights my way,
    love that lights my way,
love that lights my way...

Blessing

May the light of Christ which has come into my
    (our) world enable me (us) to walk in the light
    of the day that lasts forever. Amen.

Song:

*"We Are the Light of the World" (Jean Anthony
Greif, 1966, OCP)*
"Transfiguration" (Carey Landry, 1977, NALR)
*"Morning Has Broken" (Eleanor Farjeon,
1881-1965, OCP)*

18

A Fire Lighting Blessing

Light permits activity; light allows us to go about our daily life.

This blessing can be a meditation of appreciation for the gift of light: sunlight, firelight, candlelight, smilelight. A fire can be caused by nature or by human beings. The end product is the same: the changing of one set of substances into another; the giving up of one mode of existence (wood, paper) for another (carbon). In the process light is produced.

The occasion of this particular blessing might be the lighting of a campfire, a hearth fire, an Easter Vigil fire, a paschal candle, an ordinary candle, a peace pipe, or even a match, a cigarette, cigar, or personal pipe. The blessing accompanies the activity. It may be silent, or words similar to the following may be used.

Scripture

> God said, "Let there be light," and there was light (Gn 1:3).

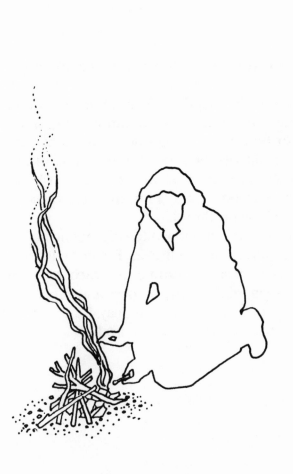

You were darkness once, but now you are light in the Lord (Eph 5:8).

You are the light for the world (Mt 5:14).

But whoever does the truth comes out into the light... (Jn 3:21).

Holy Silence

The individual or group praying this blessing might focus on the realization that each one of us has the ability from God to be light for each other. At the same time, we share in the light of those around us. This is part of the Creator's plan for us to see both physically and spiritually where we are in this beautiful universe at any given moment. The destruction wrought on our forests by unguarded fires might also be part of this meditation.

Blessing Prayer

> Here I am, O God,
>> with my eyes closed and ready for You to show
>> your love and care.
>
> As I watch this firelight (candlelight, etc.)
>> be born and grow in front of me,
>> help me to open my eyes to the wonder all
>> around me.
>
> Show me how I must live with everyone and
>> everything that surrounds me.
>
> I bless You for the gifts of light and warmth,
>> but especially as I experience your own light and
>> warmth as it comes from my sisters and brothers.
>
> Help me be a light to them. Amen.

19

A Circle Blessing in the Midst of Redwood Trees

Everyone gathers in a circle. All share in a time of holy silence. Then drum or flute music is softly played throughout the blessing. One leader recites the following prayer, another recites the next, and so on.

Prayer

> Loving Creator, we owe our existence to you.
>   All living creatures come from you.
> Today we find ourselves coming here to remember
>   the gift of life.
> As we look around ourselves we recognize the life
>   of trees and all other life forms to which we and
>   they are related.
> We bless you this day. Amen.

All Face EAST

> From the East the sun comes everyday and spreads
>   light over all living things.

It speaks to us of your love.
  As we think of all the people and things that live
  to the east of us,
we ask for wisdom and understanding that what is
  done at this place may be for the benefit of
  everything and everyone.

ALL: Amen.

All Face SOUTH

The South makes us think of warmth.
  We thank you for all the gifts that come to us
  from the South.
Help us not to waste them.
Help us to remember the needs of all our relatives,
  especially those which cannot speak for
  themselves.
May what we do here and what is done here in the
  future be a blessing.

ALL: Amen.

All Face WEST

The sun sets in the West and our day comes to an
  end.
Give us abundant waters to fill our rivers, lakes,
  and oceans.
Help us to value the gift of water.

May there be an abundance for our land and its
  wildlife and peoples for generations to come.

ALL: Amen.

All Face NORTH

As we look North we think of cool winds,
cleansing breezes that cause leaves to fall to the
earth to rest.
As we are gathered here, teach us patience and
endurance.
May we lighten one another's burden.

ALL: Amen.

Holy Silence

Final Blessing

Bless this holy place.
May the redwoods and all other trees abound.
May all people enjoy the goodness that we now
experience.
May the birds sing.
May beauty be always before us and behind us.
May all that is beautiful be above and below us.
May we be surrounded by beauty and immersed in
it.
In our youth and in our old age,
may we walk the path of beauty.

ALL: Amen.

Song:
"Hymn of the Earth" (Jim Manley, 1983, NCCC)

All spend some time looking at, admiring, touching, experiencing the uniqueness of the redwood trees. This blessing, with adaptations, could be offered whenever certain kinds of trees and plant life are scarce or are facing extinction. It should remind the people gathered in prayer that all humans have a responsibility before the Creator-Redeemer to care for all other life forms on planet earth.

20

Parental Blessing of a Child in the Womb

A blessing of a child in the womb is a beautiful expression of faith in the goodness of the Creator. Every child is a sign of hope for the world. The following blessing could be celebrated outdoors in the sunlight. Others besides the couple could be present; they could form a circle around the couple. This blessing could also be adapted as a blessing for single mothers.

The husband stands behind the wife and puts his arms around the area of the womb. The wife then puts her hands on his. He says something like this:

> O God, You who are like a Father to us,
>   it is good for us to be here.
> Bless our little one(s).
>   Help us to enjoy this special time of life, of
>   growth, of now-moving-into-future.
> Keep (name of wife), my wife, healthy.
>   Keep this/these little one(s) healthy as well.
>
> I praise You for this miracle of Life!

The wife then says:

> O God, You who are like a Mother to us,
>   it is good for us to be here.
> You have brought us to this special holy time.
> Fill my being with your goodness that I might
>   always proclaim to this/these little one(s) and all
>   my family and friends your love for us all.
> I praise You for this miracle of Life!

Anyone else present is invited to approach the couple, offer a blessing, and make the sign of the cross over the area of the womb. Then all depart to allow the couple to pray alone for a few moments.

21

Prayer While in Motion

Very often we take our power of movement for granted. We do not always feel our relatedness to everything else. The universe is alive, thanks to God, and life means movement of one kind or another. We can "walkabout" in the Australian Aboriginal way to draw strength from the land. Or we can, in our own more technological culture, move about by means of motorcycles, cars, trains, airplanes, bicycles, and skateboards; we can even jazzercise or go windsurfing. Movement is a part of our very existence.

We should give thanks for the gift of motion while at the same time appreciate more deeply our unique experience of time and place. We may look, but we do not always see. In this activity the English poet William Blake reminds us, "If the doors of perception were cleansed, everything would be seen as it is, infinite."

The following is a simple contemplative meditation that needs to be prayed from within rather than be read from a page.

Scriptures

"...it is in him that we live, and move, and exist..."
(Acts 17:28).

Prayer

O God, it is good to be alive!
As I stretch out the muscles of my arms and legs,
   I feel your strength within me!
As my body moves along, I sense more deeply who
   I am.
As I look around me, I see both stillness and
   movement.
I am surrounded by life!
   I am alive thanks to You!
Birds, flowers, trees, mountains and streams, the
   earth, the sky, all people and You belong to me!
It is good to be here!
   It is good to be alive!
Alleluia!

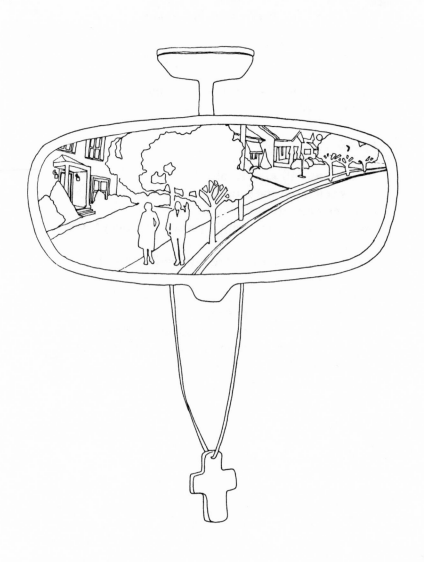

22

Prayer Before Driving to Work

Scripture

> Heaven belongs to Yahweh
> but earth he has given to the children of Adam...
> We, the living, shall bless Yahweh,
> henceforth and for ever (Ps 115:16,18).

Prayer

> Here I am, O God,
> I am getting into my car.
> My day of work is before me.
> Be with me.
> Help me to feel your presence, even as I start up
> the engine.
> Let your gentle presence vibrate through all of me.
> Move in me as I move along the streets and
> highways of my neighborhood.
> Speed me on safely as I pass by telephone poles,
> houses, dogs and cats, birds, and my other
> brothers and sisters.

Let me recognize your special presence in the
buildings, cars, and colours of our human
ingenuity.
Take me safely to my place of work.
Until I return home, let me do my best today with
everyone and everything. Amen.

APPENDICES

A

The Development of
Judaeo-Christian Feasts

PASSOVER

Agrarian	Nomadic
Pagan Ritual	
(Rite of the bread)	(Rite of the lamb)
Now Abel became a shepherd and kept flocks, while Cain tilled the soil. Time passed and Cain brought some of the produce of the soil as an offering for Yahweh, while Abel for his part brought the first-born of his flock and some of their fat as well (Gn 4:2-4).	*Same scriptural reference*

Jewish Transition

Spiritualization and Historicization of the Feast

Three times a year you will hold a festival in my honour. You will observe the feast of Unleavened Bread. For seven days you will eat unleavened bread, as I have commanded you, at the appointed time in the month of Abib, for in that month you came out of Egypt (Ex 23:14,15).

Moses summoned all the elders of Israel and said to them, "Go and choose a lamb or kid for your families, and kill the Passover victim. Then take a bunch of hyssop, dip it in the blood that is in the basin, and with blood from the basin touch the lintel and both door-posts; then let none of you venture out of the house till morning. Then, when Yahweh goes through Egypt to strike it, and sees the blood on the lintel and on both doorposts, he will pass over the door and not allow the Destroyer to enter your homes and strike" (Ex 12:21-24).

During these seven days unleavened bread may be eaten; no leavened bread may be seen among you...and on that day you will explain to your son, "This is because of what Yahweh did for me when I came out of Egypt (Ex 13:7,8).

...in the place where Yahweh your God chooses to give his name a home, there you must sacrifice the Passover, in the evening at sunset, at the hour when you came out of Egypt (Dt 15:5-7).

Two Feasts Combined

You will cook it and eat it in the place chosen by Yahweh your God, and in the morning you must return and go to your tents. For six days you will eat unleavened bread (Dt 16:7,8).

Christian Feast

Eschatologization of the Passover

Now as they were eating, Jesus took bread, and when he had said the blessing he broke it and gave it to his disciples. "Take it and eat," he said, "this is my body." Then he took a cup, and when he had given thanks he handed it to them saying, "Drink from this all of you, for this is my blood, the blood of the covenant, poured out for many and for the forgiveness of sins. From now on, I tell you, I shall never again drink wine until the day I drink the new wine with you in the kingdom of my Father (Mt 26:20-25).

For you know that the price of your ransom from the futile way of life handed down from your ancestors was paid, not in anything perishable like silver or gold, but in precious blood as of a blameless and spotless lamb, Christ (Pet 1:18,19).

Throw out the old yeast so that you can be the fresh dough, unleavened as you are. For our Passover has been sacrificed, that is, Christ; let us keep the feast, then, with none of the old yeast and no leavening of evil and wickedness, but only the unleavened bread of sincerity and truth (1 Cor 5:7,8).

The Christian Eucharist[212]

PENTECOST

Agrarian	Nomadic	Laws on How to Live Properly, Given by the gods

Pagan Ritual

Feasts of the grain harvest ↓   Animal sacrifices

Jewish Transition

Feast of Weeks

Feast of the Giving of the Covenant

You will observe the feast of Weeks, of the first-fruits of wheat harvest (Ex 34:22).

He then said, "Look, I am now making a covenant: I shall work such wonders at the head of your whole people as have never been worked in any other country or nation, and all the people round you will see what Yahweh can do, for what I shall do through you will be awe-inspiring" (Ex 34:10).

Spiritualization of the Feast

Eschatologization of the Feast

From the day after the sabbath, the day on which you bring the sheaf of offering, you will count seven full weeks. You will count fifty days, to the day after the seventh sabbath, and then you will offer Yahweh a new cereal offering. You will bring bread from your homes to present with the gesture of offering—two loaves made of two tenths of wheaten flour baked with leaven; these are first fruits for Yahweh (Lv 23:15-17).

Two Rites Fused

In addition to the bread you will offer seven unblemished lambs a year old, a young bull and two rams, as a burnt offering to Yahweh, with a cereal offering and a libation, as food burnt as a smell pleasing to Yahweh (Lv 23:18-20).

Look, the days are coming, Yahweh declares, when I shall make a new covenant with the House of Israel (and the House of Judah), but not like the covenant I made with their ancestors the day I took them by the hand to bring them out of Egypt...Within them I shall plant my Law, writing it on their hearts (Jer 31:31-33).

Christian Feast

Eschatologization of the Feast

Receive the Holy Spirit. If you forgive anyone's sins, they are forgiven; if you retain anyone's sins, they are retained (Jn 20:22,23).

I give you a new commandment: love one another; you must love one another just as I have loved you (Jn 13:34).

When Pentecost day came round, they had all met together, when suddenly there came from heaven a sound as of a violent wind which filled the entire house in which they were sitting; and there appeared to them tongues as of fire; these separated and came to rest on the head of each of them. They were filled with the Holy Spirit and began to speak different languages as the Spirit gave them power to express themselves (Acts 2:1-4).

Christian Feast of Pentecost[213]

FEAST OF TENTS

Pagan Ritual

Agrarian (Rhythm of Nature celebrated):

These went out into the countryside to harvest their vineyards: they trod the grapes and made merry and went into the temple of their god. They ate and drank there and cursed Abimelech (Jgs 9:27,28).

Jewish Transition

Spiritualization of the Harvest and Historicization of the Feast (celebrates the development of history guided by the hand of God):

You will celebrate a feast for Yahweh in this way for seven days every year. This is a perpetual law for your descendants. You will keep this feast in the seventh month. For seven days you are to live in shelters: all the citizens of Israel will live in shelters, so that your descendants may know that I made the Israelites live in shelters when I brought them out of the land of Egypt, I, Yahweh, your God (Lv 23:42-43).

Eschatologizing of the Feast (elements of the feast of the New Year and the feast of Tents are fused together):

Along the river, on either bank, will grow every kind of fruit tree with leaves that never wither and fruit that never fails; they will bear new fruit every month, because this water comes from the sanctuary. And their fruit will be good to eat and the leaves medicinal (Ezek 47:12).

The rites of this feast were spiritualized first by investing them with the historic experience of the people when they were in the desert, then with a new prophetic and eschatological meaning belonging to the messianic era. Thus the feast of Tents continued to be celebrated and became a preparation for the events that were to come, an alerting of the people summoned to the happiness of the end-time.

But I have been Yahweh, your God, since your days in Egypt, and I will make you live in tents again as in the days of Meeting (Hos 12:9).

...until the spirit is poured out on us from above, and the desert becomes productive ground, so productive you might take it for a forest. Fair judgement will fix its home in the desert, and uprightness live in the productive ground, and the product of uprightness will be peace, the effect of uprightness being quiet and security forever. My people will live in a peaceful home, in peaceful houses, tranquil dwellings. And should the forest be totally destroyed and the city gravely humiliated, you will be happy to sow wherever there is water and to let the ox and donkey roam free (Is 32:15-18).

Christian Feast

Feast becomes a person (Jesus transcends and replaces the feast.):

Then Peter spoke to Jesus. "Lord," he said, "it is wonderful for us to be here; if you want me to, I will make three shelters here, one for you, one for Moses and one for Elijah." He was still speaking when suddenly a bright cloud covered them with shadow, and suddenly from the cloud there came a voice which said, "This is my Son, the Beloved; he enjoys my favour. Listen to him" (Mt 17:4-5).

Great crowds of people spread their cloaks on the road, while others were cutting branches from the trees and spreading them in his path (Mt 21:8,9).

Jesus Spiritualizes the Feast (The feast of Tents becomes the feast of Easter.):

On the last day, the great day of the festival, Jesus stood and cried out: "Let anyone who is thirsty come to me! Let anyone who believes in me come and drink! As scripture says, 'From his heart shall flow streams of living water' " (Jn 7:37,38).

Easter and Pentecost

The Christian Sunday[214]

B

Daily Prayer in Reformed Churches

Lutheran

Matins	*Vespers*
Invitatory	Invitatory
Psalm 95	Psalm
Hymn	Lesson
Psalm	Hymn
Lessons	Sermon
Hymn	Hymn
Sermon	Canticle of Mary or
Canticle or Te	Canticle of Simeon
Deum	Collect
Collect	Lord Have Mercy
Lord Have Mercy	Collects
Lord's Prayer	Dismissal[218]
Collects	
Dismissal[217]	

Presbyterian	Methodist
Morning Prayer	*Morning Prayer*
Hymn	Scriptural
Call to Worship	Sentences
Prayer of Adoration	Invitatory
General	Psalms
Confession of Sins	Old Testament
and Assurance of	Lesson
Pardon	Hymn or Te Deum
Psalm	New Testament
Lesson	Lesson
Hymn	Hymn
Lesson	Canticle of
Creed	Zechariah or Psalm
Hymn	Creed
Thanksgiving	Three Collects
Prayer	Psalm or Hymn
Prayer of	Other Particular
Supplication	and General
Prayer of	Collects
Intercession	General
Other Collects	Thanksgiving
Lord's Prayer	Benediction[216]
Sermon	
Offering of Money	
Doxology	
Hymn	
Benediction	
Hymn[215]	

Episcopalian

Morning Prayer *(Evening Prayer is similar.)*	*Noonday Prayer*	*Night Prayer*
Seasonal Scriptural Sentences	Invitatory	Invitatory
Confession of Sins and Absolution	Hymn	Confession of Sins and Absolution
Invitatory	Psalms	Doxology
Psalms	Scriptural Sentences	Psalms
Old Testament and New Testament Lessons	Meditation	Short Scriptural Sentences
Canticle	Lord Have Mercy	Hymn
Sermon or Meditation	Lord's Prayer	Lord Have Mercy
Apostles' Creed	Collect	Lord's Prayer
Lord's Prayer	Intercessions	Collect
Suffrages	Dismissal[220]	Intercessions and Thanksgivings
Collects		Canticle of Simeon
Hymn		Dismissal[221]
Intercessions and Thanksgivings		
General Thanksgiving		
Dismissal[219]		

C

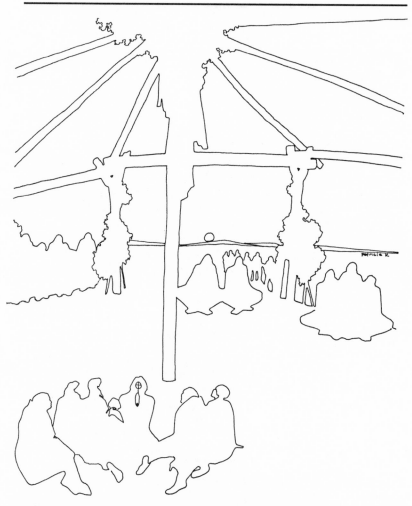

Cheyenne Sundance Lodge with its thirteen poles
surrounding the central leafy crotched pole.

D

The constant relationship of the major points of danced space.

Notes

1. J. M. Quinn, "Time," *New Catholic Encyclopedia* (New York: McGraw-Hill, 1966), 156.
2. Ibid., 157.
3. Mircea Eliade, *The Sacred and the Profane* (New York: Harcourt, Brace & World, 1959), 68-69.
4. Ibid., 68.
5. Theodore Gaster, *Thespis* (New York: Harper Torchbooks, 1961), 17.
6. Ibid.
7. Luci Shaw, ed., *Sightseers into Pilgrims* (Wheaton, Illinois: Tyndale House, 1973), 69.
8. Frank Waters, *The Book of the Hopi* (New York: Ballantine Books, Inc., 1963), 213.
9. Ibid., 168-292. Here is a table of the major Hopi celebrations of the year:

> *Winter*: This is a time for celebration of the three phases of Creation. Wuwuchim, held in November, has eight days of preparation and eight days of secret rituals in kivas followed by a public dance. Soyal, held in December, has eight days of purification, eight days of secret rituals, and four days of rabbit-hunting, feasting, and rites of blessing.

Powamu, held in February, has eight days of preparation and eight days of secret ritual.

Spring: There are no major celebrations during this Season because it is the planting time.

Summer: This is a celebration of the evolutionary process on the Road of Life. Kachin-nima, celebrated in July, is sixteen days long. Flute Ceremony (which alternates each year with the Snake-Antelope Ceremony) is held in the middle of August and includes eight days of preparation, eight days of initiation, prayer and dance. Snake-Antelope Ceremony, also held in the middle of August, has fifteen days of preparation and a sixteenth day for public dancing.

Autumn: This is a celebration of Creation's maturity and fruition. Lakon, held in late September or early October, includes four days of prayer and song, one day for initiation, and one day for public ceremony. Marawu, held shortly after the Lakon ceremonies, has six days of special prayer, one day set aside to teach salvation-history, and four days of special healing prayers. Owaqlt, held in October, has one day set aside for kiva rituals, public dance and the bestowal of food to bystanders.

10. W. D. Alexander, *A Brief History of the Hawaiian People* (New York: American Book Co., 1891), 52-53:

Here is an example of one festival taboo, the Aku and Opelu taboo. Two kinds of fish, the aku (a kind of tuna fish) and the opelu, had a sacred character, and were taboo by turns for six months at a time. At the *kapu hua*, the thirteenth day of Kaelo, in January, a human sacrifice was offered together with the fish aku, at which it was said that the *kahoalii*, a man personifying the god, plucked out and ate an eye from the fish and the human. By this ceremony the taboo was taken off the aku, and the opelu then became taboo for the next six months, not to be eaten on pain of death.

In the month of Hinaiaeleele, or our July, the taboo was taken off the opelu and reimposed on the aku. The first night of this month, Hilo, was *kapa loa*, or taboo. No fire could be kindled, and no human sound could be uttered. Toward morning the high priest went to the opelu shrine of the god of fishermen, where he sacrificed a pig and prayed. Then the people prayed. The next morning the head fisherman put out to sea; meanwhile, no fire could be lighted, nor could any canoe leave the shore or land. The fisherman cast his net after prayer and brought in a haul of opelu. These were offered in the temple. The next day the sea was free for catching opelu, but aku was illegal for six months.

11. International African Institute, *African Systems of Thought* (New York: Oxford University Press, 1965), 54-55.
12. Aylward Shorter, *African Culture and the Christian Church* (New York: Orbis Books, 1974), 52.
13. Ibid., 108-109.
14. Walter Harrelson, *From Fertility Cult to Worship* (New York: Anchor Books, 1970), 16.
15. Ibid., 18.
16. Thierry Maertens, *A Feast in Honor of Yahweh* (Notre Dame, Indiana: Fides Press, 1965), 23.
17. Roland deVaux, *Ancient Israel* (New York: McGraw-Hill Book Co., 1965), 190.
18. Ibid., 184.
19. Theodore Gaster, *Festivals of the Jewish Year* (New York: William Morrow & Co., 1953) 26-27. This the basic Hebrew calendar which is still in use today:

1. Nisan (March-April)
2. Iyar (April-May)
3. Sivan (May-June)
4. Tammuz (June-July)
5. Ab (July-August)
6. Elul (August-September)
7. Tishri (September-October)
8. Heshvan (October-November)
9. Kisley (November-December)
10. Tebeth (December-January)
11. Shebat (January-February)
12. Adar (February-March)

20. Ibid., 27.
21. Isadore Epstein, *Judaism* (London: Penguin Books, 1970), 170.
22. Gastor, *Thespis*, 47:

A solstice is a point in the sun's ecliptic at which it is farthest north or farthest south of the equator. An equinox is time when the sun crosses the equator, making night and day of equal length in all parts of the world. The vernal equinox occurs about March 21 and the autumnal equinox takes place about September 22 or 23. In pagan religions the seasonal festivals are often made to coincide with the solstice or the equinox. Among the Israelites both the Spring festival of Pentecost and the autumnal festival of Ingatherings fell in the months of the equinox, the latter being expressly associated with that event in the ritual calendar of Exodus 34:22: "You will observe the feast of Weeks, of the first-fruits of wheat harvest, and the feast of Ingatherings at the close of the year."

23. Franz Cumont, *The Mysteries of Mithra* (New York: Dover Publications, 1956), 167:

Clement of Alexandria believed that the birthday of Christ was actually the 18th day of November because it was a special sun festival dedicated in the pagan culture to Mithra's birthday celebration. The date of Christ's resurrection was associated with the vernal equinox. We have good reasons for believing that the equinoxes were also days of rejoicing, the return of the deified seasons being inaugurated by some religious salutation. The initiations took place preferably at the beginning of Spring, in March or in April, at the Paschal period, when Christians admitted their catechumens to the rite of baptism.

24. Gaster, *Thespis*, 48.
25. Maertens, *Feast*, 29.
26. Ibid., 38.
27. Ibid., 39.
28. Gaster, *Thespis*, 23.
29. Maertens, *Feast*, 87.
30. Ibid., 99.
31. Ibid.
32. Harrelson, *From Fertility*, 20.
33. Maertens, *Feast*, 110.
34. Ibid., 122-125:

Christ's attitude of soul enabled him to personalize this feast within the drama of his own experience. According to one theologian, it is possible that there was no lamb eaten at this supper, nor was unleavened bread used. Jesus did not use the two elements that had always been essential to the rite. In doing this he made it possible for Christian communities to celebrate the Passover every Sunday, even every day. Saint Paul seems to have understood the historical-spiritual concept of the Passover, for he says:

...Throw out the old yeast so that you can be fresh dough, unleavened as you are. For our Passover has been sacrificed, that is, Christ; let us keep the feast, then, with none of the old yeast and no leavening of evil and wickedness, but only the unleavened bread of sincerity and truth (1 Cor 5:7-8).

Jesus Christ is now the only Feast to be celebrated!

35. Gaster, *Festivals*, 59.
36. Ibid., 60.
37. deVaux, *Ancient Israel*, 493.
38. Gaster, *Festivals*, 62-63.
39. Harrelson, *From Fertility*, 21.
40. Ibid., 23.
41. Maertens, *Feast*, 70.
42. H. H. Rowley, *Worship in Ancient Israel* (Philadelphia: Fortress Press, 1967), 89.
43. Maertens, *Feast*, 79-80.
44. Ibid., 92-93.
45. Paul Neuenzeit, "Time," *Sacramentum Verbi* vol. 3 (New York: Herder & Herder, 1970), 911-912.
46. Ibid., 912.
47. Ibid., 912-913.
48. John R. Wilch, *Time and Event* (Leiden, Netherlands: E. J. Brill, 1969), 168.
49. Neuenzeit, *Time*, 914.
50. Ibid.
51. Ibid., 380.
52. Raymond E. Brown, *et alia*, "New Testament Eschatology," in *Jerome Biblical Commentary* (Englewood Cliffs, New Jersey: Prentice-Hall, Inc., 1968), 782.
53. Herbert A. Musurillo, *The Fathers of the Primitive Church* (New York: New American Library, 1966), 35.
54. Philip Schaff and Henry Wace, *The Nicene and Post-Nicene Fathers* vol. 12 (New York: Christian Literature Co., 1895), 201.

55. Thomas Aquinas, *Summa Theologiae* (Garden City, New York: Image Books, 1969), 144:

> Just as we can only come to know simple things by way of composite ones, so we can only come to know eternity by way of time, which is merely the numbering of before and after in change...So two things characterize eternity. First, anything existing in eternity is unending, that is to say, lacks both beginning and end (for both may be regarded as ends). Secondly, eternity itself exists as an instantaneous whole lacking successiveness.

56. Francis X. Connolly, *Wisdom of the Saints* (New York: Pocket Books, Inc., 1963), 178:

> ...a man is always dying from afore his birth, and every hour of our age, as it passeth by, cutteth his own length out of our life and maketh it shorter by so much, and our death so much the nearer. Which measuring of time and diminishing of life, with approaching towards death, is nothing else but from our beginning to our ending, one continual dying: So that wake we, sleep we, eat we, drink we, mourn we, sing we, in what wise soever live we, all the same while die we. So that we never ought to look towards death as a thing far off, considering that although he made no haste towards us, yet we never cease ourselves to make haste towards him.

57. Pierre Teilhard deChardin, *The Future of Man* (New York, Harper & Row Torchbooks, 1964), 91.
58. Jacques Maritain, *Redeeming the Time* (London: The Centenary Press, 1946), 51.
59. Pierre Teilhard deChardin, *The Hymn of the Universe* (New York: Harper & Row, 1965), 139.
60. Ibid., 133.
61. P.O.M. Project, *Survival* (Canoga Park, California: P.O.M. Project, Inc., 1967), 218.

62. Ibid., 135-137.
63. Theoderich Kampmann, *The Year of the Church* (Westminster, Maryland: Newman Press, 1966), 33, 39:

> The *Annus Domini* means "the Year of the Lord." The Lord's Day is the mainspring and foundation of the ecclesiastical year. This year can legitimately be called the Lord's year or the year of salvation, and furthermore, the year of the Church... The Church year...commemorates only the feasts of the Lord, because he becomes present in person in the solemn celebration. And what this Lord effects is the continuous offering of the salvific grace that flows from his unique redemptive act. This unique historical event becomes a religious presence in order to effect today's salvation... The year of the Lord, just like the Lord's Day, subsists wholly and exclusively because it is caused by the historical and metaphysical reality of the Christ-event. Its climax and substance...are the redeeming death and the resurrection that effects salvation.

64. Theodorich Kampmann, *Roman Calendar* (Washington, D.C.: USCC Publishing Office, 1976), 7.
65. Ibid., 2, 5.
66. Walter M. Abbott, *The Documents of Vatican II* (New York: America Press, 1966), 168.
67. James Dallen, *Liturgical Celebration: Patterns for Advent and Christmas* (Cincinnati: North American Liturgy Resources, 1974), 7.
68. Ibid., 6, 7:

> About the ninth century Advent came to be regarded as the beginning of the Church year. A fusion of Roman Gallican Advents was accepted at Rome about the tenth century and the liturgical season as we basically know it came to be. From about the fourth century the Gallican Advent was an ascetical preparation for baptisms to be

celebrated at Epiphany. This theme has since been suppressed from the season. At Rome it was a preparation for Christmas. Pope Gregory I (who served as pope from 590 C.E. until 604 C.E.) is regarded as the originator of the Roman Advent.

Charles K. Riepe, *Living the Christmas Seasons* (New York: Herder & Herder, 1964), 94, 95:

> The Church utilizes the feast of the first coming to stir up our hearts in preparation for the Second Coming. We pray by means of the advent liturgies for a still greater coming of the Lord through grace into our bodies and souls at Christmas. It is in this context that the liturgy of Advent, with its constant prayer that Jesus may "come," must be understood. Advent is dedicated to the last things, to death, judgement, heaven, and hell, but above all to Jesus' glorious coming to complete his Easter work. The Church goes so far as to set aside an entire liturgical season to the end of the world and the final coming of the Lord, so important a part of the faith does she consider these truths.

69. K. A. Heinrich Kellner, *Heortology* (London: Kegan, Paul, Trench, Truber & Co., 1908), 157:

> Even in the fourth and fifth centuries it was unknown in some parts of the Church. The introduction of Christmas to be celebrated on December 25 caused the establishment of three other festivals which relate to Christ's humanity: Circumcision, which is celebrated eight days after the Nativity; Annunciation, which is celebrated on March 25, and which is also the day of Christ's conception and so is placed nine months before December 25; Nativity of John the Baptizer, which is celebrated on June 24 and stresses Christ's kinship with the rest of humanity.

70. Ibid., 167-169.
71. W. J. O'Shea, *The Worship of the Church* (London: Dartman, Longman & Todd, 1957), 249.
72. Joseph Jungmann, *The Early Liturgy* (Notre Dame, Indiana: Notre Dame Press, 1959), 253.
73. Maertens, *Feast*, 229.
74. Jay C. Rochelle, *The Revolutionary Year* (Philadelphia: Fortress Press, 1973), x.
75. Mircea Eliade, *Rites and Symbols of Initiation* (New York: Harper Torchbooks, 1965), ix.
76. Ibid., x.
77. Eliade, *Rites and Symbols*, 2.
78. Ibid., 4.
79. Ibid., 19.
80. Ibid., 53.
81. Ibid., 54.
82. Ibid., 105.
83. Ibid., 105-106.
84. Clark Tibbitts, ed., *Handbook of Social Gerontology* (Chicago: University of Chicago Press, 1960), 6.
85. Ibid., 160.
86. Henri Nouwen, *Aging* (Garden City, New York: Doubleday & Co., 1974), 3.
87. Edward H. Peters, *The Constitution on the Church of Vatican Council II* (Glen Rock, New Jersey: Paulist Press, 1965), 26.
88. Michael Marx, ed., *Protestants and Catholics on the Spiritual Life* (Collegeville, Minn.: Liturgical Press, 1965), 69.
89. Adolphe Tanqueray, *The Spiritual Life* (Tournai, Belgium: Desclee & Cie, 1930), 297.
    Louis John Cameli, "The Spirituality of Celebration," in *Chicago Studies* vol. 16, no. 1 (Mundelein, Illinois: Civitas Dei Foundation, 1977), 64:

    Characteristically, writers have portrayed the stages in a sequential order. Persons successfully complete one state before progressing to the next. This kind

of perspective of spiritual development holds an as-
censional or ever-rising movement as typical of
spiritual development. A more contemporary view
which draws from many of the spiritual classics
situates purification, illumination, and union as
special dimensions of Christian life throughout the
whole Christian life cycle. There is growth and
movement, but it is movement about a more clearly
defined focus and growth in contact with a center.
The visual image to which this pattern corresponds
is no longer a line ascending at an angle into in-
finity but a spiral which moves to a point. In Christian life, then, persons will experience purification
of illumination or union with greater intensity at
various times. All three elements form significant
components of Christians in movement.

90. Tanqueray, *Spiritual Life*, 301.
91. Ibid., 305.
92. Ibid., 456.
93. Pierre Teilhard deChardin, *The Divine Milieu* (New York:
    Harper & Row, 1960), 138.
94. Trophime Mouiren, *The Creation* (New York: Hawthorn
    Books, 1962), 115-123.
95. Kieran Kavanaugh and Otilio Rodriguez, *The Collected
    Works of St. John of the Cross* (Washington D.C.: I.C.S.
    Publications, 1973), 669.
96. Marx, *Protestants and Catholics*, 81.
97. Henri Nouwen, *With Open Hands* (Notre Dame, Indiana:
    Ave Maria Press, 1972), 56.
98. Joseph deGuibert, *The Theology of the Spiritual Life*
    (New York: Sheed & Ward, 1953), 262.
99. Ibid., 263.
100. Henri Nouwen, *Reaching Out* (Garden City, New York:
    Doubleday & Co., 1975), 14-15.
101. Casimir Kucharek, *The Sacramental Mysteries: A
    Byzantine Approach* (Allendale, New Jersey: Alleluia
    Press, 1976), 335.

102. Ibid., 333.

103. *Rite of Christian Initiation of Adults* (Washington, D.C.: U.S.C.C. Publications Office, 1974), 7.

104. John Chapin, ed., *The Book of Catholic Quotations* (New York: Farrar, Straus & Cudahy, 1956), 153.

105. Franc Shor, ed., *Great Religions of the World* (New York: National Geographic Society, 1971), 44-48.

106. Franklin Edgerton, *The Bhagavad Gita* (New York: Harper & Row, 1964), 89.

107. Kenneth W. Morgan, ed., *The Religion of the Hindus* (New York: The Ronald Press Co., 1953), 163.

108. Ibid., 164.

109. Mircea Eliade, *The Myth of the Eternal Return* (Princeton, New Jersey: Princeton University Press, 1974), 115.

110. Ibid., 115.

111. E. Power, *The History of Religions* vol. 4 (London: Catholic Truth Society, 1910), 11-12.

112. Victor Solomon, *A Handbook on Conversions to the Religions of the World* (New York: Stravon Educational Press, 1965), 247-248.

113. deVaux, *Ancient Israel*, 458.

114. A. Z. Idelsohn, *Jewish Liturgy and Its Development* (New York: Schocken Books, 1967), 24.

115. George E. Gingas, trans., *Egeria: Diary of a Pilgrimage* (New York: Newman Press, 1970), 89, 90.

116. Leonard J. Doyle, trans., *St. Benedict's Rule for Monasteries* (Collegeville, Minn.: St. John's Abbey Press, 1948), 37, 38:

Vespers are to be sung with four Psalms every day. These shall begin with Psalm 109 and go on to Psalm 147. Omitting those which are set apart for other hours: that is to say that with the exception of Psalms 117 to 127 and Psalms 133 and 142, all the rest of these are to be said at Vespers. And since there are three Psalms too few, let the longer ones of the above number be divided, namely Psalms

138, 143, and 144. But let Psalm 116 because of its brevity to be joined to Psalm 115. The order of the Vesper Psalms being thus settled, let the rest of the Hour—lesson, responsory, hymn, verse and canticle—be carried out as we prescribed above. At Compline the same Psalms are to be repeated every day, namely Psalms 4, 90, and 133.

117. Joseph Raya, & Jose DeVinck, *Byzantine Daily Worship* (Tournai, Belgium: Desclee & Cie, 1969), 205.
118. Constantine N. Callincos, *The Greek Orthodox Catechism* (New York: Greek Archdiocese of No. & So. America, 1960), 205:

Evensong follows this Pattern:

Preparatory singing
Prooimiakos—Psalm 104
Litany of Peace—general intercessions
Psalm 141 and Psalm 142 and others sung
   antiphonally
Evening Hymn
Prophetic Readings and Old Testament
   Admonitions
Nunc Dimittis (Luke 2:29-32).

Morning Prayer is longer and somewhat more elaborate:

Exapsalmus—a set of six psalms
Collect
Kathismata—verses which stress the theme of the
   Resurrection.
Anavathmoi—short anthems
Gospel—concerning one of the eleven
   appearances of the Risen Christ
Canon—a fixed set of tropes
Exaposteilaria—praises addressed to God, Mary,
   or a saint

Lauds—sometimes the psalms of Lauds are added
   at dawn
Doxology

Eucharist usually follows Morning Prayer. Different
stichera (scriptural meditation verses) and *troparia*
(melodic text phrases interpolated between the
words of the verses of a hymn) and ecclesiastical
poetry fill out the different sections of the service.

119. William G. Storey, *et alia, Morning Praise and
   Evensong* (Notre Dame, Indiana: Fides Press, 1973), iii.
120. *The Liturgy of the Hours* (New York: Catholic Book
   Publishing Co., 1975), 17.
121. Ibid., 11.
122. Ibid., 41.
123. Here is the basic format of Morning Prayers:

   Invitatory
   Hymn
   Psalm and antiphon
   Old Testament canticle and antiphon
   Psalm and antiphon
   Short reading and response
   New Testament canticle and antiphon
   Intercessions
   Lord's Prayer
   Collect
   Dismissal

Evening Prayer follows this pattern:

   Invitatory
   Hymn
   Two psalms and antiphons
   New Testament canticle and antiphon
   Short reading and response
   Canticle of Mary and antiphon
   Intercessions

Lord's Prayer
Collect
Dismissal

124. For example, one might look at Evening Prayer I for the
first Sunday of Advent to note how the content of this
hour expresses the spirit of Advent as well as the spirit of
the natural Season of Autumn.

	Liturgical Theme	Natural Theme of Autumn
Invitatory	We lack help. God will provide it.	The lack of abundant life (apart from the harvest) will be made up for in Spring and Summer.
Hymn: Rorate Coeli *or other hymn.*	Stresses expectancy of the coming of Christ.	Autumn expects to be followed by Winter and Spring and Summer.
Antiphon 1: "Proclaim the Good News among the nations! Our God will come to save us."	We have a need for God to come.	The cycle of the Seasons constantly turns for us and all of Nature. We need the cycle to survive.
Psalm 141:1 (a prayer when one is in danger)	Our prayers now are a prelude to heaven itself.	Autumn is a prelude to the other seasons.
Psalm Prayer	May our prayers be acceptable to God.	

Antiphon 2: "Know that the Lord is coming and with him all his saints; that day will dawn with a wonderful light."	We have a darkness in our lives that needs the Light of the world.	Darkened days are with us only for a time.
Psalm 142	We are poured out and need to be filled with the Lord's goodness.	Autumn speaks of what was poured out (the harvest).
Psalm Prayer	May we receive a share of the Lord's goodness.	The harvest is Nature's goodness.
Antiphon 3: "The Lord will come with mighty power; all mortal eyes shall see him."	Our eyes, now empty, will be filled with the sight of the Lord coming.	Autumn tells us that the cycle is being repeated and harvest will come again and again.
New Testament Canticle (Philippians 2:6-11)	Christ emptied himself to become one of us and to save us. God will perfect what is lacking in holiness in us and have us whole and entire when Jesus comes. We who are empty will be filled with mercy.	Nature empties herself so that we have a harvest of benefits. Autumn alone is not enough; it is complete only along with the other seasons.
Responsory	We who are empty will be filled with mercy.	Nature empties herself and the harvest is given.

Antiphon 4: "See, the Lord is coming from afar; his splendour fills the earth."	Already we are being filled.	Nature empties herself and the harvest is given.
Canticle of Mary	God fills Mary (and us) with praise for his deeds; he fills the hungry with good things, etc. These prayers address Jesus whose joy and happiness fill all those who await his coming.	The benefits of the autumnal harvest fill the hungry with good things.
Our Father	Give us this day our daily bread.	Autumnal harvest gives us bread.
Concluding Prayer	Our hearts desire the warmth of God's love and our minds search for the light of his Word.	Even in Autumn we experience cold and darkness.
Dismissal	We go back to our daily world.	We prepare for the next autumnal harvest.

125. Pierre Tielhard deChardin, *Science and Christ* (New York: Harper & Row, 1969), 14.

126. Rex Warner, *The Confessions of St. Augustine*, New American Library, 1963), 17.

127. Langdon Gilkey, *Maker of Heaven and Earth*, Garden City (New York: Anchor Books, 1965), 58-59.

128. Lewis Browne, *The World's Great Scriptures* (New York: Macmillan Co., 1966), 298.

129. Edith Hamilton, *Mythology* (New York: New American Library, 1963), 53:

> The early Greeks knew her as Rhea, the mother of Zeus, or as the mother of the gods. As the myths changed and developed, Rhea was supplanted by Demeter. In the basic myth Demeter's only daughter Persephone, the maiden of Spring, was abducted by the god of the underworld. In her great grief, Demeter withheld her gifts from the earth. The green and flowering land became icebound and lifeless because Persephone had disappeared. Zeus intervened. The outcome was that Persephone was to go to the underworld for four months of the year, the winter time, and come back to her mother during the rest of the year. Eleusis, a town near Athens, became the center of Demeter's worship. During the Eleusinian mysteries which were celebrated every Spring the initiates would cry out:
>
> Queen of fragrant Eleusis,
>   Giver of earth's good gifts,
>   Give me your grace, O Demeter.
> You, too, Persephone, fairest,
>   Maiden all lovely, I offer
>   Song for your favor.

130. Mircea Eliade, *Patterns in Comparative Religion* (New York: Sheed & Ward, 1958), 354.
131. Ibid., 345-346.
132. T. C. McLuhan, *Touch the Earth* (New York: Pocket Books, 1972), 56.
133. Archdale King, *Rite of Eastern Christendom* (Rome: Catholic Books Agency, 1948), 315, 297:

> Christians have also recognized the female symbolism in nature. Mary, the mother of Jesus, has been traditionally associated with the earth and its

fecundity, although not in exactly the same way as the pagan Great Mother. Chaldean Rite Catholics, who live mainly in Iraq and Iran, mention Mary very often in their liturgy. They have a fixed feast of Our Lady "for the protection of the seeds" every May 15.

In their service book *Kdham wa d'Wathar* they have a vesper prayer which says: "Your body, o chaste virgin, is to us a treasure of blessing and its abundant help enriches the world;..."

K. A. Heinrich Kellner, *Heortology*, 239:

Also, Marian blessings are not unknown in Western Catholicism: "In not a few German and Slavonic dioceses a blessing of the fruits of the field take place on the 15th of August...It seems to have arisen from some popular customs connected with harvest."

134. Pennethorne Hughes, *Witchcraft* (Baltimore: Penguin Books, 1971), 25.
135. Ibid., 84.
136. Augustin George, *Praying the Psalms* (Notre Dame, Indiana: Fides Publications, 1964), 53.
137. Ibid., 55.
138. F. C. Happold, *Mysticism* (Baltimore: Penguin Books, 1964), 29.
139. Cumont, *Mysteries*, 149.
140. Cornelius Ernst, *Theological Dictionary* (New York: Herder & Herder, 1965), 407.
141. Helmut Thielicke, *Death and Life* (Philadelphia: Fortress Press, 1970), 201.
142. Lucien Deiss, *Biblical Hymns and Psalms* vol. 3 (Cincinnati: World Library of Sacred Music, 1971), 35.
143. Teilhard deChardin, *Science and Christ*, 60-61.
144. Abbott, *Documents*, 140-141.
145. Claus Westermann, *Creation* (Philadelphia: Fortress Press, 1974), 118.

146. Ibid., 122-123.
147. John Reumann, *Creation and New Creation*
(Minneapolis: Augsburg Publishing House, 1973), 89-99.
148. John G. Gibbs, *Creation and Redemption* (Leiden,
Netherlands: E. J. Brill Co., 1971), 143.
149. James M. Carmody, & Thomas E. Clarke, eds., *Word and Redeemer* (Glen Rock, New Jersey: Paulist Press, 1966),
16.
150. Ibid., 21-22:

> Thus there is one God the Father, as we have demonstrated, and one Christ Jesus our Lord who came in fulfillment of God's comprehensive design and consummates all things in himself. Man is in all respects the handiwork of God; thus he consummates man in himself: he was invisible and became visible; incomprehensible and made comprehensible; impossible and made possible; the Word, and made man; consummating all things in himself. That as in things above the heavens and in the spiritual and invisible world the Word of God is supreme, so in the visible and physical realm he may have preeminence, taking to himself the primacy and constituting himself the head of the Church, that he may draw all things to himself in due time.

151. Ibid., 46:

> ...For men's minds having finally fallen to things of sense, the Word disguised himself by appearing in a body, that he might, as man, transfer men to himself, and center their senses on himself, and, men seeing him thenceforth as man, persuade them by the works he did that he is not man only, but also God, and the Word and wisdom of the true God...For by the Word revealing himself everywhere, both above and beneath, and in the depth and in the breadth—above, in the creation;

beneath, in becoming man; in the depth, in Hades; and in the breadth, in the world—all things have been filled with the knowledge of God.

152. Ibid., 64.
153. Ibid., 120.
154. Kellner, *Heortology*, 190.
155. L. Duchesne, *Christian Worship: Its Origin and Evolution* (London: S.P.C.K., 1903), 288.
156. John Dowden, *The Church Year and Calendar* (London: Cambridge University Press, 1910), 86-87, 289:

But rogations came to be offered as supplications at times other than during the ceremony of averting blight. Mamertus, Bishop of Vienne in Gaul about 470 A.D., appointed rogations to be performed at a time of great calamity for his city which was beset with earthquakes and fires. The practice of these rogations soon spread throughout all of Gaul. Rome seems to have introduced such rogations for certain days about the year 800 A.D. In Gaul, from the end of the fifth century, the three days before the feast of Ascension were used to the time of this litanic procession. Such days were for strict fasting. These litanies for Springtime were not used in Spain; rather, there they had litanies for the beginning of November which was the time for sowing the seed. These litanies were also employed on the feast of Pentecost and at the Autumnal equinox, according to the locality. With the revision of the Roman Calendar, rogation days may be determined locally once again.

157. Mary Reed Newland, *The Year and Our Children* (New York: P. J. Kenedy & Sons, 1956), 179-180.
158. Paulinus Milner, *The Worship of the Church* (New York: Hawthorn Books, 1964), 905.
159. O'Shea, *Worship of the Church*, 233.

160. Sharon Gallagher, *Medieval Art* (New York: Tudor Publishing Co., 1969), 5.

161. John H. Wright, *The Order of the Universe in the Theology of St. Thomas Aquinas* (Rome: Gregorian University Press, 1957), 7.

162. Benen Fahy, *The Writings of St. Francis of Assisi* (Chicago: Franciscan Herald Press, 1964), 130-131:

> Most high, all powerful, all good, Lord!
> All praise is yours, all glory, all honour, and all
>   blessing.
> To you alone, Most High, do they belong.
> No mortal lips are worthy to pronounce your name.
> All praise be yours, my Lord, through all that you
>   have made,
> and first my lord, Brother Sun,
> Who brings the day; and light you give us through
>   him.
> How beautiful is he, how radiant in all his
>   splendor!
> Of you, Most High, he bears the likeness.
> All praise be yours, my Lord, through Sister Moon
>   and Stars;
> In the heavens you have made them, bright
> And precious and fair.
> All praise be yours, my Lord, through Brother
>   Wind and Air,
> And fair and stormy, all the weather's moods,
> By which you cherish all that you have made.
> All praise be yours, my Lord, through Sister Water,
> So useful, lowly, precious, and pure.
> All praise be yours, my Lord, through Brother Fire,
> Through whom you brighten up the night.
> How beautiful is he, how gay! Full of power and
>   strength.
> All praise be yours, my Lord, through Sister Earth,
>   our mother,

Who feeds us in her sovereignty and produces
various fruits with coloured flowers and herbs...

163. Eliade, *Sacred and the Profane*, 22.
164. Ibid., 37.
165. Ibid., 63, 65.
166. Ibid., 33.
167. Eliade, *Rites and Symbols*, 5, 32, 33.
168. M. Inez Hilger, *Arapaho Child Life and Its Cultural Background* (Washington, D.C.: Government Printing Office, 1952), 152.
169. E. Adamson Hoebel, *The Cheyennes* (New York: Holt, Rinehart and Winston, 1960), 13.
170. Hyemeyohsts Storm, *Seven Arrows* (New York: Harper & Row, 1972), 14-20.
171. T. C. McLuhan, *Touch the Earth*, 16-17.
172. Marx, *Protestants and Catholics*, 88-89.
173. Maria-Gabrielle Wosien, *Sacred Dance* (New York: Avon Books, 1974), 11, 12.
174. Bernard S. Mason, *Dances and Stories of the American Indians* (New York: The Ronald Press Co., 1944), 4.
175. Wosien, *Sacred Dance*, 21.
176. Ibid., 22-23.
177. Ibid., 29.
178. Ibid.
179. Ibid., 26.
180. Harvey Cox, *The Feast of Fools* (Cambridge, Mass.: Howard University Press, 1970), 55.
181. Abbott, *Documents*, 203.
182. Ibid.
183. Ibid., 231.
184. Marshall McLuhan, *Understanding Media: The Extensions of Man* (Toronto: McGraw-Hill Book Co., 1964), 80.
185. Philip Slater, *The Pursuit of Loneliness* (Boston: Beacon Press, 1972), 1.

186. W. H. Gardner and N. E. Mackenzie, eds., *The Poems of Gerard Manley Hopkins* (London: Oxford University Press, 1970), 66.
187. Teilhard deChardin, *Future of Man*, 17.
188. Pierre Teilhard deChardin, *The Phenomenon of Man* (New York: Harper Torchbooks, 1959), 297.
189. Ibid.
190. Louis Bouyer, *Liturgical Piety* (Notre Dame, Indiana: University of Notre Dame Press, 1955), 201, 202, 205, 206:

> ...Every liturgical feast is a celebration of the Lord's *transitus*, his dying and rising. This is also true of the feast of Christmas. As St. Gregory once preached, "Christ is coming from heaven. Go to meet him. While He is here on earth, may you ascend up to heaven." This feast helps us to understand the incarnation as being redemptive only in the sense that it was an incarnation in a flesh which has to undergo death, so that the death of Adam might die in the death of Christ. By means of Christ's own birth, death, and Resurrection we are born to eternal life. The birth of Christ was a necessary prerequisite to his redemptive Cross and Resurrection. In the descent of God to his people, the Church celebrates the beginning of the action which brings us back to God. However, we can say that the paschal mystery is celebrated even in the commemoration of Christ's birth because God gifts us with his Son so that through him we might be born again to become (with his Son) the gift that he can receive; the Christmas liturgy, in the Prayer over the Gifts for the fifth day within the Octave, puts it this way: "Lord, receive our gifts in this wonderful exchange: from all you have given us we bring you these gifts, and in return, you give us yourself. We ask this through Christ our Lord. Amen."

191. Ibid., 195:

> The daily celebration of the Eucharist, as well as the celebrations of the other sacraments, helps us to realize that every day we live is really a microcosm of our whole life with Christ, just as the natural day is a microcosm of our whole natural life.

192. A theology of ecology is a theology which says that stewardship should be a basic Christian preoccupation. Here is a sampling of the views of various Christians who are concerned about the subject:

Andre Dumas, "The Ecological Crisis and the Doctrine of Creation," *Catholic Mind* vol. 84, no. 1296 (New York: American Press, 1975), 25, 26:

> ...religions have always flirted with asceticism and often even become wedded to it. But this asceticism has assumed two main forms, neither of which matches the dimensions of the present ecological crisis: an other-worldly asceticism embraced by those who withdraw from the world and the entice-ments of its wealth and an inner-worldly asceticism embraced by those who prefer to save and invest that wealth. What we need now is an asceticism which is pro-worldly, which knows that we have only limited space and a short time and also knows that conviviality is essential, if our faith in creation is to aim not so much at the protection of a nature which is still intact, as at the blessing of the human beings for whom God continually structures nature, inviting these human beings to recognize His own image in themselves as attendants of their brothers and sisters. In this way, ecology invites ethical reflection and action to seek a balanced habitat of all people while respecting the autonomous iden-tity of each.

Mary Evelyn Jegen & Bruno V. Manno, eds., *The Earth is the Lord's* (New York: Paulist Press, 1978), 128:

> Commitment to stewardship of land implies personal responsibility in choice of life-style. It also requires critical examination of unjust social institutions and the denunciation of those institutions as sinful where injustices exist. That is, institutions that contribute to a grossly unbalanced distribution of land and its life-essential resources, that contribute to destruction of the delicate interrelationships of the ecological system, and that contribute to the depletion of critical and nonrenewable resources are not just unfortunate political, social and economic arrangements; they are sinful in themselves.

Lawrence Cunningham, ed., *Brother Francis* (Huntington, Indiana: Pyramid Publications, 1977), 112, 120:

> ...What people do about their ecology depends on what they think about themselves in relation to things around them. Human ecology is deeply conditioned by beliefs about our nature and destiny—that is, by religion...The greatest spiritual revolutionary in Western history, St. Francis, proposed what he thought was an alternative Christian view of nature and man's relation to it: he tried to substitute the idea of the equality of all creatures, including man, for the idea of man's limitless rule of creation. He failed. Both our present science and our present technology are so tinctured with orthodox Christian arrogance toward nature that no solution for our ecologic crisis can be expected from them alone. Since the roots of our trouble are so largely religious, the remedy must also be essentially religious, whether we call it that or not. We must rethink and refeel our nature and destiny. The profoundly religious, but heretical, sense of the

primitive Franciscans for the spiritual autonomy of all parts of nature may point a direction. I propose Francis as a patron saint for ecologists.

Warren G. Hansen, *St. Francis of Assisi: Patron of the Environment* (Chicago: Franciscan Herald Press, 1971), 51, 52:

The basic mission of the Christian Church is the mission of reconciliation...Throughout its entire history the Church has always recognized that this was its work...It is abundantly clear that man is out of harmony with nature for the same basic reason that he is out of harmony with his fellows and with his creator. This disharmony with nature is thoroughly destructive, not only to God's "Brother and Sister" creatures in nature, but indeed also to man himself. Truly man's abusive, arrogant, exploitive attitude toward nature—which lies at the root of his impending environmental crisis—is just as in need of redemption and transformation as his attitude toward his fellows, toward himself and toward God. Man cannot be truly whole until he comes to emphasize that sacramental principle, that all things in the created order are vehicles and signs of God's grace.

193. Herbert Butterfield, *Christianity and History* (New York: Charles Scribner & Sons, 1950), 117.
194. Abbott, *Documents*, 199.
195. King, *Rites*, 402.
196. Teilhard deChardin, *Hymn*, 34.
197. Christopher Hollis, *The Achievements of Vatican II* (New York: Hawthorn Publishers, 1966), 23.
198. Francois Chagneau, *Stay With Us* (New York: Newman Press, 1971), v.
199. Gerard A. Pottebaum, *The Rites of People* (Washington, D.C.: The Liturgical Conference Press, 1975), 47.
200. Abbott, *Documents*, 141.

201. Ibid., 143, 146, 150, 151.
202. A. Bugnini and C. Braga, eds., *The Commentary on the Constitution and on the Instruction on the Sacred Liturgy* (New York: Benziger Brothers, 1965), 100.
203. Pottebaum, *Rites*, 76.204.
Abbott, *Documents*, 147.
205. Bugnini and Braga, *Commentary*, 103.
206. Peter R. Akehurst, *Liturgy and Creation* (Bramcote, Notts., England: Grove Books, 1974), 19.
207. Ibid.
208. Ibid., 4.
209. Ibid., 24.
210. Abbott, *Documents*, 78-79.
211. George A. Lindbeck, *The Future of Roman Catholic Theology* (Philadelphia: Fortress Press, 1970), 16.
212. Maertens, *Feast*, 98-134.
213. Ibid., 135-151.
214. Ibid., 62-97.
215. *Book of Common Worship* (Philadelphia: Board of Christian Education of the Presbyterian Church, 1946), 11-19.
216. *Book of Offices* (London: Methodist Publishing House, 1936), 11-30.
217. *Lutheran Book of Worship* (Minneapolis: Augsburg Publishing House, 1978), 131-141.
218. Ibid., 142-153.
219. *The Book of Common Prayer* (Kingsport, Tennessee: Kingsport Press, 1977), 37-102.
220. Ibid., 103-108.
221. Ibid., 127-135.

Extended Bibliography

Abbey, Edward. *Monkey Wrench Gang*. Philadelphia: J. B. Lippincott Co., 1975.

Abbott, Walter M. *The Documents of Vatican II*. New York: American Press, 1966.

Adam, Davis. *The Edge of Glory: Prayers in the Celtic Tradition*. London: Triangle/SPCK, 1985.

Adams, Richard. *Nature Through the Seasons*. New York: Penguin Books, 1975.

Akehurst, Peter R. *Liturgy and Creation*. Bramcote, Notts., England: Grove Books, 1974.

Alexander, W. D. *A Brief History of the Hawaiian People*. New York: American Book Co., 1891.

Baur, Johannes B., ed. *Sacramentum Verbi 3*. New York: Herder and Herder, 1970.

Beck, Peggy, and Anna L. Walters. *The Sacred: Ways of Knowledge, Sources of Life*. Tsaile, Arizona: Navajo Community College Press, 1977.

Berry, Thomas. *The Dream of the Earth*. San Francisco: Sierra Club Books, 1988.

_____. "Twelve Principles for Reflecting on the Universe and the Role of the Human in the Universe Process." *Cross Currents* 37, no. 2-3 (1987).

Birnbaum, Philip. *Daily Prayer Book*. New York: Hebrew Publishing Co., 1949.

Blessings and Consecrations: A Book of Occasional Services. Nashville: Abingdon Press, 1984.

Boissiere, Robert. *Meditations with the Hopi*. Santa Fe, New Mexico: Bear and Co., 1986.

Book of Common Prayer, The. Kingsport, Tennessee: Kingsport Press, 1977.

Book of Common Worship. Philadelphia: Board of Christian Education of Presbyterian Church, 1946.

Book of Offices. London: Methodist Publishing House, 1936.

Bopp, Judy, *et alia*. *The Sacred Tree*. Lethbridge, Alberta: University of Lethbridge, 1988.

Bouyer, Louis. *Liturgical Piety*. Notre Dame, Indiana: Notre Dame University Press, 1955.

Brandon, William. *The Magic World: American Indian Songs and Poems*. New York: William Morrow and Co., Inc., 1971.

Brown, Joseph Epes. *The Sacred Pipe: Black Elk's Account of the Seven Rites of the Oglala Sioux*. Norman, Oklahoma: University of Oklahoma Press, 1953.

Brown, Raphael, trans. *The Little Flowers of St. Francis*. Garden City, New York: Image Books, 1958.

Brown, Raymond E. *et alia*. "New Testament Eschatology." In *Jerome Biblical Commentary*. Englewood Cliffs, New Jersey: Prentice-Hall, 1968.

Brown, Robert McAfee. *Spirituality and Liberation*. Philadelphia: Westminster Press, 1988.

Brown, Vinson. *Voices of the Earth and Sky*. Harrisburg, Pennsylvania: Stackpole Books, 1974.

Browne, Lewis. *The World's Great Scriptures*. New York: Macmillan Co., 1966.

Butterfield, Herbert. *Christianity and History*. New York: Charles Scribner and Sons, 1950.

Bugnini, A., and C. Braga. eds. *The Commentary on the Constitution and on the Instruction on the Sacred Liturgy*. New York: Benziger Bros., 1965.

Caduto, Michael J., and Joseph Bruchac. *Keepers of the Earth*. Golden, Colorado: Fulcrum, Inc., 1988.

Callincos, Constantine N. *The Greek Orthodox Catechism*. New York: Greek Archdiocese of North and South America, 1960.

Cameli, Louis John. "The Spirituality of Celebration." *Chicago Studies* 16., no. 1. Mundelein, Illinois: Civitas Dei Foundation, 1977.

Campbell, Joseph. *The Hero With a Thousand Faces*. Princeton: Princeton University Press, 1968.

_____. *The Way of the Animal Powers*. London: Summerfield Press, 1983.

_____. *Myths to Live By*. New York: Viking Press, 1972.

Carmody, James M., and Thomas E. Clarke, eds. *Word and Redeemer*. Glen Rock, New Jersey: Paulist Press, 1966.

Chagneau, Francois. *Stay With Us*. New York: Newman Press, 1971.

Chapin, John, ed. *The Book of Catholic Quotations*. New York: Farrar, Straus and Cudahy, 1956.

Chapungco, Anscar J. *Cultural Adaptation of the Liturgy*. New York: Paulist Press, 1982.

Cheneviere, Alain. *Vanishing Tribes: Primitive Man on Earth*. Garden City, New York: Doubleday and Co., 1987.

Clarke, W. K. Lowther. *Liturgy and Worship*. London: S.P.C.K., 1964.

Connolly, Francis X. *Wisdom of the Saints*. New York: Pocket Books, Inc., 1963.

Cornell, Joseph. *Listening to Nature*. Nevada City: Califoria: Dawn Publ., 1987.

Cowie, L. W., and John Selwyn Gummer. *The Christian Calendar*. Springfield, Massachusetts: G & C Merrion Co., 1974.

Cox, Harvey. *The Feast of Fools*. Cambridge, Mass.: Harvard University Press, 1970.

Cumont, Franz. *Oriental Religions in Roman Paganism*. New York: Dover Publications, 1958.

_____. *The Mysteries of Mithra*. New York: Dover Publications, 1956.

Cunningham, Lawrence, ed. *Brother Francis*. Huntington, Indiana: Pyramid Publications, 1977.

Dallen, James. *Liturgical Celebration: Patterns for Advent and Christmas*. Cincinnati: North American Liturgy Resources, 1974.

Day, A. Grove. *The Sky Clears: Poetry of the American Indians*. Lincoln, University of Nebraska Press, 1951.

deGuibert, Joseph. *The Theology of the Spiritual Life*. New York: Sheed and Ward, 1953.

Deiss, Lucien. *Biblical Hymns and Refrains* 1. Cincinnati: World Library of Sacred Music, 1971.

Densmore, Frances. *Teton Sioux Music* bulletin 61. Washington, D.C.: Bureau of American Ethnology, Government Printing Office, 1918.

Devall, Bill, and George Sessions. *Deep Ecology*. Layton, Utah: Peregrine Smith, 1985.

DeVaux, Roland. *Ancient Israel* vols. 1 and 2. New York: McGraw-Hill Book Co., 1965.

Doherty, Richard T. *Practical Handbook of Rites, Blessings, and Prayers*. St. Paul, Minn.: North Central Publishing Co., 1961.

Dowden, John. *The Church Year and Calendar*. London: Cambridge University Press, 1910.

Doyle, Leonard J., trans. *St. Benedict's Rule for Monasteries*, Collegeville, Minn.: St. John's Abbey Press, 1948.

Duchesne, L. *Christian Worship: Its Origin and Evolution*. London: S.P.C.K., 1903.

Dumas, Andre. "The Ecological Crisis and the Doctrine of Creation." *Catholic Mind* 84, no. 1296, New York: American Press, 1975.

Edgerton, Franklin. *The Bhagavad Gita*. New York: Harper and Row, 1964.

Editorial Staff of Catholic University of America. *New Catholic Encyclopedia* 14. New York: McGraw-Hill, 1966.

Eliade, Mircea. *Patterns in Comparative Religion*. New York: Sheed and Ward, 1958.

_____. *Rites and Symbols of Initiation*. New York: Harper Torchbooks, 1965.

_____. *The Myth of the Eternal Return*. Princeton, New Jersey: Princeton University Press, 1974.

_____. *The Sacred and the Profane*. New York: Harcourt, Brace and World, 1959.

Epstein, Isadore. *Judaism*. London: Penguin Books, 1970.

Erdoes, Richard. *Crying for A Dream*. Santa Fe, New Mexico: Bear and Co., 1990.

Ernst, Cornelius. *Theological Dictionary*. New York: Herder and Herder, 1965.

Faban, Don. *The Dynamics of Change*. Englewood Cliffs, New Jersey: Prentice-Hall, Inc., 1966.

Fahy, Behan. *The Writings of St. Francis of Assisi*. Chicago: Franciscan Herald Press, 1964.

Fox, Matthew. *Original Blessing: A Primer of Creation Spirituality*. Santa Fe, New Mexico: Bear and Co., 1983.

Freesoul, John Redtail. *Breath of the Invisible: The Way of the Pipe*. Wheaton, Illinois: Theosophical Publishing House, 1986.

Gallagher, Sharon. *Medieval Art*. New York: Tudor Publishing Co., 1969.

Gardner, W. M., and N. H. Mackenzie, eds. *The Poems of Gerard Manley Hopkins*. London: Oxford University Press, 1970.

Gaster, Theodore. *Festivals of the Jewish Year*. New York: William Morrow and Co., 1953.

_____. *Thespis*. New York: Harper Torchbooks, 1961.

George, Augustin. *Praying the Psalms*. Notre Dame, Indiana: Fides Publications, 1964.

Gibbs, John G. *Creation and Redemption*. Leiden, Netherlands: E. J. Brill, 1971.

Gilkey, Langdon. *Maker of Heaven and Earth*. Garden City, New York: Anchor Books, 1965.

Graf, Dom Ernest. *The Church's Daily Prayer*. London: Burns, Oates and Washbourne, 1938.

Greeley, Andrew. "The Spirit of Pluralism." *Spiritual Life* 22, no. 1 (Spring, 1976).

Gulpilil, David. *The Birrick: Our Ancestors of the Dreaming*. Cheltenham, Australia: L & S Publications, Inc., 1983.

Guss, David M. *The Language of the Birds: Tales, Texts, and Poems of Interspecies Communication*. San Francisco: North Point Press, 1985.

Hamilton, Edith. *Mythology*. New York: New American Library, 1963.

Hansen, Warren G. *St. Francis of Assisi: Patron of the Environment*. Chicago: Franciscan Herald Press, 1971.

Happold, F. C. *Mysticism*. Baltimore: Penguin Books, 1964.

Harrelson, Walter. *From Fertility Cult to Worship*. New York: Anchor Books, 1970.

Hatchett, Marion. *Sanctifying Life, Time and Space*. New York: Seabury Press, 1976.

Haug, Helmut, and Jurgen Rump, eds. *The Radical Bible*. Maryknoll, New York: Orbis Books, 1972.

Hays, Edward. *Prayers for a Planetary Pilgrim*. Easton, Kansas: Forest of Peace Books, 1988.

Hedgepeth, William, and Dennis Stock. *The Alternative: Communal Life in New America*. New York: Macmillan Co., 1970.

Heffern, Rich. "The Eleventh Commandment: Take Care of the Earth, Heal the Planet." *Eucharistic Minister* no. 61 (April 1989). Kansas City, Missouri: Celebration Publ.

Highwater, Jamake. *Ritual of the Wind*. New York: Viking Press, 1977.

Hilger, M. Inez. *Arapaho Child Life and Its Cultural Background*. Washington, D.C.: Government Printing Office, 1951.

_____. *Chippewa Child Life and Its Cultural Background*. Washington D.C.: Government Printing Office, 1951.

Hoebel, E. Adamson. *The Cheyennes*. New York: Holt, Rinehart and Winston, 1960.

Hollis, Christopher. *The Achievements of Vatican II*. New York: Hawthorn Publications, 1966.

Hughes, Pennethorne. *Witchcraft*. Baltimore: Penguin Books, 1971.

Idelsohn, A. Z. *Jewish Liturgy and Its Development*. New York: Schocken Books, 1967.

International African Institute. *African Systems of Thought.* New York: Oxford University Press, 1965.

Jeffers, Robinson. *Selected Poetry of Robinson Jeffers.* New York: Random House, 1959.

Jegen, Mary Evelyn, and Bruno V. Manno, eds. *The Earth is the Lord's.* New York: Paulist Press, 1978.

Jenness, Diamond. *The Ojibway Indians of Parry Island: Their Social and Religious Life.* Ottawa: King's Printer, 1935.

Jungmann, Joseph A. *The Early Liturgy.* Notre Dame, Indiana: Notre Dame Press, 1959.

Kampmann, Theoderich. *The Year of the Church.* Westminster, Maryland: Newman Press, 1966.

Kavanaugh, Kieran, and Otilio Rodriguez. *The Collected Works of St. John of the Cross.* Washington D.C.: I.C.S. Publications, 1973.

Kellner, K. A. Heinrich. *Heortology.* London: Kegan Paul, Trench, Trubner & Co., 1908.

King, Archdale. *The Rites of Eastern Christendom.* Rome: Catholic Books Agency, 1948.

Krause, Hans-Joachim. *Worship in Israel.* Richmond, Virginia: John Knox Press, 1966.

Kucharek, Casimir. *The Sacramental Mysteries: A Byzantine Approach.* Allendale, New Jersey: Alleluia Press, 1976.

LaChapelle, Dolores. *Earth Festivals.* Silverton, Colorado: Finn Hill Arts, 1976.

_____. *Earth Wisdom.* Silverton, Colorado: Finn Hill Arts, 1978.

_____. *Sacred Land, Sacred Sex, Rapture of the Deep.* Silverton, Colorado: Finn Hill Arts, 1988.

Lame Deer, John, and Richard Erdoes. *Lame Deer, Seeker of Visions.* New York: Pocket Books, 1972.

Land and Hunger: A Biblical Worldview. New York: Bread for the World Educational Fund, 1981.

Lappe, Frances Moore, and Jospeh Collins. *Food First: Beyond the Myth of Scarcity.* New York: Ballantine Books, 1977.

Larson, Jeanne, and Madge Micheels-Cyrus. *Seeds of Peace*. Philadelphia: New Society Publications, 1987.

Laubin, Reginold and Gladys. *Indian Dancers of North America*. Norman, Oklahoma: University of Oklahoma Press, 1976.

Lawrence, D. H. *The Plumed Serpent*. New York: Alfred A. Knopf, 1951

LeBlanc, Etienne, and Mary Rose Talbot. *How Green is Green?* Notre Dame, Indiana: Ave Maria Press, 1974.

Lindbeck, George A. *The Future of Roman Catholic Theology*. Philadelphia: Fortress Press, 1970.

Linzey, Andrew, and Tom Regan, eds. *Love the Animals*. New York: Crossroads, 1989.

Liturgy of the Hours, The. New York: Catholic Book Publishing Co., 1975.

Lonsdale, Steven. *Animals and the Origins of Dance*. New York: Thames and Hudson, Inc., 1981.

Luckert, Karl W. *Coyoteway: A Navajo Holyway Healing Ceremonial*. Tucson: University of Arizona Press, 1979.

Lutheran Book of Worship. Minneapolis, Minn.: Augsburg Publishing House, 1978.

Maertens, Thierry. *A Feast in Honor of Yahweh*. Notre Dame, Indiana: Fides Publications, 1965.

Magnuson, Osgood *et alia*. *Living Waters*. League City, Texas: National Association of Conservation Districts, 1983.

Mails, Thomas E. *Secret Native American Pathways: A Guide to Inner Peace*. Tulsa, Oklahoma: Council Oak Books, 1988.

_____. *Sundancing at Rosebud and Pineridge*. Sioux Falls, South Dakota: Center for Western Studies, 1978.

Manley, Jim. *Seed Songs of Earth and Spirit*. New York: National Council of Churches of Christ in the U.S.A., 1983.

Maritain, Jacques. *Redeeming the Time*. London: The Centenary Press, 1946.

Marx, Michael, ed. *Protestants and Catholics on the Spiritual Life*. Collegeville, Minn.: Liturgical Press, 1965.

Mason, Bernard S. *Dances and Stories of the American Indian*. New York: The Ronald Press Co., 1964.

McIntyre, Joan. *Mind in the Waters*. San Francisco: Sierra Club Books, 1974.

McLuhan, Marshall. *Understanding Media: The Extensions of Man*. Toronto: McGraw-Hill Book Co., 1964.

McLuhan, T. C. *Touch the Earth*. New York: Pocket Books, 1972.

Michel, John. *The Earth Spirit: Its Ways, Shrines and Mysteries*. New York: Avon Books, 1975.

Milner, Paulinus. *The Worship of the Church*. New York: Hawthorn Books, 1964.

Montenat, Christian *et alia*. *How to Read the World: Creation in Evolution*. New York: Crossroad Publication Co., 1985.

Montilus, Guerin. *Dompin: The Spirituality of African Peoples*. Nashville: Winston-Derek Publishing Co., 1989.

Morgan, Kenneth W., ed. *The Religion of the Hindus*. New York: The Ronald Press Co., 1953.

Mossi, John, ed. *Bread Blessed and Broken*. New York: Paulist Press, 1974.

Mouiren, Trophime. *The Creation*. New York: Hawthorn Books, 1962.

Musurillo, Herbert A. *The Fathers of the Primitive Church*. New York: New American Library, 1966.

Nabokov, Peter, and Robert Easton. *Native American Architecture*. New York: Oxford University Press, 1989.

Newland, Mary Reed. *The Year of Our Children*. New York: P. J. Kenedy and Sons, 1956.

Not Man Apart: Lines from Robinson Jeffers. New York: Ballantine Books, 1965.

Nouwen, Henri J. M. *Aging*. Garden City, New York: Doubleday and Co., 1974.

_____. *Reaching Out*. Garden City, New York: Doubleday and Co., 1975.

_____. *With Open Hands*. Notre Dame, Indiana: Ave Maria Press, 1972.

O Fiannachta, Padraig. *Saltair*. Translated by Desmond Forristal. Dublin: The Columba Press, 1988.

Osborne, Hayward. *Lord of the Harvest*. London: Josef Weinberger Ltd., 1974.

O'Shea, William. *The Worship of the Church*. London: Darton, Longman and Todd, 1957.

Osterreicher, John M., ed. *The Bridge* 1. New York: Pantheon Books, 1955.

Parsch, Pius. *The Church's Year of Grace*. Collegeville, Minnesota: The Liturgical Press, 1954.

Peck, M. Scott, with Marilyn von Waldner and Patricia Kay. *What Return Can I Make?* New York: Simon and Schuster, 1985.

Peters, Edward H., ed. *The Constitution of the Church of Vatican Council II*. Glen Rock, New Jersey: Paulist Press, 1965.

Pintauro, Joe. *Earth Mass*. New York: Harper and Row, 1973.

Pottebaum, Gerard A. *The Rites of People*. Washington, D.C.: The Liturgical Conference Press, 1975.

P.O.M. Project. *Survival*. Canoga Park, California: P.O.M. Project, Inc., 1967.

Power, E. *The History of Religions* 1. London: Catholic Truth Society, 1910.

Prayers We Have in Common: Agreed Liturgical Texts Proposed by the International Consultation on English Texts. Philadelphia: Fortress Press, 1970.

Raya, Joseph, and Jose deVinck. *Byzantine Daily Worship*. Tournai, Belgium: Desclee and Cie., 1969.

Reumann, John. *Creation and New Creation*. Minneapolis: Augsburg Publishing House, 1973.

Riepe, Charles K. *Living the Christian Seasons*. New York: Herder and Herder, 1964.

Rite of Christian Initiation of Adults. Washington, D.C.: U.S.C.C. Publications Office, 1974.

Rochelle, Jay. *The Revolutionary Year*. Philadelphia: Fortress Press, 1973.

Roman Calendar. Washington, D.C.: U.S.C.C. Publications Office, 1976.

Rowley, H. H. *Worship in Ancient Israel*. Philadelphia: Fortress Press, 1973.

Sacred Congregation for Divine Worship. *General Instruction of the Liturgy of the Hours*. New York: Catholic Book Publications, 1975.

Savary, Louis. *A Time for Salvation*. New York: Regina Press, 1972.

Schaff, Philip, and Henry Wace. *The Nicene and Post-Nicene Fathers* 12. New York: Christian Literature Co., 1895.

Schaffran, Janey, and Pat Kozak. *More Than Words: Prayer and Ritual for Inclusive Communities*. Oak Park, Illinois: Meyer-Stone Books, 1988.

Scharper, Philip and Sally, eds. *The Gospel in Art by the Peasants of Solentiname*. Maryknoll, New York: Orbis Books, 1984.

Schultz, Paul, and George Tinker. *Rivers of Life: Native Spirituality for Native Churches*. Minneapolis: Publishing House of Evangelical Lutheran Church in America, 1988.

Seattle (Chief). *How Can One Sell the Air: A Manifesto for the Earth*. Summertown, Tennessee: Book Publishing Company, 1980.

Seed, John *et alia*. *Thinking Like a Mountain: Towards a Council of All Beings*. Philadelphia: New Society Publications, 1988.

Sender, Ramon, and Alicia Bay Laurel. *Being of the Sun*. New York: Harper and Row, 1973.

Sharkey, John. *Celtic Mysteries*. New York: Thames and Hudson, 1979.

Shaw, Luci, ed. *Sightseers into Pilgrims*. Wheaton Illinois: Tyndale House Publishers, 1973.

Sheen, Canon. *The Magic of Spring*. Dublin: Mercier Press, 1973.

Shor, Franc, ed. *Great Religions of the World*. New York: National Geographic Society, 1971.

Shorter, Aylward. *African Culture and the Christian Church*. New York: Orbis Books, 1974.

_____. *Prayer in the Religious Tradition of Africa*. Oxford: Oxford University Press, 1975.

Simons, Thomas G. *Blessings: A Reappraisal of Their Nature, Purpose, and Celebration*. San Jose, California: Resource Publications, Inc., 1981.

_____. *Blessings for God's People: A Book of Blessings for All Occasions*. Notre Dame, Indiana: Ave Maria Press, 1983.

Slater, Philip. *The Pursuit of Loneliness*. Boston: Beacon Press, 1972.

Snyder, Gary. *Earth House Hold*. New York: New Directions Publishing Corp., 1969.

_____. *The Old Ways*. San Francisco: City Lights Books, 1977.

_____. *Turtle Island*. New York: New Directions Publishing Corp., 1974.

_____. *He Who Hunted Birds in His Father's Village: The Dimensions of a Haida Myth*. Bolinas, California: Grey Fox Press, 1979.

Solomon, Victor. *A Handbook on Conversions to the Religions of the World*. New York: Stravon Educational Press, 1965.

Spangler, David. *Festivals in the New Age*. Forres, Moray, Scotland: Findhorn Foundation, 1975.

Steltenkamp, Michael F. *The Sacred Vision: Native American Religion and Its Practice Today*. Ramsey, New Jersey: Paulist Press, 1982.

Stolzman, William. *The Pipe and Christ*. Chamberlain, South Dakota: St. Joseph's Indian School, 1986.

Storey, William G., *et alia*, eds. *Morning Praise and Evensong*. Notre Dame, Indiana: Fides Publications, 1973.

Storm, Hyemeyohsts. *Seven Arrows*. New York: Harper and Row, 1972.

Streit, Jacob. *Sun and Cross*. Edinburgh: Floris Books, 1984.

Swimme, Brian. *The Universe is a Green Dragon*. Santa Fe, New Mexico: Bear and Co., 1984.

Tanqueray, Adolphe. *The Spiritual Life*. Tournai, Belgium: Desclee and Cie., 1930.

Teilhard deChardin, Pierre. *Science and Christ*. New York: Harper and Row, 1969.

_____. *The Divine Milieu*. New York: Harper and Row, 1960.

_____. *The Future of Man*. New York: Harper Torchbooks, 1964.

_____. *The Hymn of the Universe*. New York: Harper Torchbooks, 1959.

Thielicke, Helmut. *Death and Life*. Philadelphia: Fortress Press, 1970.

Thomas Aquinas. *Summa Theologiae*. Garden City, New York: Image Books, 1969.

Tibbitts, Clark, ed. *Handbook of Social Gerontology*. Chicago: University of Chicago Press, 1960.

Turner, Victor. *Celebration: Studies in Festivity and Ritual*. Washington, D.C.: Smithsonian Institution Press, 1982.

Twohy, Patrich J. *Finding a Way Home: Indian and Catholic Spiritual Paths of the Plateau Tribes*. Inchelium, Washington: St. Michael's Mission, 1983.

United Methodist Council of Bishops. *In Defense of Creation: The Nuclear Crisis and a Just Peace*. Nashville: Graded Press, 1986.

Warner, Rex. *The Confessions of St. Augustine*. New York: New American Library, 1963.

Waters, Frank. *The Book of the Hopi*. New York: Ballantine Books, Inc., 1963.

Westermann, Claus. *Creation*. Philadelphia: Fortress Press, 1974.

Wilch, John R. *Time and Event*. Leiden, Netherlands: E. J. Brill, 1969.

Wosien, Maria-Gabrielle. *Sacred Dance*. New York: Avon Books, 1974.

Wright, David F. "Interim Breviaries: An Evaluation." *Worship* 146, no. 4 (1972).

Wright, John R. *The Order of the Universe in the Theology of St. Thomas Aquinas*. Rome: Gregorian University Press, 1946.

Yeadon, Davis. *When the Earth Was Young: Songs of the American Indian*. Garden City, New York: Doubleday and Co., 1978.

Zeilinger, Ron. *Sacred Ground: Reflections on Lakota Spirituality and the Gospel.* Chamberlain, South Dakota: Tipi Press, 1987.

Video Recording

Krutein, Wernher, and David Pomeranz. *It's In Every One Of Us.* San Francisco: New Era Media, 1987.

Music Publishing Companies

Agape Music. Carol Stream, Illinois 60187.

Canadian Conference of Catholic Bishops (CCCB). Parent Avenue, Ottawa, Ontario, Canada (for Catholic Book of Worship, CBW)

Damean Music. c/o NALR, 2110 West Peoria Avenue, Phoeniz, AZ 85029

Desert Flower Music. P. O. Box 1735, Ridgecrest, CA 93555

FEL. 2545 Chandler Avenue, Suite 5, Las Vegas, NV 89120

Franciscan Communications. 1229 So. Santee St., Los Angeles, CA 90015

GIA. 7404 South Mason Avenue, Chicago, IL 60638.

NALR. 2110 West Peoria Avenue, Phoenix, AZ 85029.

OCP. P. O. Box 18030, Portland, OR 97218.

J. S. Paluch Company, Inc. 1800 West Winnemac Avenue, Chicago, IL 60640.

Raven Music. 4107 Woodland Park Avenue North, Seattle, WA 98103.

WLP. 5040 Ravenswood Avenue, Chicago, IL 60640.

LOVING OUR NEIGHBOR, THE EARTH
Creation-Spirituality Activities for 9-11 Year Olds
Christie L. Jenkins
Paperbound, $14.95, 125 pages, 8 1/2" x 11", perforated
ISBN: 0-89390-204-7

The environmental crisis is a profoundly religious issue — it goes
to our relationship with the creator, creation, and each other.
Yet virtually no resources exist to help parochial school teachers
and parish catechists address such topics as the greenhouse
effect, loss of the ozone layer, deforestation, soil erosion,
contaminated ground water and the like. This book of activities
is a corrective — at least for those working with 9-11 year olds.
Twenty different lessons and activities you can use in science
classes, religion classes, catechetical sessions, or for camp
activities.

Ask for this title at your dealer, or use the order form on the
next to last page to order from:

 Resource Publications, Inc.
160 E. Virginia St. #290
San Jose , CA 95112-5848

Fanfare for a Feather
and 76 Other Ways
to Celebrate Practically Anything

Vivienne Margolis, Kerry Smith, and Adele Weiss

FANFARE FOR A FEATHER
77 Ways to Celebrate Practically Anything
Vivienne Margolis, Kerry Smith, and Adelle Weiss
Paperbound, $9.95, 154 pages, 5½″ x 8½″
ISBN: 0-89390-202-0

This whimsical book is a collection of non-religious exercises which has a serious purpose: improving your sense of well-being by introducing you to the wonders in one corner of your kitchen. Or in your backyard. Or out your office window. Or wherever you happen to be. Use these impromptu celebrations anytime you need to loosen up, lighten up, and live a little! 77 illustrations. Great for individuals, catechists, and workshop leaders.

PENCIL
We have finally come to the time when the pencil is an endangered spieces. Just yesterday, I asked my granddaughter for a pencil. She handed me a ballpoint pen, "Pilot B.P.S. Fine."
"No," I said. "I want a PENCIL. You know, it has lead in it and an eraser on the other end." She said,"Oh, a pencil. I've heard about those things. But what is it?"
Ceremony: Find a pencil, a very, very small one, an almost gone one. Mount it on a card. Put a frame around the card. Hang it someplace. Who knows, it may be worth a million someday. — from *Fanfare for a Feather: 77 Ways to Celebrate Practically Anything*.

FEEDING THE SPIRIT: How to Create
Your Own Ceremonial Rites, Festivals, and Celebrations
Nacy Brady Cunningham
Paperbound, $7.95 118 pages, 5½" x 8½"
ISBN 0-89390-117-2

Combine ancient rites and modern-day practicality with these 24
ceremonies you can celebrate in your own home. Ceremonies
such as Dream Making, Color Meditation, and Moon Magic will
inspire you to create your own rituals; the solstice and equinox
celebrations will add a special air to each season. You'll find
ordinary events in our daily life suddenly transformed into special
moments that ourch the spirit. Feeding The Spirit will help you
nourish your soul and recapture a joy in living.

SEASONAL STORIES FOR FAMILY FESTIVALS
Armandine Kelly
Paperbound $7.95, 128 pages, 5½" x8½.
ISBN 0-89390-096-6

With *Seasonal Stories for Family Festivals* you'll find out how deeply
the great Christian feasts are connected to the natural world and
human traditions that cross religious lines. Read these stories out
loud or to yourself — just for the wealth of information. Read about
the Full Rose Moon, The Flower Moon, How January Got its
Name, the Wedding, and much, much more.

DANCING WITH CREATION
Martha Ann Kirk, CCVI
Paperbound, $7.95
104 pages, 5½" x 8½"
ISBN 0-89390-042-7

12 complete choreographies, along with a clear explanation of the background behind these specific dance examples, and behind the custom of dancing as it was developed among our Native American peoples and the Mexican people. Excellent dance and religious education resource.

ORDER FORM --

Order from your local religious bookstore, or mail this form to:

Resource Publications, Inc.
160 E. Virginia St., #290
San Jose, CA 95112
408 286-8505
FAX 408 287-8748

Qty	Title	Price	Total
___	_____	_____	_____
___	_____	_____	_____
___	_____	_____	_____
___	_____	_____	_____
___	_____	_____	_____
___	_____	_____	_____

☐ My check or purchase order is enclosed.
☐ Charge my: ☐ Visa ☐ MC Exp. date _____

Subtotal _____
CA Residents Add 6% Sales Tax _____
*Postage and Handling _____
Total Amount Enclosed _____

Card # _____ - _____ - _____ - _____
Signature: _____
Name: _____
Institution: _____
Street: _____
City: _____ St ____ Zip _____

*Postage and Handling
$1.50 for orders under $10.00
$2.00 for orders of $10.00-$25.00
9% (max. $7.00) of order for orders over $25.00

Code: CTE

If you are active in worship or ministry, *Modern Liturgy* is your magazine! Every issue explores the history and theology of liturgy, integrating it with our contemporary culture to help you see what good ritual is, where it comes from, why it is important, and how to do it. In addition, you receive abundant and imaginative liturgical resource ideas, including dramas, stories, gestures, songs, decoration, and design—all in plenty of time for your seasonal planning. Add to this the profiles and interviews with leaders and experts, the reviews of available resources, and regular columns for ministry skills and you get an *essential* resource.

How To Subscribe

Subscribe today so *Modern Liturgy* can start making your job easier. Just check the box on the order form (back of this page) and fax or mail it in today. Or, call TOLL FREE 1-800-736-7600 (8-5 Pacific time weekdays) and ask us to rush you your first issue and an invoice for a one year subscription. Whether you mail or phone your order, if you are not satisfied with what you get in your first issue, simply send back the invoice marked "cancel". Your first issue is yours either way. If you do find ML helpful, you will enjoy a full year of great resource ideas for only $40 (ten issues).

Single Copies are Available

Modern Liturgy is on display at participating dealers where you can purchase individual copies.

Special Rates for Groups

Special rates are also available for prepaid Team (group) subscriptions. Send ML to yourself and to each of your key team members, at each one's home address or parish address. Enclose a list of names and addresses along with your payment according to this schedule:

    One or two subscriptions, $40 per year each
    3 to 5 subscriptions, $25 each
    6 to 9 subscriptions, $20 each
    10 or more subscriptions, $15 each